DICT[illegible]

OF DIFFICULT

WORDS

5000 ENGLISH

WORDS

MANIK JOSHI

<u>Dedication</u>

THIS BOOK IS

DEDICATED

TO THOSE

WHO REALIZE

THE POWER OF ENGLISH

AND WANT TO

LEARN IT

SINCERELY

Copyright Notice

****

IMPORTANT NOTE

This Book is Part of a Series
SERIES Name: "English Word Power"
[A Twenty-Book Series]
BOOK Number: 20
BOOK Title: "Dictionary of Difficult Words"
****

Table of Contents

5000 Difficult Words in English

Letter A -- 275 Difficult English Words

Letter B -- 242 Difficult English Words

Letter C -- 438 Difficult English Words

Letter D -- 321 Difficult English Words

Letter E -- 238 Difficult English Words

Letter F -- 233 Difficult English Words

Letter G -- 171 Difficult English Words

Letter H -- 149 Difficult English Words

Letter I -- 266 Difficult English Words

Letter J -- 51 Difficult English Words

Letter K -- 19 Difficult English Words

Letter L -- 132 Difficult English Words

Letter M -- 175 Difficult English Words

Letter N -- 66 Difficult English Words

Letter O -- 109 Difficult English Words

Letter P -- 393 Difficult English Words

Letter Q -- 22 Difficult English Words

Letter R -- 303 Difficult English Words

Letter S -- 787 Difficult English Words

Letter T -- 205 Difficult English Words

Letter U -- 172 Difficult English Words

Letter V -- 98 Difficult English Words

Letter W -- 112 Difficult English Words

Letter XYZ -- 23 Difficult English Words

TOTAL -- 5000 DIFFICULT ENGLISH WORDS

SYMBOLS USED IN THIS DICTIONARY

adj. -- adjective // adv. -- adverb // n. -- noun // prep. -- preposition //
pron. -- pronoun // v. -- verb // sb -- somebody // sth -- something

Difficult English Words -- A

0001 -- abandon (v.) -- to discard; to dump; to leave sb/sth permanently || related word: **abandoned (adj.), abandonment (n.)**

0002 -- abase (v.) -- to do sth that makes people have less respect for you; to degrade || related word: **abasement (n.)**

0003 -- abashed (adj.) -- ashamed in a social situation; embarrassed

0004 -- abate (v.) -- to become very weak; to fade away; to subside || related word: **abatement (n.)**

0005 -- abdicate (v.) -- to step down from the position of being king; to renounce; to give up || related word: **abdication (n.)**

0006 -- aberrant (adj.) -- abnormal, unsocial or weird; nonstandard || related word: **aberration (n.)**

0007 -- abet (v.) -- to assist, encourage or support sb in doing sth illegal, immoral, etc.

0008 -- abhor (v.) -- to extremely hate or dislike sb/sth for ethical reasons; to detest || related words: **abhorrent (adj.), abhorrence (n.)**

0009 -- abide (v.) -- to reside somewhere

0010 -- abiding (adj.) -- (of feelings, ideas, etc.) long lasting

0011 -- abject (adj.) -- having no hope or self-esteem; miserable || related word: **abjectly (adv.)**

0012 -- abjure (v.) -- to give up a belief or idea publicly; to renounce

0013 -- ablaze (adj.) -- on fire; afire | full of strong feelings, bright lights, etc.

0014 -- ablutions (n.) -- action of cleaning or washing yourself

0015 -- abnegate (v.) -- to reject sth that you like; to renounce || related word: **abnegation (n.)**

0016 -- abode (n.) -- the place where you reside/live; residence

0017 -- abolish (v.) -- to get rid of a law, rule, etc. officially; to eliminate || related words: **abolition (n.), abolitionist (n.)**

0018 -- abominate (v.) -- to hate intensely || related words: **abominable (adj.), abomination (n.)**

0019 -- aboriginal (adj.) -- primitive

0020 -- abortive (adj.) -- (of an action) unsuccessful

0021 -- abound (v.) -- to be plentiful

0022 -- about-turn (n.) -- reversal of a plan or opinion, etc.

0023 -- above board (adj./adv.) -- honest or genuine / honestly or genuinely

0024 -- abrasion (n.) -- cut or scratch

0025 -- abrasive (adj.) -- rough | rude || related words: **abrasively (adv.), abrasiveness (n.)**

0026 -- abreast (adv.) -- side by side

0027 -- abridge (v.) -- to shorten a book, etc. || related words: **abridged (adj.), abridgement (n.)**

0028 -- abrogate (v.) -- to officially cancel a law || related word: **abrogation (n.)**

0029 -- abrupt (adj.) -- sudden | impolite || related words: **abruptly (adv.), abruptness (n.)**

0030 -- abscond (v.) -- to run away; to escape

0031 -- abseil (v.) -- to descend a steep cliff

0032 -- absolution (n.) -- forgiveness

0033 -- absolutism (n.) -- rule by dictator; autocracy || related word: **absolutist (adj./n.)**

0034 -- absolve (v.) -- to officially forgive somebody

0035 -- abstain (v.) -- to give up or stay away from sth bad, illegal or immoral | to decide not to cast your vote in election | related words: **abstainer (n.), abstention (n.)**

0036 -- abstemious (adj.) -- self-disciplined

0037 -- abstinence (n.) -- restraint from eating or drinking because of ethical reasons | related word: **abstinent (adj.)**

0038 -- **abstracted (adj.)** -- absentminded || related word: **abstractedly (adv.)**

0039 -- **abstruse (adj.)** -- that cannot be understood easily; obscure

0040 -- **abundant (adj.)** -- plentiful || related word: **abundantly (adv.)**

0041 -- **abut (v.)** -- to be next to sth; to adjoin

0042 -- **abysmal (adj.)** -- extremely bad || related word: **abysmally (adv.)**

0042 -- **abyss (n.)** -- enormously deep hole

0044 -- **accede (v.)** -- to give approval to a plan, request, etc. | to become ruler

0045 -- **accentuate (v.)** -- to highlight something; to emphasize || related word: **accentuation (n.)**

0046 -- **accession (n.)** -- the state of becoming a ruler

0047 -- **acclaim (v.)** -- to praise or greet sb/sth in public || related word: **acclamation (n.)**

0048 -- **acclimatize (acclimate) (v.)** -- to get used to new climate, situation, etc. || related word: **acclimatization (acclimation) (n.)**

0049 -- **accolade (n.)** -- honor for a marvelous achievement

0050 -- **accommodate (v.)** -- to give a place to stay | to adjust | to oblige or help || related words: **accommodating (adj.), accommodation (n.)**

0051 -- **accord (n./v.)** -- official agreement | to agree officially

0052 -- **accost (v.)** -- to suddenly come close and talk to sb

0053 -- **accouter (accouter) (v.)** -- to put on special clothes, equipments, etc. | related word: **accoutrements (n.)**

0054 -- **accredit (v.)** -- to officially recognize sb/sth || related words: **accredited (adj.), accreditation (n.)**

0055 -- **accretion (n.)** -- addition of a layer in a gradual way; newly but slowly added layer

0056 -- **accrue (v.)** -- to mount up; to accumulate || related word: **accrual (n.)**

0057 -- **acculturate (v.)** -- to adjust yourself in different culture || related word: **acculturation (n.)**

0058 -- **acerbic (adj.)** -- bitter in speech || related word: **acerbity (n.)**

0059 -- **Achilles heel (n.)** -- weak point in character

0060 -- **acme (n.)** -- the highest point in development; peak

0061 -- **acolyte (n.)** -- helper of a leader

0062 -- **acoustic (adj.)** -- connected with sound | designed to make natural sound || related words: **acoustically (adv.), acoustician (n.), acoustics (n.)**

0063 -- **acquiesce (v.)** -- to agree without arguing || related words: **acquiescent (adj.), acquiescence (n.)**

0064 -- **acrid (adj.)** -- bitter

0065 -- **acrimony (n.)** -- bitterness or hostility || related words: **acrimonious (adj.), acrimoniously (adv.)**

0066 -- **acrobat (n.)** -- circus performer || related words: **acrobatic (adj.), acrobatically (adv.), acrobatics (n.)**

0067 -- **acronym (n.)** -- short form of a group of words

0068 -- **acuity (n.)** -- the ability to hear, see or think in a clear way

0069 -- **acumen (n.)** -- intelligence

0070 -- **ad hominem (adj./adv.)** -- (of criticism, etc.) targeted to sb's character

0071 -- **ad infinitum (adv.)** -- infinitely or repeatedly

0072 -- **ad nauseam (adv.)** -- repeatedly in a boring way

0073 -- **adamant (adj.)** -- too determined; obstinate || related word: **adamantly (adv.)**

0074 -- **adamantine (adj.)** -- unbreakable

0075 -- **addendum (n.)** -- extra section in a book; appendix

0076 -- **addle (v.)** -- to confuse || related word: **addled (adj.)**

0077 -- **adduce (v.)** -- to cite sth

0078 -- **adhere (v.)** -- to stick fast to sth | to follow a particular set of rules || related word: **adherence (n.)**

0079 -- **adherent (n.)** -- supporter of a particular set of beliefs

0080 -- **adhesive (adj./n.)** -- sticky | glue || related word: **adhesion (n.)**

0081 -- **adieu (exclamation)** -- goodbye

0082 -- **adjure (v.)** -- to seriously request or urge sb to do something

0083 -- **adlib (v.)** -- to speak without preparation

0084 -- **admonish (v.)** -- to speak harshly to sb; to warn || related words: **admonitory (adj.), admonition (n.)**

0085 -- **adore (v.)** -- to admire or love || related words: **adorable (adj.), adoring (adj.), adoringly (adv.), adorably (adv.), adoration (n.)**

0086 -- **adorn (v.)** -- to decorate || related word: **adornment (n.)**

0087 -- **adrift (adj.)** -- floating | without aim

0088 -- **adroit (adj.)** -- able to deal with people cleverly || related words: **adroitly (adv.), adroitness (n.)**

0089 -- **adumbrate (v.)** -- to summarize

0090 -- **advent (n.)** -- arrival of an important person or event

0091 -- **adventitious (adj.)** -- unplanned; accidental

0092 -- **aesthete (n.)** -- admirer of art and beauty || related words: **aesthetic (adj./n.), aesthetically (adv.), aesthetics (n.), aestheticism (n.)**

0093 -- **affable (adj.)** -- friendly || related words: **affably (adv.), affability (n.)**

0094 -- **affinity (n.)** -- attraction or resemblance

0095 -- **afflict (v.)** -- to create trouble for sb || related word: **affliction (n.)**

0096 -- **affluent (adj.)** -- wealthy || related word: **affluence (n.)**

0097 -- **affray (n.)** -- fight or violence in a public place

0098 -- **affront (n./v.)** -- insulting remark | to insult or upset sb

0099 -- **aficionado (n.)** -- sb who is too much interested in a particular activity, subject, etc.: enthusiast

0100 -- **aflame (adj.)** -- on fire | colorful and brightly lit | excited

0101 -- **agglomerate (adj./n./v.)** -- formed into a mass | collection or mass | to collect and form a group || related word: **agglomeration (n.)**

0102 -- **aggrandizement (n.)** -- increase in the power of country or person

0103 -- **aggravate (v.)** -- to make sth worse || related words: **aggravated (adj.), aggravating (adj.), aggravation (n.)**

0104 -- **aggrieved (adj.)** -- angry or hurt

0105 -- **aggro (n.)** -- irritating problems, too aggressive behavior

0106 -- **aghast (adj.)** -- shocked

0107 -- **agile (adj.)** -- quick to notice sth; swift in movement || related word: **agility (n.)**

0108 -- **agog (adj.)** -- excited while trying to find out sth

0109 -- **agonize (v.)** -- to worry a lot || related words: **agonized (adj.), agonizing (adj.), agonizingly (adv.)**

0110 -- **agony (n.)** -- pain

0111 -- **agrarian (adj.)** -- related to farming

0112 -- **aground (adv.)** -- ashore

0113 -- **ail (v.)** -- to create problems | to make sb ill

0114 -- **airy-fairy (adj.)** -- impractical; idealistic

0115 -- **ajar (adj.)** -- (of a door, window, etc.) slightly open

0116 -- **al fresco (adj./adv.)** -- outdoors

0117 -- **alacrity (n.)** -- quickness in an excited way

0118 -- **albatross (n.)** -- something that creates difficulty and get in the way of progress

0119 -- **alchemy (n.)** -- magical power that can transform things

0120 -- **alien (adj.)** -- foreign | hostile

0121 -- **alienate (v.)** -- to lose your support with sb; to feel isolated || related word: **alienation (n.)**

0122 -- **alight (adj./v.)** -- on fire; shining brightly | to get down from the bus, etc.

0123 -- **allay (v.)** -- to reduce the intensity of feelings, emotions, etc.

0124 -- **allegiance (n.)** -- faithfulness towards your senior or a group you belong to

0125 -- **alleviate (v.)** -- to reduce the intensity of sth bad || related word: **alleviation (n.)**

0126 -- **allure (n.)** -- attraction or fascination | related words: **alluring (adj.), alluringly (adv.), allurement (n.)**

0127 -- **allusion (n.)** -- indirect reference or remark || related word: **allusive (adj.)**

0128 -- **alluvial (adj.)** -- made of sand deposited by river or sea || related word: **alluvium (n.)**

0129 -- **aloft (adv.)** -- in the air; overhead

0130 -- **also-ran (n.)** -- unsuccessful person

0131 -- **altercation (n.)** -- a quarrel in a public place

0132 -- **altruism (n.)** -- selflessness || related word: **altruistic (adv.)**

0133 -- **ambidextrous (adj.)** -- able to use both the hands equally well

0134 -- **ambience (n.)** -- surroundings or atmosphere of a place || related word: **ambient (adj.)**

0135 -- **ambivalence (n.)** -- state of two minds, showing mixed feelings || related words: **ambivalent (adj.), ambivalently (adv.)**

0136 -- **amble (v.)** -- to walk slowly

0137 -- **ambrosia (n.)** -- delicious thing to eat

0138 -- **ambulatory (adj.)** -- connected with walking; mobile

0139 -- **amenable (adj.)** -- agreeable or controllable

0140 -- **amicable (adj.)** -- pleasant and friendly || related word: **amicably (adv.)**

0141 -- **amiss (adj.)** -- wrong

0142 -- **amity (n.)** -- peaceful and friendly relationship

0143 -- **amnesia (n.)** -- loss of memory || related word: **amnesiac (n.)**

0144 -- **amorous (adj.)** -- expressing feeling of love passionately || related word: **amorously (adv.)**

0145 -- **amorphous (adj.)** -- formless or shapeless

0146 -- **amplify (v.)** -- to increase sound ; to add more information to a story, etc. || related word: **amplification (n.)**

0147 -- **anachronism (n.)** -- old-fashioned person or thing || related word: **anachronistic (adj.)**

0148 -- **analgesia (n.)** -- inability to feel pain || related word: **analgesic (adj./n.)**

0149 -- **analogy (n.)** -- a comparison that shows similarities or correlation between two things

0150 -- **anathema (n.)** -- sth that you hate strongly

0151 -- **anecdote (n.)** -- a short and real story or event

0152 -- **angst (n.)** -- deep fear, tension or anxiety; nervousness

0153 -- **anguish (n.)** -- severe suffering || related word: **anguished (adj.)**

0154 -- **animated (adj.)** -- full of life; energetic || related word: **animatedly (adv.)**

0155 -- **animism (n.)** -- belief that natural objects possess soul || related words: **animistic (adj.), animist (n.)**

0156 -- **animosity (n.)** -- enmity

0157 -- **animus (n.)** -- hatred

0158 -- **annals (n.)** -- historical records; yearly record of events

0159 -- **annex (v.)** -- to forcefully take over another country || related word: **annexation (n.)**

0160 -- **annihilate (v.)** -- to defeat or destroy completely || related word: **annihilation (n.)**

0161 -- **annotate (v.)** -- to add notes to explain sth || related words: **annotated (adj.), annotation (n.)**

0162 -- **annul (v.)** -- to cancel sth officially || related word: **annulment (n.)**

0163 -- **anodyne (adj.)** -- inoffensive, harmless

0164 -- **anoint (v.)** -- to smear somebody with water or oil as part of a religious ceremony

0165 -- **anomalous (adj.)** -- abnormal, unusual or unexpected || related words: **anomalously (adv.), anomaly (n.)**

0166 -- **anomie (n.)** -- unsocial or immoral behaviour

0167 -- **anorexia (n.)** -- fear of being fat || related word: **anorexic (adj./n.)**

0168 -- **antagonize (v.)** -- to irritate or annoy sb | to make sb no longer friendly with you || related words: **antagonistic (adj.), antagonistically (adv.), antagonist (n.), antagonism (n.)**

0169 -- **antecedent (adj./n.)** -- previous | something that has been followed by something else

0170 -- **antediluvian (adj.)** -- primitive; outdated

0171 -- **anthology (n.)** -- compilation of stories, poems, etc. from different sources

0172 -- **antipathy (n.)** -- hostility || related word: **antipathetic (adj.)**

0173 -- **antiquated (adj.)** -- old-fashioned

0174 -- **antiquity (n.)** -- the ancient past; an object, a work of art, etc. from the ancient past

0175 -- **antithesis (n.)** -- exact opposite | contrast || related word: **antithetical (adj.)**

0176 -- **apathy (n.)** -- lack of interest || related words: **apathetic (adj.), apathetically (adv.)**

0177 -- **aphorism (n.)** -- a short phrase that expresses sth sensible || related word: **aphoristic (adj.)**

0178 -- **aplomb (n.)** -- self-confidence in a difficult situation

0179 -- **apnea (apnoea) (n.)** -- temporary loss of breath during sleep

0180 -- **apocalypse (n.)** -- complete or severe destruction || related word: **apocalyptic (adj.)**

0181 -- **apocryphal (adj.)** -- dubious; mythical

0182 -- **apoplexy (n.)** -- loss of the ability to feel

0183 -- **apostate (n.)** -- sb who has changed their religious beliefs || related word: **apostasy (n.)**

0184 -- **apostle (n.)** -- strong supporter or follower of an idea or a policy

0185 -- **appalled (adj.)** -- shocked, distressed || related words: **appalling (adj.), appallingly (adv.)**

0186 -- **apparent (adj.)** -- obvious; noticeable

0187 -- **apparition (n.)** -- spirit or ghost

0188 -- **appease (v.)** -- to calm down sb by accepting their demands || related word: **appeasement (n.)**

0189 -- **append (v.)** -- to add sth as an attachment || related word: **appendage (n.)**

0190 -- **appetizing (adj.)** -- mouth-watering

0191 -- **applaud (v.)** -- to clap in order to praise sb; to praise | related word: **applause (n.)**

0192 -- **appliqué (n.)** -- ornamental needlework || related word: **appliquéd (adj.)**

0193 -- **apportion (v.)** -- to divide and distribute || related word: **apportionment (n.)**

0194 -- **apposite (adj.)** -- suitable

0195 -- **appraise (v.)** -- to assess the quality of something; to evaluate | related words: **appraisal (n.), appraiser (n.)**

0196 -- **appreciable (adj.)** -- noticeable || related word: **appreciably (adv.)**

0197 -- **appurtenance (n.)** -- small part of sth; accessory

0198 -- **apropos (prep.)** -- concerning

0199 -- **aquifer (n.)** -- a layer of rock that can hold or transmit water.

0200 -- **arable (adj.)** -- related to growing crops

0201 -- **arbiter (n.)** -- a person who is authorized to settle a dispute

0202 -- **arbitrary (adj.)** -- illogical | uncontrolled || related words: **arbitrarily (adv.), arbitrariness (n.)**

0203 -- **arbitrate (v.)** -- to officially settle a dispute between two parties || related word: **arbitration (n.)**

0204 -- **arboreal (adj.)** -- connected with trees

0205 -- **arcane (adj.)** -- mysterious; puzzling

0206 -- **archetype (n.)** -- a typical example

0207 -- **ardent (adj.)** -- enthusiastic; excited || related word: **ardently (adv.)**

0208 -- **ardor (ardour) (n.)** -- passion

0209 -- **arduous (adj.)** -- difficult and tiring; laborious || related word: **arduously (adv.)**

0210 -- **argot (n.)** -- special words used by a particular profession; jargon

0211 -- **arid (adj.)** -- dry | ordinary || related word: **aridity (n.)**

0212 -- **Armageddon (n.)** -- an extremely terrible war

0213 -- **armistice (n.)** -- break in fighting; ceasefire

0214 -- **arm-twisting (n.)** -- persuasion by force

0215 -- **arouse (v.)** -- to cause particular emotion | to awaken someone from sleep || related word: **arousal (n.)**

0216 -- **arraign (v.)** -- to charge sb for a crime || related word: **arraignment (n.)**

0217 -- **arrant (adj.)** -- (of sth bad) absolute or complete

0218 -- **arrogant (adj.)** -- very proud || related word: **arrogantly (adv.)**

0219 -- **artifact (artefact) (n.)** -- historical object

0220 -- **ascend (v.)** -- to go/lead/move up; to rise

0221 -- **ascendancy (n.)** -- dominance or supremacy || related words: **ascendant (n.), ascension (n.)**

0222 -- **ascetic (adj./n.)** -- enormously self-disciplined | strict in self-discipline || related word: **asceticism (n.)**

0223 -- **ascribe (v.)** -- to state or believe that sth is caused or done by a particular thing/person or written by a particular person | to think sb/sth should have a particular quality || related words: **ascribable (adj.), ascription (n.)**

0224 -- **ashen (adj.)** -- light in colour, whiter than usual

0225 -- **asinine (adj.)** -- foolish

0226 -- **askew (adj./adv.)** -- not straight, bent

0227 -- **aslant (adv.)** -- at an angle; sloping

0228 -- **asperity (n.)** -- harshness of tone || related word: **aspersions (n.)**

0229 -- **aspire (v.)** -- to aim big

0230 -- **assail (v.)** -- to attack sb violently; to criticize sb strongly

0231 -- **assault (n./v.)** -- violent attack | to attack sb violently

0232 -- **assent (n./v.)** -- official agreement | to agree officially

0233 -- **assertive (adj.)** -- self-confident || related words: **assertively (adv.), assertiveness (n.)**

0234 -- **assiduous (adj.)** -- hard-working || related words: **assiduously (adv.), assiduity (n.)**

0235 -- **assign (v.)** -- to allocate

0236 -- **assimilate (v.)** -- to incorporate; to include || related word: **assimilation (n.)**

0237 -- **assuage (v.)** -- to lessen painful feeling

0238 -- **astonish (v.)** -- to extremely surprise sb

0239 -- **astound (v.)** -- to shock or surprise sb too much || related words: **astounded (adj.), astounding (adj.), astoundingly (adv.)**

0240 -- **astride (adv./prep.)** -- with a leg on each side of sth

0241 -- **astringent (adj.)** -- harsh; severe || related word: **astringency (n.)**

0242 -- **astronomical (adj.)** -- (of a price) excessive || related word: **astronomically (adv.)**

0243 -- **astute (adj.)** -- very clever; shrewd || related words: **astutely (adv.), astuteness (n.)**

0244 -- **asunder (adv.)** -- not together

0245 -- **atavistic (adj.)** -- connected with primitive humans

0246 -- **ataxia (n.)** -- loss of control of bodily movements || related word: **ataxic (adj.)**

0247 -- **atone (v.)** -- to express regret and make up for sth || related word: **atonement (n.)**

0248 -- **atrocity (n.)** -- terrible and violent act; evil || related words: **atrocious (adj.), atrociously (adv.), atrociousness (n.)**

0249 -- **attenuate (v.)** -- to make sth less forceful or effective || related words: **attenuated (adj.), attenuation (n.)**

0250 -- **attire (n.)** -- clothes || **related word:** attired **(adj.)**

0251 -- **attuned (adj.)** -- completely familiar with sth

0252 -- **audacity (n.)** -- boldness; rudeness || related words: **audacious (adj.), audaciously (adv.)**

0253 -- **auditory (adj.)** -- related to hearing

0254 -- **augment (v.)** -- to increase || related word: **augmentation (n.)**

0255 -- **augur (v.)** -- to foretell, foresee or predict || related word: **augury (n.)**

0256 -- **aura (n.)** -- noticeable quality of surrounding areas

0257 -- **aural (adj.)** -- related to hearing and listening || related word: **aurally (adv.)**

0258 -- **austere (adj.)** -- having strict attitude; having simple style; having uncomfortable way of life || related words: **austerely (adv.), austerity (n.)**

0259 -- **autism (n.)** -- loss of ability to form relationship or communicate with people || related word: **autistic (adj.)**

0260 -- **autocrat (n.)** -- a ruler with absolute power | || related word: **autocratic (adj.), autocratically (adv.) autocracy (n.),**

0261 -- **avarice (n.)** -- greed || related word: **avaricious (adj.)**

0262 -- **avenue (n.)** -- path; a way of making progress

0263 -- **aver (v.)** -- to firmly express a truth

0264 -- **averse (adj.)** -- not liking sth || related word: **aversion (n.)**

0265 -- **avert (v.)** -- to prevent or foil sth undesirable from happening

0266 -- **avid (adj.)** -- enthusiastic || related words: **avidly (adv.), avidity (n.)**

0267 -- **avow (v.)** -- to say sth openly; to affirm || related words: **avowed (adj.), avowedly (adv.), avowal (n.)**

0268 -- **awash (adj.)** -- flooded with water; containing large amount of something

0269 -- **awe (n./v.)** -- admiration and wonder | to respect || related word: **awed (adj.)**

0270 -- **awe-inspiring (adj.)** -- splendid

0271 -- **awesome (adj.)** -- amazing || related word: **awesomely (adv.)**

0272 -- **awestruck (adj.)** -- fascinated

0273 -- **awful (adj./adv.)** -- too bad; excessive | extremely || related word: **awfulness (n.)**

0274 -- **awry (adj./adv.)** -- wrong; untidy

0275 -- **axiom (n.)** -- a principle that is believed to be true || related word: **axiomatic (adj.)**

Difficult English Words -- B

0276 -- **babble (n./v.)** -- confused talks | to talk nonsense

0277 -- **bacchanalian (adj.)** -- wild and drunken

0278 -- **backbiting (n.)** -- unkind talks about sb in his/her absence

0279 -- **backlash (n.)** -- strong and adverse reaction esp. to a social or political change

0280 -- **backslapping (n.)** -- great enthusiasm and admiration among a group

0281 -- **back-stabbing (n.)** -- the action of unfair criticism of your friend in their absence

0282 -- **badger (v.)** -- to ask sb about/for something in an annoying and a repeated manner

0283 -- **baffle (v.)** -- to totally confuse sb || related words: **baffling (adj.), bafflement (n.)**

0284 -- **bailout (n.)** -- financial assistance to an organization, etc. that is facing financial crisis

0285 -- **bait (n./v.)** -- food used to catch fish, animals, etc; temptation | to entice, to lure; to provoke

0286 -- **balderdash (n.)** -- senseless or meaningless talks or writing

0287 -- **bald-faced (adj.)** -- shameless

0288 -- **baldly (adv.)** -- in brief; in a few words

0289 -- **baleful (adj.)** -- having a harmful effect; threatening || related word: **balefully (adv.)**

0290 -- **Balkanize (v.)** -- to divide a large place into smaller parts in order to separate people with different ideologies || related word: **Balkanization (n.)**

0291 -- **ballad (n.)** -- a song that is slow and sentimental; a poem that narrates a story || related word: **balladeer (n.)**

0292 -- **ballpark (n.)** -- estimated range

0293 -- **balmy (adj.)** -- pleasantly warm | crazy

0294 -- **bamboozle (v.)** -- to trick and confuse sb

0295 -- **banal (adj.)** -- dull, boring || related word: **banality (n.)**

0296 -- **bandolier (n.)** -- a shoulder-belt that carries bullets

0297 -- **bandwagon (n.)** -- a popular activity

0298 -- **bandy (adj.)** -- (of legs) curving

0299 -- **bane (n.)** -- something that causes great distress; curse || related word: **baneful (adj.)**

0300 -- **banish (v.)** -- to forcefully send sb out of their country; to expel | to get rid of sth || related word: **banishment (n.)**

0301 -- **bankroll (n./v.)** -- a large sum of money | to support sb/sth financially

0302 -- **banter (n./v.)** -- chitchat; amusement | to chitchat || related word: **bantering (adj.)**

0303 -- **barb (n.)** -- a remark that is hurtful; insult

0304 -- **barbarian (n.)** -- uncivilized, cruel or aggressive person || related words: **barbarous (adj.), barbaric (adj.), barbarically (adv.), barbarism (n.), barbarity (n.)**

0305 -- **barbiturate (n.)** -- a drug for making you feel relaxed

0306 -- **bard (n.)** -- poet

0307 -- **barge (v.)** -- to move awkwardly or forcefully

0308 -- **barmy (adj.)** -- crazy or wacky

0309 -- **baron (n.)** -- leading businessman; tycoon

0310 -- **barrack (v.)** -- to criticize in noisy way || related word: **barracking (n.)**

0311 -- **Barrel (v.)** -- to move very fast in an uncontrollable manner

0312 -- **barter (v.)** -- to exchange products or services for other products or services

0313 -- **bash (n./v.)** -- celebration; hard or violent hit | to hit or knock hard; to criticize severely

0314 -- **bashful (adj.)** -- very shy || related words: **bashfully (adv.), bashfulness (n.)**

0315 -- **bashing (n.)** -- physical assault | severe criticism

0316 -- **bastion (n.)** -- a place where there is huge support for particular belief; stronghold

0317 -- **batter (v.)** -- to harm sb/sth by hitting them repeatedly || related word: **battering (n.)**

0318 -- **battered (adj.)** -- in bad condition because of repeated use | attacked or injured

0319 -- **battleaxe (n.)** -- an extremely impolite older woman

0320 -- **baulk (v.)** -- to hesitate to do sth | to stop sb from doing or getting sth

0321 -- **bawdy (adj.)** -- indecent in humorous way

0322 -- **bawl (n./v.)** -- a loud cry or shout | to cry or shout in a noisy and angry way

0323 -- **bead (n.)** -- drop of liquid | a perforated piece of glass, stone, etc,|| related word: **beaded (adj.)**

0324 -- **beatific (adj.)** -- extremely happy

0325 -- **beatify (v.)** -- to declare that a particular dead person is very holy || related word: **beatification (n.)**

0326 -- **beat-up (adj.)** -- damaged and old; worn out

0327 -- **beckon (v.)** -- to gesture | to seem to be very attractive

0328 -- **becoming (adj.)** -- suitable | making sb look more attractive

0329 -- **bedeck (v.)** -- to decorate

0330 -- **bedevil (v.)** -- to cause trouble or harm to sb

0331 -- **bedlam (n.)** -- a state of complete confusion or disorder

0332 -- **bedraggled (adj.)** -- untidy and wet due to rain, mud, etc.

0333 -- **bedrock (n.)** -- fundamental principle; basis

0334 -- **befall (v.)** -- (of sth bad) to happen to sb

0335 -- **befit (v.)** -- to be proper and suitable

0336 -- **befog (v.)** -- to make sb confused

0337 -- **befuddle (v.)** -- to confuse sb in a way that they cannot behave normally || related word: **befuddled (adj.)**

0338 -- **beget (v.)** -- to bring about sth; to produce | to become father of a child || related word: **begetter (n.)**

0339 -- **begrudge (v.)** -- to be resented by sth | to be unwilling to give, pay, etc. something

0340 -- **beguile (v.)** -- to trick; to tempt || related words: **beguiling (adj.), beguilingly (adv.)**

0341 -- **behemoth (n.)** -- powerful union, organization, etc.

0342 -- **behold (v.)** -- to see, look or observe

0343 -- **beholden (adj.)** -- obliged

0344 -- **belated (adj.)** -- delayed || related word: **belatedly (adv.)**

0345 -- **beleaguered (adj.)** -- under attack

0346 -- **belie (v.)** -- to disprove or contradict

0347 -- **bellicose (adj.)** -- aggressive or quarrelsome || related word: **bellicosity (n.)**

0348 -- **belligerent (adj./n.)** -- unfriendly | indulged in war || related words: **belligerently (adv.), belligerence (n.)**

0349 -- **bellow (v.)** -- to shout loudly

0350 -- **bellwether (n.)** -- sign or indicator for future change

0351 -- **bemoan (v.)** -- to complain about sth; to mourn

0352 -- **bemuse (v.)** -- to confuse or puzzle sb || related words: **bemused (adj.), bemusedly (adv.)**

0353 -- **benevolent (adj.)** -- generous || related words: **benevolently (adv.), benevolence (n.)**

0354 -- **benighted (adj.)** -- unknowledgeable | disadvantaged || related words: **benightedness (n.)**

0355 -- **benign (adj.)** -- kind or gentle; harmless || related word: **benignly (adv.)**

0356 -- **berate (v.)** -- to angrily criticize sb

0357 -- **bereaved (adj.)** -- having lost your loved one because of his/her death || related word: **bereavement (n.)**

0358 -- **bereft (adj.)** -- lacking sth | very sad and lonely

0359 -- **berserk (adj.)** -- crazy and uncontrollable; erratic

0360 -- **beseech (v.)** -- to plead or beg || related words: **beseeching (adj.), beseechingly (adv.)**

0361 -- **beset (v.)** -- to unpleasantly affect sth; to threaten

0362 -- **besiege (v.)** -- to lay siege to sth

0363 -- **besmirch (v.)** -- to damage reputation of sb/sth

0364 -- **besotted (adj.)** -- love-struck; infatuated

0365 -- **bestial (adj.)** -- inhuman or cruel | connected with animals || related word: **bestially (adv.), bestiality (n.)**

0366 -- **bestir (v.)** -- to make an effort physically or mentally; to rouse

0367 -- **betray (v.)** -- to deceive; to be disloyal to sb || related word: **betrayal (n.)**

0368 -- **betrothal (n.)** -- engagement || related word: **betrothed (adj.)**

0369 -- **bevy (n.)** -- a large group of same/similar type of people or things

0370 -- **bewail (v.)** -- to regret or lament | to cry loudly over sth

0371 -- **bewilder (v.)** -- to confuse sb completely || related words: **bewildered (adj.), bewildering (adj.), bewilderingly (adv.), bewilderment (n.)**

0372 -- **bewitch (v.)** -- to enormously impress sb | to gain control over sb by music || related words: **bewitching (adj.), bewitchingly (adv.) bewitchment (n.)**

0373 -- **biblical (adj.)** -- extremely large or great

0374 -- **bicameral (adj.)** -- (of parliament) having two parts or houses

0375 -- **bicker (v.)** -- to unnecessarily argue over unimportant things | to flash intermittent light || related word: **bickering (n.)**

0376 -- bifurcate (v.) -- to divide into two parts || related word: **bifurcation (n.)**

0377 -- bigot (n.) -- sb who is stubborn about their unreasonable beliefs; prejudiced; extremist || related words: **bigoted (adj.), bigotry (n.)**

0378 -- bile (n.) -- anger; rage || related word: **bilious (adj.)**

0379 -- bilk (v.) -- to deceive sb financially

0380 -- billet (n./v.) -- base or camp | to send soldiers to camp

0381 -- billow (n./v.) -- moving mass of smoke, cloud etc. | (of smoke, cloud, etc.) to swell

0382 -- bimbo (n.) -- very attractive but unintelligent woman

0383 -- binge (n./v.) -- a particular intense activity | to drink, eat or do sth too much

0384 -- blabbermouth (n.) -- too talkative person who often says secret things

0385 -- blabber (n./v.) -- foolish or senseless talk | to talk foolishly or excessively

0386 -- bland (adj.) -- ordinary, plain or unremarkable || related words: **blandly (adv.), blandness (n.)**

0387 -- blandishments (n.) -- activities or talks to please sb

0388 -- blare (n./v.) -- an unpleasant noise or harsh sound | to make an unpleasant noise or harsh sound || related word: **blaring (adj.)**

0389 -- blasé (adj.) -- uncaring or unimpressed to sth because you have already seen, heard, experienced, it a lot of times.

0390 -- blatant (adj.) -- unashamed; too obvious || related word: **blatantly (adv.)**

0391 -- blather (n./v.) -- nonsense talk | to talk nonsense

0392 -- blaze (n./v.) -- large fire; strong feelings | to burn or shine brightly

0393 -- Bleachers (n.) -- rows of seats at a sports ground or stadium

0394 -- **bleak (adj.)** -- depressing | cold || related words: **bleakly (adv.),** **bleakness (n.)**

0395 -- **bleary (adj.)** -- unfocused; sleepy; unclear || related words: **blearily (adv.), bleariness (n.)**

0396 -- **bleat (n./v.)** -- sound made by goat or sheep; complaint | to complain || related word: **bleating (n.)**

0397 -- **blemish (n./v.)** -- stain; | to stain

0398 -- **blench (v.)** -- to act frantically

0399 -- **blight (n./v.)** -- a type of plant disease | to spoil or ruin sth

0400 -- **bling (adj./n.)** -- fashionable | fashionable clothes or jewelry

0401 -- **blip (n.)** -- a temporary fault; short high sound; flashing point of light on screen of radar

0402 -- **bliss (n.)** -- great happiness || related word: **blissful (adj.)**

0403 -- **blister (n./v.)** -- swelling | to swell || related word: **blistered (adj.)**

0404 -- **blistering (adj.)** -- too hot | very impressive or critical || related word: **blisteringly (adv.)**

0405 -- **blithe (adj.)** -- extremely happy; carefree || related word: **blithely (adv.)**

0406 -- **blithering (adj.)** -- complete; utter

0407 -- **blitz (n./v.)** -- an extensive activity; sudden military attack | to attack a place with bombs

0408 -- **blizzard (n.)** -- severe snowstorm

0409 -- **bloat (v.)** -- to inflate: to swell || related word: **bloated (adj.)**

0410 -- **blob (n/v.)** -- a drop of thick liquid or a spot of color | to put a drop of thick liquid

0411 -- **bloke (n.)** -- man || related word: **blockish (blokeish) (adj.)**

0412 -- **bloom (n./v.)** -- state of flowering or freshness | to blossom; to flourish; to produce buds or flowers

0413 -- **bloomer (n.)** -- serious or stupid mistake

0414 -- **blooper (n.)** -- embarrassing mistake

0415 -- **blotch (n.)** -- irregular mark or spot

0416 -- **Bloviate (v.)** -- to talk or write in a lengthy but ineffective way

0417 -- **blowback (n.)** -- unexpected political result

0418 -- **blub (v.)** -- to cry

0419 -- **blubber (v.)** -- to uncontrollably cry and shed tears

0420 -- **bludge (n./v.)** -- a job that can be done easily | to beg

0421 -- **bludgeon (v.)** -- to hit hard | to force sb to do sth

0422 -- **bludger (n.)** -- an idle person

0423 -- **bluff (n./v.)** -- trick | to trick sb

0424 -- **blunder (n./v.)** -- big, careless mistake | to make a big, careless mistake

0425 -- **blunt (adj./v.)** -- critical in saying sth; not having sharp edges | to weaken sth; to make sth less sharp

0426 -- **bluntly (adv.)** -- openly and rudely

0427 -- **blur (n./v.)** -- unclear shape, etc. | to make sth less clear || related word: **blurry (adj.) blurred (adj.)**

0428 -- **blurb (n.)** -- short description of a book or other product used in promotional campaign

0429 -- **blurt (v.)** -- to say sth suddenly and impolitely

0430 -- **blush (v.)** -- to feel embarrassed

0431 -- **bluster (n./v.)** -- loud, aggressive talk | to talk aggressively without having any effect; to blow in full force

0432 -- **blustery (adj.)** -- stormy

0433 -- **bob (n./v.)** -- a movement in which you head or sth goes up and down repeatedly | to move up and down

0434 -- **body double (n.)** -- an expert in dangerous skills and who works in movies in place of an actor

0435 -- **bog (n./v.)** -- soft, wet, muddy ground; marsh | to prevent from making progress

0436 -- **bohemian (adj./n.)** -- having unconventional habits | sb who lives life in unconventional way

0437 -- **boisterous (adj.)** -- energetic or noisy; lively || related word: **boisterously (adv.)**

0438 -- **bolster (v.)** -- to strengthen

0439 -- **bombast (n.)** -- words with no important meaning but sounds very impressive || related word: **bombastic (adj.)**

0440 -- **bonhomie (n.)** -- warmth; friendliness

0441 -- **boomerang (v.)** -- (of sb's plan) to bounce back

0442 -- **boondoggle (n.)** -- an unnecessary work that wastes time and money

0443 -- **boor (n.)** -- bad tempered person

0444 -- **bootleg (adj./v.)** -- produced and sold in an illegal way | to copy and sell other works in an illegal way || related words: **bootlegger (n.), bootlegging (n.)**

0445 -- **bootlicker (n.)** -- flatterer || related word: **bootlicking (n.)**

0446 -- **booty (n.)** -- valuable goods especially ill-gotten or stolen ones

0447 -- **booze (n./v.)** -- alcohol drink | to drink alcohol || related words: **boozy (adj.), boozer (n.)**

0448 -- **booze-up (n.)** -- an extensive activity of drinking alcohol by many people

0449 -- **borough (n.)** -- a region with its own administrative unit

0450 -- **botch (n./v.)** -- failure | to do sth in a very bad way

0451 -- **boudoir (n.)** -- private room for woman

0452 -- **boulevard (n.)** -- a wide street or road

0453 -- **bounteous (adj.)** -- generous; plentiful || related word: **bountiful (adj.)**

0454 -- **bounty (n.)** -- gift or reward in the form of money | generosity

0455 -- **bourgeoisie (n.)** -- the middle class

0456 -- **bout (n.)** -- short period of intense activity | an attack of illness

0457 -- **bovine (adj.)** -- related to cows | of a person (dull-witted)

0458 -- **bow (n./v.)** -- action of bending | to bend

0459 -- **bower (n.)** -- a shady place under trees

0460 -- **bracing (adj.)** -- energizing or refreshing

0461 -- **brag (v.)** -- to talk about himself in a proud way || related word: **braggart (n.)**

0462 -- **brandish (v.)** -- to hold and wave a weapon

0463 -- **brash (adj.)** -- impatient and impolite | too bright || related words: **brashly (adv.), brashness (n.)**

0464 -- **brat (n.)** -- rude child | related word: **bratty (adj.)**

0465 -- **bravado (n.)** -- boldness

0466 -- **brawl (n./v.)** -- fight among a group of people in a public place | to be a part of brawl || related word: **brawler (n.)**

0467 -- **brawny (adj.)** -- physically big and strong

0468 -- **brazen (adj.)** -- bold or shameless || related words: **brazenly (adv.), brazenness (n.)**

0469 -- **breakneck (adj.)** -- very swift and dangerous

0470 -- **Breezy (adj.)** -- showing a relaxed manner | pleasantly windy

0471 -- **brew (v.)** -- to make a drink

0472 -- **brickbat (n.)** -- critical remark; insult

0473 -- **bridle (v.)** -- to show your irritation by moving your head up and down.

0474 -- **brim (n./v.)** -- edge | to overflow || related word: **brimful (adj.)**

0475 -- **brink (n.)** -- very close to a new situation

0476 -- **brinkmanship (n.)** -- dangerous activity in politics with a view to make sb do sth

0477 -- **brisk (adj.)** -- fast; fresh || related words: **briskly (adv.), briskness (n.)**

0478 -- **bristle (n./v.)** -- a short stiff hair | to get annoyed; (of hair) to stand up on the back because of anger or fear

0479 -- **brittle (adj.)** -- easily broken in spite of being hard | (of a sound) unpleasantly hard and sharp || related word: **brittleness (n.)**

0480 -- **broach (v.)** -- to mention about an embarrassing subject

0481 -- **brood (n./v.)** -- offspring | to think too much about sth that makes you upset

0482 -- **brooding (adj.)** -- frightening

0483 -- **brook (n.)** -- stream

0484 -- **browbeat (v.)** -- to frighten sb to make them do sth

0485 -- **brusque (adj.)** -- impolite; curt || related words: **brusquely (adv.), brusqueness (n.)**

0486 -- **buccaneer (n.)** -- successful but dishonest person, especially in business

0487 -- **bucolic (adj.)** -- related to countryside; rural

0488 -- **Budding (adj.)** -- (of a person) showing signs of getting successful

0489 -- **budge (v.)** -- to slightly move or shift | to change your ideas, thoughts, etc.

0490 -- **buff (n.)** -- sb who is extremely fond of doing particular activity; expert

0491 -- **buffet (v.)** -- to knock || related word: **buffeting (n.)**

0492 -- **Buffoon (n.)** -- an amusing person

0493 -- **Bugbear (n.)** -- serious problem or worry

0494 -- **bulbous (adj.)** -- round and ugly

0495 -- **bulge (n./v.)** -- lump; fat | to stick out; to swell || related word: **bulging (n.)**

0496 -- **bulldoze (v.)** -- to bully | to destroy buildings, etc using bulldozer | to force sth somewhere

0497 -- **bullish (adj.)** -- optimistic

0498 -- **bully (n./v.)** -- sb who frightens others | to frighten || related word: **bullying (n.)**

0499 -- **bulwark (n.)** -- safeguard

0500 -- **bumble (v.)** -- to behave awkwardly || related word: **bumbling (adj.)**

0501 -- **bummer (n.)** -- disappointment

0502 -- **bumptious (adj.)** -- too proud; arrogant

0503 -- **bunfight (n.)** -- angry disagreement | exciting social event

0504 -- **bung (v.)** -- to throw sth without care

0505 -- **bungle (n./v.)** -- failure | to do sth in a bad way || related words: **bungling (adj.), bungler (n.)**

0506 -- **bunion (n.)** -- painful swelling on foot

0507 -- **buoy (v.)** -- to keep sth afloat | to make sb cheerful | to keep prices at a high level || related words: **buoyant (adj.), buoyancy (n.)**

0508 -- **burble (v.)** -- to talk nonsense | to make a continuous murmuring sound

0509 -- **burgeon (v.)** -- to grow rapidly || related word: **burgeoning (adj.)**

0510 -- **burlesque (n.)** -- parody

0511 -- **burly (adj.)** -- (of a man) strongly built

0512 -- **burnish (v.)** -- to polish metal || related word: **burnished (adj.)**

0513 -- **bushels (n.)** -- a large amount

0514 -- **bustle (n./v.)** -- intense activity | to be very busy || related word: **bustling (adj.)**

0515 -- **butler (n.)** -- main male servant or helper

0516 -- **buttress (v.)** -- to support or strengthen

0517 -- **byzantine (adj.)** -- very complicated and difficult to change

Difficult English Words -- C

0518 -- **cachet (n.)** -- reputation

0519 -- **cack-handed (adj.)** -- awkward

0520 -- **cackle (n./v.)** -- unpleasant laugh | to laugh in an unpleasant way

0521 -- **cacophony (n.)** -- mixture of different types of unpleasant sounds || related word: **cacophonous (adj.)**

0522 -- **cad (n.)** -- dishonest man

0523 -- **cadaver (n.)** -- dead body

0524 -- **cadaverous (adj.)** -- very pale

0525 -- **caddy (n.)** -- small bag

0526 -- **cadence (n.)** -- rhythm

0527 -- **cadge (v.)** -- to ask sb for sth in order to avoid making payment || related word: **cadger (n.)**

0528 -- **cagey (adj.)** -- secretive || related word: **cagily (adv.)**

0529 -- **cajole (v.)** -- to persuade

0530 -- **calibrate (v.)** -- to standardize

0531 -- **calisthenics (callisthenics) (n.)** -- extensive physical exercise

0532 -- **callous (adj.)** -- insensitive || related words: **callously (adv.), callousness (n.)**

0533 -- **callow (adj.)** -- inexperienced

0534 -- **calumny (n.)** -- defamation

0535 -- **camaraderie (n.)** -- friendship

0536 -- **camouflage (n./v.)** -- disguise | to hide

0537 -- **canard (n.)** -- false information

0538 -- **candid (adj.)** -- truthful || related word: **candidly (adv.)**

0539 -- **candor (candour) (n.)** -- frankness

0540 -- **cannibal (n.)** -- a person who eats human flesh || related words: **cannibalistic (adj.), cannibalism (n.)**

0541 -- **canny (adj.)** -- prudent and cautious || related word: **cannily (adv.)**

0542 -- **canon (n.)** -- norm

0543 -- **canopy (n.)** -- covering

0544 -- **caper (n./v.)** -- short jump; illegal activity | to jump or run excitedly

0545 -- **capitulate (v.)** -- to accept your defeat; to yield || related word: **capitulation (n.)**

0546 -- **caprice (n.)** -- inconsistent behavior || related words: **capricious (adj.), capriciously (adv.), capriciousness (n.)**

0547 -- **capsize (v.)** -- to overturn

0548 -- **captivate (v.)** -- to fascinate || related word: **captivating (adj.)**

0549 -- **carbuncle (n.)** -- painful swelling

0550 -- **carcass (n.)** -- dead body of a large animal

0551 -- **cardinal (adj.)** -- fundamental

0552 -- **careen (v.)** -- to move in zigzag motion

0553 -- **caress (n./v.)** -- gentle touch | to touch sb affectionately

0554 -- **caretaker (adj./n.)** -- in charge | in charge of a place, etc.

0555 -- **caricature (n./v.)** -- sketch | to make a sketch || related word: **caricaturist (n.)**

0556 -- **carnal (adj.)** -- related to body || related word: **carnally (adv.)**

0557 -- **carnival (n.)** -- public celebration

0558 -- **carnivore (n.)** -- flesh-eating animal || related word: **carnivorous (adj.)**

0559 -- **carouse (v.)** -- to enjoy in a noisy way

0560 -- **carp (v.)** -- to complain

0561 -- **carrion (n.)** -- dead and rotten body of an animal

0562 -- **cartel (n.)** -- group of companies with a common interest

0563 -- **carve (v.)** -- to cut stone, wood, etc. in order to give them particular shape

0564 -- **cascade (n./v.)** -- flow | to fall or flow in large amounts

0565 -- **Cassandra (n.)** -- forecaster of bad events

0566 -- **castigate (v.)** -- to severely criticize sb/sth || related word: **castigation (n.)**

0567 -- **cataclysm (n.)** -- disaster || related word: **cataclysmic (adj.)**

0568 -- **catastrophe (n.)** -- great tragedy; disaster || related words: **catastrophic (adj.), catastrophically (adv.)**

0569 -- **catatonic (adj.)** -- unable to move or react

0570 -- **categorical (adj.)** -- clearly said or expressed || related word: **categorically (adv.)**

0571 -- **catharsis (n.)** -- action of showing strong feelings to get relaxed || related word: **cathartic (adj.)**

0572 -- **catnap (n.)** -- a sleep for a short time

0573 -- **caucus (n./v.)** -- assembly | to discuss sth in a group

0574 -- **caustic (adj.)** -- mocking; corrosive || related word: **caustically (adv.)**

0575 -- **cauterize (v.)** -- to burn a wound in order to save it from getting infected

0576 -- **cavalier (adj.)** -- not caring about feelings of sb/sth || related word: **cavalierly (adv.)**

0577 -- **cavalry (n.)** -- army that uses horses

0578 -- **caveat (n.)** -- warning

0579 -- **cavernous (adj.)** -- spacious

0580 -- **cavil (v.)** -- to complain without good reason

0581 -- **cavort (v.)** -- to jump, move or run excitedly

0582 -- **cede (v.)** -- to unwillingly give up your rights, etc.

0583 -- **celestial (n.)** -- outer space

0584 -- **certitude (n.)** -- certainty

0585 -- **cessation (n.)** -- pause

0586 -- **cesspit (n.)** -- drain | gathering of dishonest people

0587 -- **chaff (n./v.)** -- outer covering of seeds | to mock

0588 -- **chagrin (n.)** -- disappointment || related word: **chagrined (adj.)**

0589 -- **chamberlain (n.)** -- manager of king's home

0590 -- **chancy (adj.)** -- risky

0591 -- **changeover (n.)** -- switch from one thing to another

0592 -- **chant (n./v.)** -- hymn | to shout; to say prayer || related word: **chanting (n.)**

0593 -- **chaos (n.)** -- disorder

0594 -- **chaperone (n./v.)** -- caretaker | to act as a caretaker

0595 -- **char (v.)** -- to burn

0596 -- **charade (n.)** -- pretence

0597 -- **charisma (n.)** -- appealing personality || related words: **charismatic (adj.), charismatically (adv.)**

0598 -- **charlatan (n.)** -- con, imposter, fraud

0599 -- **charred (adj.)** -- completely burnt

0600 -- **charwoman (n.)** -- female servant

0601 -- **chary (adj.)** -- extremely cautious

0602 -- **chaste (adj.)** -- simple, innocent, or faithful || related word: **chastely (adv.)**

0603 -- **chasten (v.)** -- to clearly tell sb that they have done sth wrong

0604 -- **chastise (v.)** -- to punish or scold || related word: **chastisement (n.)**

0605 -- **chastity (n.)** -- faithfulness in married life

0606 -- **chattel (n.)** -- ownership of sth

0607 -- **chauvinism (n.)** -- a belief that no other country is better than your country || related words: **chauvinistic (adj.), chauvinistically (adv.), chauvinist (n.)**

0608 -- **checkered (chequered) (adj.)** -- having both successful and failing periods

0609 -- **cheeky (adj.)** -- rude || related words: **cheekily (adv.), cheekiness (n.)**

0610 -- **cheer (n./v.)** -- joyfulness | to be very happy || related words: **cheering (adj./n.), cheerful (adj.), cheerfully (adv.), cheerfulness (n.),**

0611 -- **cherish (v.)** -- to treasure

0612 -- **cherub (n.)** -- angel || related word: **cherubic (adj.)**

0613 -- **chic (adj.)** -- fashionable

0614 -- **chicanery (n.)** -- trick

0615 -- **chide (v.)** -- to scold

0616 -- **chime (n./v.)** -- ringing sound | to ring

0617 -- **chimera (n.)** -- daydream

0618 -- **chink (n./v.)** -- crack | to make a light ringing side

0619 -- **chirp (n./v.)** -- high short sound | to tweet; to speak cheerfully

0620 -- **chirpy (adj.)** -- cheerful || related words: **chirpily (adv.), chirpiness (n.)**

0621 -- **chiseled (chiselled) (adj.)** -- (of sb's face) very attractive

0622 -- **chivalrous (adj.)** -- courteous or polite || related words: **chivalrously (adv.), chivalry (n.)**

0623 -- **chivvy (v.)** -- to persuade sb to do sth promptly

0624 -- **choke (v.)** -- to suffocate, especially because of strong emotions || related word: **choked (adj.)**

0625 -- **chomp (v.)** -- to chew

0626 -- **chop (v.)** -- to cut or reduce

0627 -- **choppy (adj.)** -- irregular; not still

0628 -- **chore (n.)** -- task

0629 -- **chortle (n./v.)** -- loud laugh | to laugh loudly

0630 -- **chorus (n./v.)** -- singing group | to say or sing sth in group

0631 -- **chronic (adj.)** -- continual || related word: **chronically (adv.)**

0632 -- **chronicle (n./v.)** -- diary | to write diary || related word: **chronicler (n.)**

0633 -- **chubby (adj.)** -- slightly fat in an attractive way || related word: **chubbiness (n.)**

0634 -- **chuck (v.)** -- to throw

0635 -- **chuckle (n./v.)** -- quiet laugh | to laugh quietly

0636 -- **chug (v.)** -- to swallow

0637 -- **chum (n.)** -- friend

0638 -- **chummy (adj.)** -- sociable || related words: **chummily (adv.), chumminess (n.)**

0639 -- **chump (n.)** -- silly person

0640 -- **chunk (n.)** -- a piece or portion of sth

0641 -- **chunky (adj.)** -- thick, short and heavy

0642 -- **churlish (adj.)** -- bad-mannered || related words: **churlishly (adv.), churlishness (n.)**

0643 -- **churn (v.)** -- to stir up

0644 -- **cipher (n.)** -- code

0645 -- **circa (prep.)** -- roughly

0646 -- **circuitous (adj.)** -- roundabout || related word: **circuitously (adv.)**

0647 -- **circumlocution (n.)** -- language that is full of unnecessary words || related word: **circumlocutory (adj.)**

0648 -- **circumnavigate (v.)** -- to go around the world || related word: **circumnavigation (n.)**

0649 -- **circumscribe (v.)** -- to restrict freedom of sb | related word: **circumscription (n.)**

0650 -- **circumspect (adj.)** -- cautious || related words: **circumspectly (adv.), circumspection (n.)**

0651 -- **circumvent (v.)** -- to avoid or escape || related word: **circumvention (n.)**

0652 -- **citadel (n.)** -- strong castle

0653 -- **civvies (n.)** -- ordinary clothes

0654 -- **clack (n./v.)** -- short loud sound | to bang

0655 -- **clad (adj.)** -- wearing a particular dress

0656 -- **clairvoyance (n.)** -- the power of telling the future || related word: **clairvoyant (adj./n.)**

0657 -- **clamber (v.)** -- to move with difficulty

0658 -- **clammy (adj.)** -- unpleasantly moist

0659 -- **clamor (clamour) (n./v.)** -- loud shout | to shout loudly || related word: **clamorous (adj.)**

0660 -- **clampdown (n.)** -- crack down

0661 -- **clan (n.)** -- large family

0662 -- **clandestine (adj.)** -- done in a secret way

0663 -- **clang (n./v.)** -- ringing sound | to make a ringing sound

0664 -- **clanger (n.)** -- a mistake that can easily be noticed

0665 -- **clank (n./v.)** -- loud and sharp sound | to make a loud and sharp sound

0666 -- **clasp (n./v.)** -- tight hold | to hold sth strongly

0667 -- **classy (adj.)** -- of high quality

0668 -- **clatter (n./v.)** -- loud noise that originates when two thing knocks together | (of two objects) to knock and make a noise

0669 -- **cleanse (v.)** -- to purify

0670 -- **cleave (v.)** -- to cut or split; to stick

0671 -- **cleft (n.)** -- crack

0672 -- **clement (adj.)** -- pleasant

0673 -- **clench (v.)** -- to press tightly

0674 -- **cliché (n.)** -- a boring phrase || related word: **clichéd (adj.)**

0675 -- **clime (n.)** -- a region with particular type of climate

0676 -- **clinch (n./v.)** -- embrace | to settle; to be successful

0677 -- **clincher (n.)** -- sth that is used to end an argument

0678 -- **cling (v.)** -- to adhere or hold

0679 -- **clink (n./v.)** -- sharp ringing sound | to make a sharp ringing sound

0680 -- **clique (n.)** -- a group of particular type of people || related word: **cliquey (adj.)**

0681 -- **cloak (n./v.)** -- cover | to cover || related word: **cloaked (adj.)**

0682 -- **clobber (n./v.)** -- clothes and other objects of a particular person | to defeat or hit

0683 -- **clod (n.)** -- silly person | a lump of earth

0684 -- **cloistered (adj.)** -- safe; sheltered

0685 -- **clout (n./v.)** -- power | to hit sb with your hand

0686 -- **clown (n./v.)** -- entertainer | to entertain sb with your way of behaving || related word: **clownish (adj.)**

0687 -- **cloy (v.)** -- to be too sweet || related word: **cloying (adj.), cloyingly (adv.)**

0688 -- **clump (n./v.)** -- a group of things that are very close to each other; sound of heavy steps | to form a group; to walk with heavy steps

0689 -- **clumsy (adj.)** -- awkward || related words: **clumsily (adv.), clumsiness (n.)**

0690 -- **clunk (n./v.)** -- sound of crash | to hit with loud sound

0691 -- **clunker (n.)** -- big mistake

0692 -- **clunky (adj.)** -- awkward and weighty

0693 -- **clutter (n./v.)** -- mess | to be untidy || related word: **cluttered (adj.)**

0694 -- **coalesce (v.)** -- to join together || related word: **coalescence (n.)**

0695 -- **coax (v.)** -- to persuade || related word: **coaxing (n.)**

0696 -- **cobble (v.)** -- to repair shoes || related word: **cobbler (n.)**

0697 -- **cocky (adj.)** -- very proud || related word: **cockiness (n.)**

0698 -- **cod (adj.)** -- unreal

0699 -- **coddle (v.)** -- to care about sb too much

0700 -- **codify (v.)** -- to arrange sth into a system || related word: **codification (n.)**

0701 -- **coerce (v.)** -- to frighten || related words: **coercive (adj.), coercion (n.)**

0702 -- **coffer (n.)** -- treasury

0703 -- **cogent (adj.)** -- logical || related words: **cogently (adv.), cogency (n.)**

0704 -- **cogitate (n.)** -- to think in a careful way || related word: **cogitation (n.)**

0705 -- **cognition (n.)** -- the process of developing knowledge

0706 -- **cognitive (adj.)** -- related to understanding || related words: **cognizance (n.), cognizant (n.)**

0707 -- **cognoscenti (n.)** -- an expert of a particular subject

0708 -- **cohabit (v.)** -- to live together || related word: **cohabitation (n.)**

0709 -- **cohere (v.)** -- to work or fit together; to be consistent || related words: **coherent (adj.), coherently (adv.), coherence (n.)**

0710 -- **cohesion (n.)** -- consistency | unity || related words: **cohesive (adj.), cohesiveness (n.)**

0711 -- **cohort (n.)** -- a group

0712 -- **coincide (v.)** -- to happen at the same time, especially in a surprising way; to concur || related words: **coincident (adj.), coincidental (adj.), coincidentally (adv.), coincidence (n.)**

0713 -- **collaborate (v.)** -- to work together || related words: **collaborative (adj.), collaboratively (adv.), collaboration (n.), collaborator (n.)**

0714 -- **collate (v.)** -- to collect facts about sb/sth || related word: **collation (n.)**

0715 -- **collateral (adj./n.)** -- additional | guarantee

0716 -- **colloquial (adj.)** -- (of speech) informal || related words: **colloquially (adv.), colloquialism (n.)**

0717 -- **colloquium (n.)** -- conference

0718 -- **colloquy (n.)** -- conversation

0719 -- **collude (v.)** -- to conspire || related words: **collusive (adj.), collusion (n.)**

0720 -- **colossal (adj.)** -- very large in size || related word: **colossus (n.)**

0721 -- **comestible (adj./n.)** -- edible | food

0722 -- **comeuppance (n.)** -- punishment that sb deserves

0723 -- **comfy (adj.)** -- secure; comfortable

0724 -- **commemorate (v.)** -- to remember sb from the past || related words: **commemorative (adj.), commemoration (n.)**

0725 -- **commend (v.)** -- to praise || related words: **commendable (adj.), commendation (n.)**

0726 -- **commensurate (adj.)** -- appropriate || related word: **commensurately (adv.)**

0727 -- **commiserate (v.)** -- to express sympathy: to console || related word: **commiseration (n.)**

0728 -- **communal (adj.)** -- shared || related words: **communally (adv.), communalism (n.)**

0729 -- **commune (n.)** -- community

0730 -- **communion (n.)** -- close relationship

0731 -- **communiqué (n.)** -- official message

0732 -- **commute (n./v.)** -- regular journey | to travel regularly

0733 -- **compassion (n.)** -- kindness || related words: **compassionate (adj.), compassionately (adv.)**

0734 -- **compatible (adj.)** -- well-suited || related word: **compatibly (adv.)**

0735 -- **compendium (n.)** -- a collection of various information in a book

0736 -- **complacent (adj.)** -- self-contented || related word: **complacently (adv.)**

0737 -- **complaisant (adj.)** -- obedient || related word: **complaisance (n.)**

0738 -- **complement (n./v.)** -- a thing that is used to improve sth else | to add new quality to sth || related word: **complementary (adj.)**

0739 -- **complication (n.)** -- new and difficult problem: hurdle

0740 -- **complicit (adj.)** -- involved in doing sth wrong || related word: **complicity (n.)**

0741 -- **compliment (n./v.)** -- praise | to praise || related word: **complimentary (adj.)**

0742 -- **comply (v.)** -- to obey

0743 -- **comport (v.)** -- to behave in a particular way || related word: **comportment (n.)**

0744 -- **composed (n.)** -- calm and quiet

0745 -- **composite (adj.)** -- combined

0746 -- **comprehend (v.)** -- to understand or realize || related words: **comprehensible (adj.), comprehension (n.), comprehensibility (n.)**

0747 -- **comprehensive (adj.)** -- complete || related word: **comprehensively (adv.)**

0748 -- **compulsive (adj.)** -- uncontrollable || related word: **compulsively (adv.)**

0749 -- **compunction (n.)** -- guilt

0750 -- **con (n./v.)** -- trick, trap or scam | to trick

0751 -- **concatenation (n.)** -- well-linked things

0752 -- **conceal (v.)** -- to hide || related word: **concealment (n.)**

0753 -- **concede (v.)** -- to give up; to accept your defeat

0754 -- **conceit (n.)** -- pride || related words: **conceited (adj.), conceitedly (adv.)**

0755 -- **conceive (v.)** -- to believe or imagine || related words: **conceivable (adj.), conceivably (adv.)**

0756 -- **conception (n.)** -- start; formation

0757 -- **conceptualize (v.)** -- to make an idea || related words: **conceptual (adj.), conceptually (adv.)**

0758 -- **concessionaire (n.)** -- sb who gets concession in business to sell a product, service, etc. || related word: **concessionary (adj.)**

0759 -- **concierge (n.)** -- gatekeeper

0760 -- **conciliate (v.)** -- to calm down || related words: **conciliatory (adj.), conciliation (n.)**

0761 -- **conciliator (n.)** -- mediator

0762 -- **conclave (n.)** -- gathering

0763 -- **concoct (v.)** -- to fabricate or mix || related word: **concoction (n.)**

0764 -- **concomitant (adj./n.)** -- associated | two or more things that happens at the same time

0765 -- **concord (n.)** -- peace

0766 -- **concourse (n.)** -- open space

0767 -- **concur (v.)** -- to agree; to correspond; to coexist || related words: **concurrent (adj.), concurrently (adv.), concurrence (n.),**

0768 -- **concuss (v.)** -- to forcefully hit on the head || related word: **concussed (adj.)**

0769 -- **condescend (v.)** -- to be very proud of yourself || related word: **condescending (adj.), condescension (n.)**

0770 -- **condign (adj.)** -- (of punishment) appropriate

0771 -- **condone (v.)** -- to overlook

0772 -- **conducive (adj.)** -- helpful

0773 -- **conduit (n.)** -- medium or way; means

0774 -- **confabulation (n.)** -- conversation

0775 -- **confederate (n.)** -- an associate in doing sth illegal || related word: **confederacy (n.)**

0776 -- **confer (v.)** -- to give sb an honor or award || related word: **conferment (n.)**

0777 -- **confess (v.)** -- to plead guilty

0778 -- **confetti (n.)** -- small pieces of colored paper

0779 -- **confide (v.)** -- to tell secret to sb || related word: **confidant (n.)**

0780 -- **configuration (n.)** -- pattern

0781 -- **confine (v.)** -- to imprison or restrict || related words: **confined (adj.), confinement (n.)**

0782 -- **confiscate (v.)** -- to take possession of sth || related word: **confiscation (n.)**

0783 -- **conflagration (n.)** -- a large fire

0784 -- **conflate (v.)** -- to merge || related word: **conflation (n.)**

0785 -- **conflicted (adj.)** -- confused

0786 -- **confluence (n.)** -- coming together; meeting

0787 -- **conform (v.)** -- to comply; to do the expected things || related words: **conformable (adj.), conformability (n.), conformist (n.)**

0788 -- **conformation (n.)** -- structure of an animal

0789 -- **confound (v.)** -- to confuse

0790 -- **confront (v.)** -- to deal with sb/sth || related words: **confrontational (adj.), confrontation (n.)**

0791 -- **congeal (v.)** -- to coagulate

0792 -- **congenial (adj.)** -- friendly

0793 -- **congenital (adj.)** -- inherited || related word: **congenitally (adv.)**

0794 -- **conglomerate (n.)** -- large firm or corporation

0795 -- **conglomeration (n.)** -- mixture or collection

0796 -- **congregate (v.)** -- to assemble || related words: **congregational (adj.), congregation (n.)**

0797 -- **congruent (adj.)** -- fitting or similar || related word: **congruence (n.)**

0798 -- **conjecture (n./v.)** -- guess | to guess || related word: **conjectural (adj.)**

0799 -- **conjoin (v.)** -- to be next to sth

0800 -- **conjugal (adj.)** -- marital

0801 -- **conjure (v.)** -- to perform tricks connected with appearance or disappearance of sth || related words: **conjuring (n.), conjuror (n.)**

0802 -- **connive (v.)** -- to conspire || related word: **conniving (adj.)**

0803 -- **connoisseur (n.)** -- specialist

0804 -- **connote (v.)** -- to indicate more than one meaning || related word: **connotation (n.)**

0805 -- **conquer (v.)** -- to defeat or overpower || related words: **conqueror (n.), conquest (n.)**

0806 -- **consanguinity (n.)** -- relationship by birth in a particular family

0807 -- **conscientious (adj.)** -- careful || related words: **conscientiously (adv.), conscientiousness (n.)**

0808 -- **conscript (n./v.)** -- sb who has been recruited in the armed forces | to recruit sb in the armed forces || related word: **conscription (n.)**

0809 -- **consecrate (v.)** -- to make holy || related word: **consecration (n.)**

0810 -- **consequent (adj.)** -- resulting || related words: **consequential (adj.), consequentially (adv.), consequently (adv.)**

0811 -- **considerate (adj.)** -- thoughtful || related words: **considerately (adv.), consideration (n.)**

0812 -- **consign (v.)** -- to deliver || related word: **consignment (n.)**

0813 -- **consolidate (v.)** -- to strengthen || related word: **consolidation (n.)**

0814 -- **consonance (n.)** -- agreement

0815 -- **consort (n./v.)** -- spouse of a ruler | to spend time with people who involves in immoral or illegal activities

0816 -- **consortium (n.)** -- group

0817 -- **conspicuous (adj.)** -- noticeable || related words: **conspicuously (adv.), conspicuousness (n.)**

0818 -- **constellation (n.)** -- a group of similar things, especially stars

0819 -- **consternation (n.)** -- anxiety

0820 -- **constrain (v.)** -- to control, force or restrict || related words: **constrained (adj.), constraint (n.)**

0821 -- **constrict (v.)** -- to tighten || related words: **constricted (adj.). constriction (n.)**

0822 -- **construe (v.)** -- to interpret

0823 -- **consul (n.)** -- diplomat || related word: **consular (adj.)**

0824 -- **consummate (adj.)** -- expert, perfect || related words: **consummately (adv.), consummation (n.)**

0825 -- **contagion (n.)** -- infection || related words: **contagious (adj.), contagiously (adv.)**

0826 -- **contaminate (v.)** -- to pollute || related word: **contamination (n.)**

0827 -- **contemplate (v.)** -- to consider || related word: **contemplation (n.)**

0828 -- **contemporary (adj.)** -- belonging to the same or present time

0829 -- **contemptuous (adj.)** -- disapproving || related word: **contemptuously (adv.)**

0830 -- **contend (v.)** -- to compete; to maintain || related word: **contender (n.)**

0831 -- **contention (n.)** -- serious disagreement; conflict || related word: **contentious (n.)**

0832 -- **contiguous (adj.)** -- bordering || related word: **congruity (n.)**

0833 -- **contingency (n.)** -- eventuality; emergency

0834 -- **contort (v.)** -- to twist sth out of its shape || related word: **contorted (adj.)**

0835 -- **contour (n.)** -- outline

0836 -- **contraband (n.)** -- smuggled goods

0837 -- **contravene (v.)** -- to do sth illegal; to disregard || related word: **contravention (n.)**

0838 -- **contretemps (n.)** -- argument or disagreement

0839 -- **contrite (adj.)** -- regretful || related words: **contritely (adv.), contrition (n.)**

0840 -- **contrivance (n.)** -- trick

0841 -- **contrive (v.)** -- to do sth in spite of difficulties

0842 -- **contrived (adj.)** -- artificial

0843 -- **controvert (v.)** -- to invalidate

0844 -- **contusion (n.)** -- bruise

0845 -- **conundrum (n.)** -- puzzle

0846 -- **convalesce (v.)** -- to recover || related words: **convalescent (adj.), convalescence (n.)**

0847 -- **convene (v.)** -- to organize || related word: **convener (n.)**

0848 -- **converge (v.)** -- to join; to congregate || related words: **convergent (adj.), convergence (n.)**

0849 -- **conversant (adj.)** -- familiar

0850 -- **converse (n./v.)** -- opposite | to discuss || related word: **conversely (adv.)**

0851 -- **conviction (n.)** -- determination or passion; confirmation of guilt

0852 -- **convivial (adj.)** -- friendly || related word: **conviviality (n.)**

0853 -- **convoke (v.)** -- to arrange for formal meeting || related word: **convocation (n.)**

0854 -- **convolution (n.)** -- complication || related word: **convoluted (adj.)**

0855 -- **convulse (v.)** -- to shake uncontrollably || related words: **convulsive (adj.), convulsively (adv.), convulsion (n.)**

0856 -- **coo (v.)** -- to say sth quietly

0857 -- **coop (n.)** -- cage

0858 -- **cope (v.)** -- to deal with sth complicated

0859 -- **copious (adj.)** -- plentiful || related word: **copiously (adv.)**

0860 -- **copout (n.)** -- escape

0861 -- **coquette (n.)** -- flirt || related words: **coquettish (adj.), coquettishly (adv.)**

0862 -- **cordial (adj.)** -- friendly || related words: **cordially (adv.), cordiality (n.)**

0863 -- **cordon (n.)** -- barricade

0864 -- **cornerstone (n.)** -- foundation

0865 -- **cornucopia (n.)** -- large amount

0866 -- **corollary (n.)** -- natural result

0867 -- **coronation (n.)** -- crown-ceremony

0868 -- **coroner (n.)** -- investigative officer who investigates sb's death

0869 -- **corporeal (adj.)** -- physical

0870 -- **corpus (n.)** -- a collection of texts

0871 -- **corral (v.)** -- to keep a group in a particular place

0872 -- **corroborate (v.)** -- to confirm or uphold || related words: **corroborative (adj.), corroboration (n.)**

0873 -- **corrode (v.)** -- to be destroyed by chemical action || related words: **corrosive (adj.), corrosion (n.)**

0874 -- **cortege (n.)** -- funeral procession

0875 -- **coruscate (v.)** -- to be very energetic || related words: **coruscating (adj.), coruscatingly (adv.)**

0876 -- **coterie (n.)** -- small group of like-minded people

0877 -- **couch (v.)** -- to express sth

0878 -- **countenance (n./v.)** -- expression of sb's face | to agree

0879 -- **counterfeit (n./v.)** -- fake | to make fake copy || related word: **counterfeiting (n.), counterfeiter (n.)**

0880 -- **counter-intuitive (adj.)** -- just opposite of something in an unexpected way || related word: **counter-intuitively (adv.)**

0881 -- **countermand (v.)** -- to cancel the order; to revoke

0882 -- **coup (n.)** -- action of taking over government of the country; rebellion

0883 -- **coup de grace (n.)** -- death blow

0884 -- **couture (n.)** -- tailoring

0885 -- **covenant (n./v.)** -- legal agreement connected with paying money | to have to pay money because of legal agreement

0886 -- **covet (v.)** -- to desire for sth that you have no right || related words: **covetous (adj.), covetousness (n.)**

0887 -- **cower (v.)** -- to move backwards

0888 -- **cozy (cosy) (adj./v.)** -- warm, pleasant and comfortable | to behave in a friendly way || related words: **cozily (adv.), coziness (n.)**

0889 -- **crackpot (adj./n.)** -- crazy | crazy person

0890 -- **cradle (v.)** -- to hold in hand

0891 -- **crafty (adj.)** -- cunning || related words: **craftily (adv.), craftiness (n.)**

0892 -- **craggy (adj.)** -- with strong facial expressions

0893 -- **cram (v.)** -- to enclose in small space || related word: **crammed (adj.)**

0894 -- **cramp (v.)** -- to restrict || related word: **cramped (adj.)**

0895 -- **crank (n.)** -- a person who has strange ideas or beliefs || related word: **cranky (adj.)**

0896 -- **cranny (n.)** -- gap

0897 -- **crass (adj.)** -- stupid || related words: **crassly (adv.), crassness (n.)**

0898 -- **crave (v.)** -- to desire || related word: **craving (n.)**

0899 -- **craven (adj.)** -- fearful || related word: **cravenly (adv.)**

0900 -- **creaky (adj.)** -- in bad condition because of being too old

0901 -- **credence (n.)** -- credibility

0902 -- **creditable (adj.)** -- respectable || related word: **creditably (adv.)**

0903 -- **credo (n.)** -- beliefs

0904 -- **credulous (adj.)** -- believing sth blindly || related word: **credulity (n.)**

0905 -- **creed (n.)** -- faith

0906 -- **creek (n.)** -- stream

0907 -- **creeping (adj.)** -- occurring in gradual and unnoticeable way

0908 -- **creepy (adj.)** -- frightening

0909 -- **crescendo (n.)** -- very loud noise

0910 -- **crestfallen (adj.)** -- disappointed

0911 -- **cretin (n.)** -- foolish person || related word: **cretinous (adj.)**

0912 -- **crib (v.)** -- to immorally or illegally copy sth

0913 -- **crimp (v.)** -- to crease; to restrict

0914 -- **cringe (v.)** -- to be embarrassed; to cower

0915 -- **crinkle (n./v.)** -- wrinkle | to be covered with wrinkles || related word: **crinkly (adj.)**

0916 -- **cripple (v.)** -- to make sb physically disabled || related word: **crippling (adj.)**

0917 -- **crone (n.)** -- old and ugly woman

0918 -- **crony (n.)** -- friend || related word: **cronyism (n.)**

0919 -- **crook (n./v.)** -- criminal | to bend finger

0920 -- **crooked (adj.)** -- dishonest || related word: **crookedly (adv.)**

0921 -- **croon (v.)** -- to sing in a quiet and gentle way

0922 -- **crouch (v.)** -- to bend your body || related word: **crouched (adj.)**

0923 -- **crud (n.)** -- unpleasant substance

0924 -- **cruddy (adv.)** -- of low quality

0925 -- **crude (adj.)** -- basic or natural | offensive || related words: **crudely (adv.), crudeness (n.), crudity (n.)**

0926 -- **crumb (n.)** -- small piece

0927 -- **crumble (v.)** -- to break into small pieces || related word: **crumbly (adv.)**

0928 -- **crummy (adj.)** -- worthless

0929 -- **crumple (v.)** -- to wrinkle || related word: **crumpled (adj.)**

0930 -- **crusade (n./v.)** -- campaign | to try to achieve sth in determined way || related word: **crusader (n.)**

0931 -- **crusty (adj./n.)** -- crisp | homeless person

0932 -- **cryptic (adj.)** -- mysterious; very strange || related word: **cryptically (adv.)**

0933 -- **cubicle (n.)** -- compartment

0934 -- **cuddle (n./v.)** -- hug or embrace | to hug or embrace

0935 -- **cudgel (n./v.)** -- stick | to hit with stick

0936 -- **culinary (adj.)** -- related to cooking

0937 -- **cull (n./v.)** -- killing of large number of animals of particular type | to kill large number of animals of particular type

0938 -- **culminate (v.)** -- to end or finish; to conclude || related word: **culmination (n.)**

0939 -- **culpable (adj.)** -- guilty || related words: **culpably (adv.), culpability (n.)**

0940 -- **cultivate (v.)** -- to grow plants; to develop particular way of behaving || related words: **cultivated (adj.), cultivation (n.), cultivator (n.)**

0941 -- **culvert (n.)** -- drain

0942 -- **curative (adj.)** -- remedial; medicinal

0943 -- **curb (n./v.)** -- restriction | to control sth illegal, immoral, etc.

0944 -- **curdle (v.)** -- to sour | to frighten

0945 -- **curmudgeon (n.)** -- old and irritating person || related word: **curmudgeonly (adj.)**

0946 -- **cursory (adj.)** -- brief || related word: **cursorily (adv.)**

0947 -- **curt (adj.)** -- impolite and sudden || related words: **curtly (adv.), curtness (n.)**

0948 -- **curtail (v.)** -- to restrict or limit || related word: **curtailment (n.)**

0949 -- **cushion (v.)** -- to reduce the effect of sth bad

0950 -- cushy (adj.) -- easy

0951 -- cusp (n.) -- a pointed end

0952 -- cuss (n./v.) -- curse | to curse

0953 -- cussed (adj.) -- obstinate || related words: **cussedly (adv.), cussedness (n.)**

0954 -- cynic (n.) -- a person who expects that bad things will happen or assumes everyone selfish || related words: **cynical (adj.), cynically (adv.), cynicism (n.)**

0955 -- cynosure (n.) -- very important person or thing

Difficult English Words -- D

0956 -- **dabble (v.)** -- to casually participate in an activity

0957 -- **daft (adj.)** -- stupid and funny || related word: **daftness (n.)**

0958 -- **dainty (adj.)** -- elegant || related words: **daintily (adv.),** **daintiness (n.)**

0959 -- **dally (v.)** -- to waste time || related word: **dalliance (n.)**

0960 -- **damnable (adj.)** -- irritating

0961 -- **damnation (n.)** -- being in or sending to hell || related word: **damned (adj./adv.)**

0962 -- **damning (adj.)** -- critical

0963 -- **damp (adj.)** -- moist || related words: **damply (adv.),** **dampness (n.)**

0964 -- **dampen (adj./n./v.)** -- wet | the condition of being wet | to make sth wet

0965 -- **damsel (n.)** -- unmarried woman

0966 -- **dandy (adj./n.)** -- excellent | a person who gives too much importance to his/her appearance

0967 -- **dangle (v.)** -- to hang loosely || related word: **dangly (adj.)**

0968 -- **dank (adj.)** -- moist; damp || related word: **dankness (n.)**

0969 -- **dapper (adj.)** -- well-dressed

0970 -- **dappled (adj.)** -- spotted

0971 -- **daredevil (adj./n.)** -- wicked | unreasonably bold

0972 -- **daring (adj./n.)** -- brave | willingness || related word: **daringly (adv.)**

0973 -- **dart (v.)** -- to rush

0974 -- **dashing (adj.)** -- attractive; stylish

0975 -- **dastardly (adj.)** -- wicked

0976 -- **daub (v.)** -- to smear

0977 -- **daunt (v.)** -- to frighten || related words: **daunting (adj.),** **dauntingly (adv.)**

0978 -- **dauntless (adj.)** -- determined

0979 -- **dawdle (v.)** -- to delay

0980 -- **dawn (n./v.)** -- sunrise | (of the sun) to rise

0981 -- **dazed (adj.)** -- confused

0982 -- **dazzle (v.)** -- to get confused because of bright light | to impress || related words: **dazzling (adj.), dazzlingly (adv.)**

0983 -- **de facto (adj.)** -- in effect

0984 -- **de jure (adj./adv.)** -- by law

0985 -- **deadbeat (n.)** -- a worthless person

0986 -- **deaden (v.)** -- to make a feeling, etc. less intense; to reduce || related word: **deadening (adj.)**

0987 -- **deadlock (n.)** -- stalemate || related word: **deadlocked (adj.)**

0988 -- **deadpan (adj.)** -- expressionless

0989 -- **debacle (n.)** -- disaster

0990 -- **debar (v.)** -- to prohibit

0991 -- **debase (v.)** -- to humiliate; to devalue || related word: **debasement (n.)**

0992 -- **debauchery (n.)** -- sin

0993 -- **debilitate (v.)** -- to weaken sb physically or mentally || related word: **debility (n.)**

0994 -- **debonair (adj.)** -- stylish

0995 -- **debrief (v.)** -- to officially ask questions || related word: **debriefing (n.)**

0996 -- **debunk (v.)** -- to expose true character of sth

0997 -- **debut (n./v.)** -- first public appearance | to make first public appearance

0998 -- decadence (n.) -- wickedness, corruptness || related word: **decadent (adj.)**

0999 -- decamp (v.) -- to escape

1000 -- decapitate (v.) -- to behead || related word: **decapitation (n.)**

1001 -- decimate (v.) -- to kill or destroy || related word: **decimation (n.)**

1002 -- decipher (v.) -- to decode

1003 -- declamation (n.) -- formal or strong expression of your opinions

1004 -- declutter (v.) -- to remove unnecessary or useless things from home, etc.

1005 -- decommission (v.) -- to stop using weapons of mass destruction: to ban nuclear power station

1006 -- deconsecrate (v.) -- to no longer use a building for religious activities || related words: **deconsecrating (adj.), deconsecration (n.)**

1007 -- decorous (adj.) -- well-mannered || related word: **decorously (adv.)**

1008 -- decorum (n.) -- good behavior

1009 -- decoy (n.) -- a person, thing, etc that is used to trap

1010 -- decree (n./v.) -- ruling | to give an official order

1011 -- decrepit (adj.) -- old and weak || related word: **decrepitude (n.)**

1012 -- decry (v.) -- to criticize severely

1013 -- deduce (v.) -- to assume || related word: **deducible (n.)**

1014 -- deface (v.) -- to ruin the appearance || related word: **defacement (n.)**

1015 -- defame (v.) -- to damage sb's reputation

1016 -- defer (v.) -- to postpone

1017 -- defiant (adj.) -- disobedient || related word: **defiantly (adv.)**

1018 -- definitive (adj.) -- perfect and unchangeable || related word: **definitively (adv.)**

1019 -- **deflate (v.)** -- to devalue; to collapse || related words: **deflationary (adj.), deflation (n.)**

1020 -- **deflect (v.)** -- to turn away; to suddenly change direction; to avert || related word: **deflection (n.)**

1021 -- **defoliate (v.)** -- to destroy leaves || related word: **defoliation (n.)**

1022 -- **defraud (v.)** -- to cheat

1023 -- **defray (v.)** -- to pay the owed amount

1024 -- **defrock (v.)** -- to remove a priest from his duty

1025 -- **deft (adj.)** -- skillful || related words: **deftly (adv.), deftness (n.)**

1026 -- **defunct (adj.)** -- outdated

1027 -- **defy (v.)** -- to disobey

1028 -- **degrade (v.)** -- to humiliate || related word: **degrading (adj.)**

1029 -- **deify (v.)** -- to treat a particular person as a god || related word: **deification (n.)**

1030 -- **deign (v.)** -- to not give respect to sb; to behave arrogantly

1031 -- **dejected (adj.)** -- very unhappy and without hope || related words: **dejectedly (adv.), dejection (n.)**

1032 -- **delectable (adj.)** -- very tasty

1033 -- **delectation (n.)** -- feeling of extreme pleasure

1034 -- **deleterious (adj.)** -- deadly

1035 -- **delineate (v.)** -- to outline; to explain || related word: **delineation (n.)**

1036 -- **delinquency (n.)** -- wrongdoing || related word: **delinquent (adj./n.)**

1037 -- **delirious (adj.)** -- restless and excited || related words: **deliriously (adv.), delirium (n.)**

1038 -- **deliverance (n.)** -- rescue

1039 -- **deluge (n./v.)** -- flood | to flood

1040 -- **delve (v.)** -- to try to find out sth in a bag, etc.

1041 -- **demagogue (n.)** -- cunning leader || related words: **demagogic (adj.), demagogy (n.)**

1042 -- **demean (v.)** -- to humiliate || related word: **demeaning (adj.)**

1043 -- **demeanor (demeanour) (n.)** -- a particular type of behavior

1044 -- **demimonde (n.)** -- odd people

1045 -- **demobilize (v.)** -- to dismiss sb from armed forces || related word: **demobilization (n.)**

1046 -- **demonize (v.)** -- to ruin sb's reputation || related word: **demonization (n.)**

1047 -- **demur (v.)** -- to object

1048 -- **demure (adj.)** -- modest || related word: **demurely (adv.)**

1049 -- **demystify (v.)** -- to explain about a complicated thing || related word: **demystification (n.)**

1050 -- **denigrate (v.)** -- to insult || related word: **denigration (n.)**

1051 -- **denizen (n.)** -- native

1052 -- **denomination (n.)** -- a unit to measure money

1053 -- **denouement (n.)** -- conclusion

1054 -- **denounce (v.)** -- to severely criticize sb for sth wrong they have done || related word: **denunciation (n.)**

1055 -- **denude (v.)** -- to uncover

1056 -- **deplete (v.)** -- to reduce or exhaust; to diminish || related word: **depletion (n.)**

1057 -- **deplorable (adj.)** -- shocking || related word: **deplorably (adv.)**

1058 -- **deplore (v.)** -- to condemn sb in public

1059 -- **deploy (v.)** -- to send soldiers for military action | to make effective use of sth || related word: **deployment (n.)**

1060 -- **deport (v.)** -- to expel || related words: **deportation (n.), deportee (n.)**

1061 -- deportment (n.) -- your way of behaving

1062 -- depose (v.) -- to overthrow a ruler

1063 -- deposition (n.) -- formal statement in court | removal of ruler

1064 -- deprave (v.) -- to degrade, to make sb evil || related words: **depraved (adj.), depravity (n.)**

1065 -- deprecate (v.) -- to severely criticize || related words: **deprecating (adj.), deprecatingly (adv.)**

1066 -- depredation (n.) -- destructive act

1067 -- deprive (v.) -- to prevent sb from having sth

1068 -- deprived (adj.) -- disadvantaged; poor

1069 -- depute (v.) -- to assign

1070 -- deracinate (v.) -- to make sth feel very uncomfortable || related word: **deracinated (adj.), deracination (n.)**

1071 -- deranged (adj.) -- suffering from mental illness; crazy || related word: **derangement (n.)**

1072 -- derelict (n.) -- neglected person || related word: **dereliction (n.)**

1073 -- deride (v.) -- to make fun of sb; to laugh at sb || related words: **derisive (adj.), derisory (adj.), derision (n.)**

1074 -- derogatory (adj.) -- insulting; offensive

1075 -- derring-do (n.) -- bold actions

1076 -- descry (v.) -- to see sb/sth in a sudden way

1077 -- desecrate (v.) -- to disrespect a holy thing or place || related word: **desecration (n.)**

1078 -- desensitize (v.) -- to make sb unaware of sth || related word: **desensitization (n.)**

1079 -- desist (v.) -- to cease to do sth

1080 -- desolate (adj./v.) -- isolated; unhappy | to make sb hopeless || related word: **desolation (n.)**

1081 -- desperado (n.) -- wrongdoer; criminal

1082 -- despicable (adj.) -- horrible

1083 -- despise (v.) -- to hate

1084 -- despoil (v.) -- to ruin a place

1085 -- despondent (adj.) -- hopeless || related words: **despondently (adv.), despondency (n.)**

1086 -- despot (n.) -- dictator || related word: **despotic (adj.)**

1087 -- destitute (adj.) -- without money, food, etc. || related word: **destitution (n.)**

1088 -- desultory (adj.) -- aimless || related word: **desultorily (adv.)**

1089 -- deter (v.) -- to discourage or restrain || related word: **deterrent (n.)**

1090 -- detest (v.) -- to hate || related words: **detestable (adj.), detestation (n.)**

1091 -- detour (n./v.) -- bypass || to move using bypass

1092 -- detriment (n.) -- damage || related word: **detrimental (adj.)**

1093 -- detritus (n.) -- garbage

1094 -- deviate (v.) -- to do abnormal or unusual activities || related words: **deviant (adj./n.), deviance (n.), deviancy (n.)**

1095 -- devilishly (adv.) -- extremely

1096 -- devious (adj.) -- deceitful || related words: **deviously (adv.), deviousness (n.)**

1097 -- devise (v.) -- to invent

1098 -- devolution (n.) -- the act of transferring authority from higher to lower level || related word: **devolved (adj.)**

1099 -- devour (v.) -- to consume | to destruct

1100 -- devout (adj.) -- religious || related word: **devoutly (adv.)**

1101 -- dexterity (n.) -- handiness || related words: **dexterous (adj.), dexterously (adv.)**

1102 -- diabolical (adj.) -- too bad || related word: **diabolically (adv.)**

1103 -- **diametrically (adv.)** -- entirely

1104 -- **diatribe (n.)** -- critical speech

1105 -- **dicey (adj.)** -- risky; unsafe

1106 -- **didactic (adj.)** -- educational || related word: **didactically (adv.)**

1107 -- **diddle (v.)** -- to deceive, trick or cheat sb

1108 -- **diehard (adj.)** -- having traditional views

1109 -- **diffident (adj.)** -- introvert and shy || related words: **diffidently (adv.), diffidence (n.)**

1110 -- **digress (v.)** -- to deviate from the topic you were talking about || related word: **digression (n.)**

1111 -- **dilapidated (adj.)** -- neglected || related word: **dilapidation (n.)**

1112 -- **dilate (v.)** -- to expand || related word: **dilation (n.)**

1113 -- **dilatory (adj.)** -- negligent; delaying

1114 -- **diligence (n.)** -- attentiveness; hard-work || related words: **diligent (adj.), diligently (adv.)**

1115 -- **dilly-dally (v.)** -- to delay

1116 -- **diminish (v.)** -- to decrease; to weaken; to lower

1117 -- **din (n.)** -- noise

1118 -- **ding (v.)** -- to chime

1119 -- **dingy (adj.)** -- dirty || related word: **dinginess (n.)**

1120 -- **dire (adj.)** -- terrible

1121 -- **disapprobation (n.)** -- condemnation; disapproval

1122 -- **disarming (adj.)** -- pleasant || related word: **disarmingly (adv.)**

1123 -- **disarrange (v.)** -- to mess up; to spoil

1124 -- **disarray (n.)** -- big confusion

1125 -- **disband (v.)** -- to separate || related word: **disbandment (n.)**

1126 -- **disbar (n.)** -- to ban a lawyer

1127 -- **discern (v.)** -- to determine || related word: **discernible (adj.)**

1128 -- **discerning (adj.)** -- judicious || related word: **discernment (n.)**

1129 -- **discomfit (v.)** -- to humiliate || related word: **discomfiture (n.)**

1130 -- **disconcert (v.)** -- to displease or disturb || related words: **disconcerted (adj.), disconcerting (adj.), disconcertingly (adv.)**

1131 -- **discontent (n.)** -- disappointment or dissatisfaction || related words: **discontented (adj.), discontentedly (adv.)**

1132 -- **discord (n.)** -- dispute

1133 -- **discordant (adj.)** -- without being in agreement; inharmonious

1134 -- **discourse (n.)** -- serious dialogue

1135 -- **discredit (n./v.)** -- disgrace | to disgrace || related word: **discreditable (adj.)**

1136 -- **discreet (adj.)** -- cautious; thoughtful || related word: **discreetly (adv.)**

1137 -- **discrepancy (n.)** -- disagreement

1138 -- **discursive (adj.)** -- not following particular pattern

1139 -- **disdain (n./v.)** -- disregard | to disrespect or mock || related words: **disdainful (adj.), disdainfully (adv.)**

1140 -- **disembark (v.)** -- to get off || related word: **disembarkation (n.)**

1141 -- **disembodied (adj.)** -- ghostly

1142 -- **disenchanted (adj.)** -- very sad and disappointed || related word: **disenchantment (n.)**

1143 -- **disenfranchise (v.)** -- to take away sb's right to cast vote

1144 -- **disgorge (v.)** -- to eject

1145 -- **disgruntled (adj.)** -- very unhappy

1146 -- **disheveled (dishevelled) (adj.)** -- untidy; messy

1147 -- **disillusion (v.)** -- to dishearten; to disappoint || related word: **disillusioned (adj.)**

1148 -- **disinclination (n.)** -- unwillingness || related word: **disinclined (adj.)**

1149 -- **disinformation (n.)** -- false information

1150 -- **disingenuous (adj.)** -- insincere; deceitful || related word: **disingenuously (adv.)**

1151 -- **disintegrate (adj.)** -- to break; to destroy || related words: **disintegrated (adj.), disintegration (n.)**

1152 -- **disinter (v.)** -- to dig up

1153 -- **disjointed (adj.)** -- disorganized; unsystematic

1154 -- **dislodge (v.)** -- to displace

1155 -- **dismal (adj.)** -- miserable || related word: **dismally (adv.)**

1156 -- **dismantle (v.)** -- to destroy sth in systematic way | to take apart a machine into pieces || related word: **dismantling (n.)**

1157 -- **dismay (n./v.)** -- shock and disappointment | to shock or disappoint || related word: **dismayed (adj.)**

1158 -- **dismember (v.)** -- to cut up dead body | to divide a region || related word: **dismemberment (n.)**

1159 -- **dismissive (adj.)** -- rude; mocking || related word: **dismissively (adv.)**

1160 -- **dismount (v.)** -- to get down from horse, cycle, etc.

1161 -- **disorientate (v.)** -- to confuse || related words: **disorientated (adj.), disorientation (n.)**

1162 -- **disparage (v.)** -- to mock; to demean || related words: **disparaging (adj.), disparagingly (adv.), disparagement (n.)**

1163 -- **disparate (adj.)** -- unrelated

1164 -- **disparity (n.)** -- inequality

1165 -- **dispassionate (adj.)** -- calm and unbiased || related word: **dispassionately (adv.)**

1166 -- **dispel (v.)** -- to make a feeling disappear

1167 -- **dispensable (adj.)** -- unnecessary

1168 -- **dispensation (n.)** -- action of providing sth | political or religious system

1169 -- dispense (v.) -- to provide

1170 -- disposal (n.) -- sale of assets | throwing away

1171 -- dispose (v.) -- to organize | to influence sb's behavior

1172 -- disposed (adj.) -- likely | having a particular opinion about sb/sth

1173 -- disposition (n.) -- character or personality; arrangement

1174 -- disquiet (n.) -- unrest || related word: **disquieting (adj.)**

1175 -- disquisition (n.) -- long speech or text

1176 -- disregard (n./v.) -- insult | to pay no heed to sb/sth

1177 -- disrobe (v.) -- to undress

1178 -- disrupt (v.) -- to disturb || related words: **disruptive (adj.), disruption (n.)**

1179 -- disseminate (v.) -- to make sth public || related word: **dissemination (n.)**

1180 -- dissent (v.) -- to disagree || related word: **dissension (n.)**

1181 -- dissenter (n.) -- a rebel

1182 -- dissident (adj./n.) -- opposing the government | protester || related word: **dissidence (n.)**

1183 -- dissimulate (v.) -- to not let sb know your real feelings || related word: **dissimulation (n.)**

1184 -- dissipate (v.) -- to waste | to make sth disappear gradually || related word: **dissipation (n.)**

1185 -- dissipated (adj.) -- indulged in harmful activities

1186 -- dissolute (adj.) -- immoral

1187 -- dissolution (n.) -- ending

1188 -- dissonance (n.) -- disagreement || related word: **dissonant (adj.)**

1189 -- dissuade (v.) -- to discourage

1190 -- distend (v.) -- to swell || related word: **distension (n.)**

1191 -- distil (v.) -- to clean || related word: **distillation (n.)**

1192 -- distort (v.) -- to make the facts untrue | to disfigure || related word: **distortion (n.)**

1193 -- distract (v.) -- to divert || related words: **distracting (adj.), distraction (n.)**

1194 -- distraught (adj.) -- extremely worried and upset

1195 -- distress (n./v.) -- disappointment; suffering | to bother || related words: **distressed (adj.), distressing (adj.), distressingly (adv.)**

1196 -- ditch (n.) -- to get rid of

1197 -- dither (n./v.) -- anxiety; hesitation | to hesitate

1198 -- ditty (n.) -- simple song

1199 -- diva (n.) -- opera singer

1200 -- diverge (v.) -- to depart || related words: **divergent (adj.), divergence (n.)**

1201 -- divest (v.) -- to get rid of

1202 -- divulge (v.) -- to tell the secret

1203 -- dizzy (adj.) -- faint || related words: **dizzying (adj.), dizzily (adv.), dizziness (n.)**

1204 -- docile (adj.) -- submissive; controllable || related words: **docilely (adv.), docility (n.)**

1205 -- docket (n.) -- list

1206 -- doctrine (n.) -- policy

1207 -- doddering (adj.) -- walking awkwardly

1208 -- doddle (n.) -- an easy task

1209 -- dodge (n./v.) -- dishonest trick | to avoid

1210 -- dodgy (adj.) -- deceitful; risky; bad

1211 -- doff (v.) -- to take off your hat

1212 -- dogfight (n.) -- struggle or fighting

1213 -- **dogged (adj.)** -- having strong character; determined || related words: **doggedly (adv.), doggedness (n.)**

1214 -- **dogma (n.)** -- strong and unreasonable belief || related words: **dogmatic (adj.), dogmatically (adv.), dogmatism (n.)**

1215 -- **doldrums (n.)** -- sadness; depression

1216 -- **dole (n.)** -- money for unemployed people

1217 -- **doleful (adj.)** -- unhappy || related word: **dolefully (adv.)**

1218 -- **dollop (n.)** -- lump of food

1219 -- **dolorous (adj.)** -- depressed

1220 -- **domesticate (v.)** -- to tame | to cultivate || related words: **domesticated (adj.), domestication (n.)**

1221 -- **dominion (n.)** -- control

1222 -- **doodle (v.)** -- to sketch

1223 -- **doom (n./v.)** -- devastation | to fail || related word: **doomy (adj.)**

1224 -- **doozy (n.)** -- unusual thing

1225 -- **dork (n.)** -- stupid person || related word: **dorky (adj.)**

1226 -- **doss (v.)** -- to waste time

1227 -- **dossier (n.)** -- file

1228 -- **doting (adj.)** -- loving

1229 -- **double-entendre (n.)** -- a phrase with double meaning

1230 -- **doublespeak (n.)** -- insincere talk

1231 -- **dour (adj.)** -- harsh || related word: **dourly (adv.)**

1232 -- **douse (v.)** -- to make sth wet | to extinguish a fire

1233 -- **dovetail (v.)** -- to join together

1234 -- **dowdy (adj.)** -- old-fashioned; boring

1235 -- **downbeat (adj.)** -- unenthusiastic; hopeless

1236 -- **downcast (adj.)** -- very sad

1237 -- **downplay (v.)** -- to not give much importance to sth

1238 -- **downright (adj./adv.)** -- complete | completely

1239 -- **downtown (n.)** -- city center

1240 -- **downtrodden (adj.)** -- oppressed

1241 -- **downturn (n.)** -- recession

1242 -- **doyen (n.)** -- the most respected person in a group

1243 -- **drab (adj.)** -- dull; colorless || related word: **drabness (n.)**

1244 -- **dragnet (n.)** -- extensive search for an unlawful person

1245 -- **drained (adj.)** -- exhausted; completely tired

1246 -- **drape (v.)** -- to wrap

1247 -- **draught (n.)** -- cool air

1248 -- **drawdown (n.)** -- reduction in supply

1249 -- **drawl (v.)** -- to use longer vowel sounds when saying sth

1250 -- **drawn (adj.)** -- weak and tired

1251 -- **dread (n./v.)** -- fear | to be extremely anxious; to afraid || related word: **dreaded (adj.)**

1252 -- **dreadful (n.)** -- fearful | extremely unpleasant

1253 -- **dreadfully (adv.)** -- in an extremely unpleasant way | extremely

1254 -- **dreary (adj.)** -- dull; depressing || related words: **drearily (adv.), dreariness (n.)**

1255 -- **drench (v.)** -- to completely soak sb/sth

1256 -- **dripping (adj.)** -- completely soaked/wet

1257 -- **drippy (adj.)** -- silly | that can fall in drops

1258 -- **drivel (n./v.)** -- nonsense | to talk nonsense

1259 -- **drizzle (n./v.)** -- light rain | to pour water in low quantity || related word: **drizzly (adv.)**

1260 -- **drool (v.)** -- to salivate

1261 -- **droop (v.)** -- to hang down; to become unhappy || related word: **droopy (adj.)**

1262 -- **drop-dead (adj.)** -- attractive

1263 -- **drove (n.)** -- herd

1264 -- drowsy (adj.) -- sleepy or tired || related words: **drowsily (adv.), drowsiness (n.)**

1265 -- drubbing (n.) -- defeat

1266 -- drudge (n.) -- sb who does boring or menial jobs || related word: **drudgery (n.)**

1267 -- dubious (adj.) -- doubtful or insincere || related word: **dubiously (adv.)**

1268 -- ducky (adj.) -- pleasant

1269 -- dud (adj./n.) -- failure | useless thing

1270 -- duff (adj.) -- ineffective

1271 -- dumbo (n.) -- silly person

1272 -- dunce (n.) -- foolish child

1273 -- dunk (v.) -- to dip

1274 -- dwell (v.) -- to settle or reside

1275 -- dwindle (v.) -- to decrease gradually

1276 -- dyslexia (n.) -- a mental disorder connected with reading and writing || related word: **dyslexic (adj./n.)**

Difficult English Words -- E

1277 -- **earmark (n./v.)** -- typical quality | to set sth aside

1278 -- **earnest (adj.)** -- sincere

1279 -- **eavesdrop (v.)** -- to overhear sth || related word: **eavesdropper (n .)**

1280 -- **ebullient (adj.)** -- cheerful || related words: **ebulliently (adv.), ebullience (n.)**

1281 -- **eccentric (adj./n.)** -- strange | odd person || related words: **eccentrically (adv.), eccentricity (n.)**

1282 -- **echelon (n.)** -- rank

1283 -- **eclectic (adj.)** -- diverse || related words: **eclectically (adv.), eclecticism (n.)**

1284 -- **ecstasy (n.)** -- delight || related words: **ecstatic (adj.), ecstatically (adv.)**

1285 -- **eddy (n./v.)** -- movement in circle | to spin

1286 -- **edgy (adj.)** -- nervous || related words: **edgily (adv.), edginess (n.)**

1287 -- **edict (n.)** -- law

1288 -- **edify (v.)** -- to educate; to provide information || related words: **edifying (adj.), edification (n.)**

1289 -- **eerie (adj.)** -- frightening || related words: **eerily (adv.), eeriness (n.)**

1290 -- **effeminate (adj.)** -- behaving like a girl || related word: **effeminacy (n.)**

1291 -- **effervescent (adj.)** -- lively || related word: **effervescence (n.)**

1292 -- **efficacious (adj.)** -- effective || related word: **efficacy (n.)**

1293 -- **effrontery (n.)** -- impudence

1294 -- **effulgent (adj.)** -- bright || related word: **effulgence (n.)**

1295 -- **effusive (adj.)** -- filled with emotions; very enthusiastic || related words: **effusively (adv.), effusion (n.)**

1296 -- **egalitarian (adj./n.)** -- believing in equality | supporter of equality || related word: **egalitarianism (n.)**

1297 -- **egregious (adj.)** -- too bad

1298 -- **egress (n.)** -- exit

1299 -- **ejaculate (v.)** -- to say something loudly

1300 -- **élan (n.)** -- style

1301 -- **elated (adj.)** -- delighted || related word: **elation (n.)**

1302 -- **elegant (adj.)** -- stylish || related words: **elegantly (adv.), elegance (n.)**

1303 -- **elegy (n.)** -- sad song || related word: **elegiac (adj.)**

1304 -- **elevate (v.)** -- to raise or lift || related words: **elevated (adj.), elevation (n.)**

1305 -- **elicit (v.)** -- to obtain || related word: **elicitation (n.)**

1306 -- **elite (adj./n.)** -- influential | group of powerful people || related words: **elitism (n.), elitist (adj./n.)**

1307 -- **elixir (n.)** -- a liquid having miraculous power

1308 -- **elongate (v.)** -- to increase the length || related words: **elongated (adj.), elongation (n.)**

1309 -- **elope (v.)** -- to run away with sb with an intention to get married

1310 -- **eloquent (adj.)** -- well-expressed || related words: **eloquently (adv.), eloquence (n.)**

1311 -- **elucidate (v.)** -- to explain || related word: **elucidation (n.)**

1312 -- **elude (v.)** -- to avoid sth cleverly

1313 -- **elusive (adj.)** -- obscure || related words: **elusively (adv.), elusiveness (n.)**

1314 -- **emaciated (adj.)** -- ill and weak || related word: **emaciation (n.)**

1315 -- **emanate (v.)** -- to originate || related word: **emanation (n.)**

1316 -- **emancipate (v.)** -- to free from legal restrictions || related words: **emancipated (adj.), emancipation (n.)**

1317 -- **emasculate (v.)** -- to reduce the power or energy || related word: **emasculation (n.)**

1318 -- **embalm (v.)** -- to preserve a dead body by using chemicals || related word: **embalmer (n.)**

1319 -- **embargo (n./v.)** -- official ban | to imposes an official ban

1320 -- **embark (v.)** -- to go on board || related word: **embarkation (n.)**

1321 -- **embattled (adj.)** -- under attack

1322 -- **embellish (v.)** -- to decorate || related word: **embellishment (n.)**

1323 -- **ember (n.)** -- ash

1324 -- **embezzle (v.)** -- to get money from your employer deceitfully || related word: **embezzlement (n.), embezzler (n.)**

1325 -- **embitter (v.)** -- to disappoint or irate sb || related word: **embittered (n.)**

1326 -- **emblazon (v.)** -- to decorate sth with noticeable items

1327 -- **emblem (n.)** -- symbol | perfect example || related word: **emblematic (adj.)**

1328 -- **embody (v.)** -- to represent | to possess || related word: **embodiment (n.)**

1329 -- **embolden (v.)** -- to encourage

1330 -- **emboss (v.)** -- to imprint || related word: **embossed (adj.)**

1331 -- **embroil (v.)** -- to involve in difficult situation

1332 -- **emend (v.)** -- to correct the mistakes in manuscript, etc. || related word: **emendation (n.)**

1333 -- **emetic (n.)** -- vomit-causing substance

1334 -- **emigrate (v.)** -- to go abroad || related word: **emigration (n.)**

1335 -- **eminence (n.)** -- importance and admiration; excellence || related word: **eminent (adj.)**

1336 -- emotive (adj.) -- emotional

1337 -- emphatic (adj.) -- forceful || related word: **emphatically (adv.)**

1338 -- empirical (adj.) -- practical || related word: **empirically (adv.)**

1339 -- emporium (n.) -- large shop

1340 -- emulate (v.) -- to follow; to assume sb as your role model || related word: **emulation (n.)**

1341 -- enamored (enamoured) (adj.) -- liking or loving sb/sth too much; charmed

1342 -- encamp (v.) -- to set a camp || related word: **encampment (n.)**

1343 -- encapsulate (v.) -- to summarize || related word: **encapsulation (n.)**

1344 -- encase (v.) -- to cover sth to keep it in safe condition

1345 -- enchant (v.) -- to delight or gladden | to put sb under magic spell || related words: **enchanted (adj.), enchanting (adj.), enchantingly (adv.), enchantment (n.), enchanter (n.), enchantress (n.)**

1346 -- enclave (n.) -- closed society

1347 -- encomium (n.) -- text or speech that is used to praise sb

1348 -- encroach (v.) -- to influence sb's right or time in an unacceptable way || to take over sb's land unlawfully || related word: **encroachment (n.)**

1349 -- encumber (v.) -- to prevent sb from making progress | to burden || related word: **encumbrance (n.)**

1350 -- endanger (v.) -- to put sb in dangerous situation

1351 -- endearing (adj.) -- charming or attractive || related words: **endearingly (adv.), endearment (n.)**

1352 -- endeavor (endeavour) (n./v.) -- great attempt | to make a great attempt

1353 -- endemic (adj.) -- widespread

1354 -- **endogamy (n.)** -- marriage that takes place within your community

1355 -- **endorse (v.)** -- to approve

1356 -- **endow (v.)** -- to award; to donate || related word: **endowment (n.)**

1357 -- **endure (v.)** -- to keep on continuing | to suffer sth painful || related word: **endurable (adj.)**

1358 -- **enduring (adj.)** -- continuing for a long time | related word: **enduringly (adv.)**

1359 -- **enervate (v.)** -- to weaken || related word: **enervation (n.)**

1360 -- **enfeeble (v.)** -- to weaken || related word: **enfeebled (adj.)**

1361 -- **enfranchise (v.)** -- to give right to vote || related word: **enfranchisement (n.)**

1362 -- **engaging (adj.)** -- attractive || related word: **engagingly (adv.)**

1363 -- **engender (v.)** -- to stimulate

1364 -- **engorge (v.)** -- to swell

1365 -- **engrave (v.)** -- to cut up metal, etc. to form a design; to carve || related words: **engraver (n.), engraving (n.)**

1366 -- **engross (v.)** -- to hold sb's attention || related words: **engrossed (adj.), engrossing (adj.)**

1367 -- **engulf (v.)** -- to cover sth wholly

1368 -- **enhance (v.)** -- to increase or improve || related words: **enhanced (adj.), enhancement (n.)**

1369 -- **enigma (n.)** -- riddle or mystery || related words: **enigmatic (adj.), enigmatically (adv.)**

1370 -- **enjoin (v.)** -- to instruct

1371 -- **enlighten (v.)** -- to explain clearly; to understand || related words: **enlightening (adj.), enlightened (adj.), enlightenment (n.)**

1372 -- **enliven (v.)** -- to add exciting qualities in sth

1373 -- **enmesh (v.)** -- to trap

1374 -- **ennui (n.)** -- boredom

1375 -- **enrage (v.)** -- to make sb full of anger

1376 -- **enrapture (v.)** -- to delight || related word: **enraptured (adj.)**

1377 -- **enrich (v.)** -- to make sb richer | to make sth better in quality || related word: **enrichment (n.)**

1378 -- **ensconce (v.)** -- to establish

1379 -- **ensemble (n.)** -- group

1380 -- **enshrine (v.)** -- to officially declare sth

1381 -- **enshroud (v.)** -- to cover sth wholly

1382 -- **ensnare (v.)** -- to trap

1383 -- **ensue (v.)** -- to follow || related word: **ensuing (adj.)**

1384 -- **entail (v.)** -- to involve as a necessary part of sth

1385 -- **entangle (v.)** -- to trap

1386 -- **entente (n.)** -- good relations

1387 -- **enthrall (enthral) (v.)** -- to delight or excite || related word: **enthralling (adj.)**

1388 -- **enthrone (v.)** -- to swear in as a king, queen, etc. || related word: **enthronement (adj.)**

1389 -- **entice (v.)** -- to tempt; to lure || related words: **enticing (adj.), enticingly (adv.), enticement (n.)**

1390 -- **entitle (v.)** -- to officially give sb the right for sth || related word: **entitlement (n.)**

1391 -- **entity (n.)** -- an individual unit

1392 -- **entomb (v.)** -- to bury

1393 -- **entourage (n.)** -- followers

1394 -- **entrails (n.)** -- intestinal parts

1395 -- **entrant (n.)** -- candidate

1396 -- **entrap (v.)** -- to capture illegally; to trap || related word: **entrapment (n.)**

1397 -- **entreat (v.)** -- to plead; to beg || related word: **entreaty (n.)**

1398 -- **entrench (v.)** -- to establish firmly || related word: **entrenchment (n.)**

1399 -- **entwine (v.)** -- to twist

1400 -- **enumerate (v.)** -- to list || related word: **enumeration (n.)**

1401 -- **enunciate (v.)** -- to express clearly || related word: **enunciation (n.)**

1402 -- **envisage (v.)** -- to visualize; to imagine

1403 -- **ephemeral (adj.)** -- short-lived

1404 -- **epicure (n.)** -- a person who is fond of high quality food || related word: **epicurean (adj.)**

1405 -- **epidemic (n.)** -- sudden increase; outbreak

1406 -- **epidural (n.)** -- anesthetic

1407 -- **epigraph (n.)** -- short phrase

1408 -- **epithet (n.)** -- nickname

1409 -- **epitomize (v.)** -- to be a perfect example; to exemplify || related word: **epitome (n.)**

1410 -- **equanimity (n.)** -- calmness

1411 -- **equinox (n.)** -- period when day and night have equal length (March 20 and Sep 22)

1412 -- **equivocation (n.)** -- avoidance

1413 -- **eradicate (v.)** -- to completely destroy sth bad; to wipe out || related word: **eradication (n.)**

1414 -- **ergo (adv.)** -- therefore

1415 -- **ergonomic (adj.)** -- connected with improvement in working conditions || related words: **ergonomically (adv.), ergonomics (n.)**

1416 -- **erode (v.)** -- to decay || related word: **erosion (n.)**

1417 -- **errand (n.)** -- a task related to delivery of sth

1418 -- **errant (adj.)** -- misbehaving

1419 -- **erratic (adj.)** -- inconsistent || related word: **erratically (adv.)**

1420 -- **erstwhile (adj.)** -- former

1421 -- **erudite (adj.)** -- learned; possessing excellent academic knowledge || related word: **erudition (n.)**

1422 -- **escapade (n.)** -- dangerous adventure

1423 -- **eschew (v.)** -- to avoid

1424 -- **esoteric (adj.)** -- understood by people with particular interest; obscure

1425 -- **espouse (v.)** -- to support a opinion, etc. || related word: **espousal (n.)**

1426 -- **esprit-de-corps (n.)** -- respect for each other in a particular group

1427 -- **estranged (adj.)** -- alienated || related word: **estrangement (n.)**

1428 -- **etch (v.)** -- to cut sth to form design or mark || related word: **etching (n.)**

1429 -- **eternal (adj.)** -- everlasting || related word: **eternally (adv.)**

1430 -- **ethereal (adj.)** -- otherworldly

1431 -- **ethnic (adj./n.)** -- racial | sb from ethnic society || related word: **ethnically (adv.)**

1432 -- **ethos (n.)** -- culture, morality

1433 -- **eulogize (v.)** -- to praise || related words: **eulogistic (adj.), eulogy (n.)**

1434 -- **euthanize (v.)** -- to give 'mercy killing' to sb || related word: **euthanasia (n.)**

1435 -- **evade (v.)** -- to avoid and escape

1436 -- **evangelize (v.)** -- to try to persuade others to accept your beliefs, especially Christianity || related words: **evangelical (adj.), evangelistic (adj.), evangelist (n.), evangelicalism (n.), evangelism (n.)**

1437 -- **evasive (adj.)** -- giving unclear reply || related words: **evasively (adv.), evasiveness (n.)**

1438 -- **evince (v.)** -- to show your qualities

1439 -- **eviscerate (v.)** -- to remove the guts

1440 -- **evoke (v.)** -- to remind || related words: **evocative (adj.),** **evocation (n.)**

1441 -- **exacerbate (v.)** -- to worsen || related word: **exacerbation (n.)**

1442 -- **exacting (adj.)** -- challenging

1443 -- **exalt (v.)** -- to admire | to promote an undeserving person

1444 -- **exaltation (n.)** -- delight || related word: **exalted (adj.)**

1445 -- **exasperate (v.)** -- to annoy || related words: **exasperated** **(adj.), exasperating (adj.), exasperatedly (adv.),**

1446 -- **excavate (v.)** -- to dig || related word: **excavation (n.)**

1447 -- **exceedingly (adv.)** -- extremely

1448 -- **exchequer (n.)** -- treasury

1449 -- **exclaim (v.)** -- to say sth in a loud and emotional way

1450 -- **excommunicate (v.)** -- to expel sb from Church || related word: **excommunication (n.)**

1451 -- **excoriate (v.)** -- to criticize; to scratch sb's skin || related word: **excoriation (n.)**

1452 -- **excruciating (adj.)** -- severe || related word: **excruciatingly** **(adv.)**

1453 -- **exculpate (v.)** -- to acquit || related word: **exculpation (n.)**

1454 -- **excursion (n.)** -- pleasure trip

1455 -- **execrable (adj.)** -- too bad

1456 -- **exemplar (n.)** -- perfect example of sth || related word: **exemplary (adj.)**

1457 -- **exemplify (v.)** -- to demonstrate; to be an example of sth || related word: **exemplification (n.)**

1458 -- **exempt (n./v.)** -- free from restrictions, making payment, etc. | to officially permit sb not to pay for a service, etc. || related word: **exemption (n.)**

1459 -- exert (v.) -- to use your talent, power, effort etc. || related word: **exertion (n.)**

1460 -- exfoliate (v.) -- to make skin smoother by removing dead cells || related word: **exfoliation (n.)**

1461 -- exhaust (v.) -- to weaken; to tire out

1462 -- exhaustive (adj.) -- extensive or complete || related word: **exhaustively (adv.)**

1463 -- exhibit (n./v.) -- an item on display; a proof given in court | to display; to show

1464 -- exhilarate (v.) -- to excite or delight || related words: **exhilarated (adj.), exhilarating (adj.), exhilaration (n.)**

1465 -- exhort (v.) -- to encourage || related word: **exhortation (n.)**

1466 -- exhume (v.) -- to unearth a dead body || related word: **exhumation (n.)**

1467 -- exigency (n.) -- an emergency

1468 -- exiguous (adj.) -- not enough

1469 -- exodus (n.) -- migration

1470 -- ex-officio (adj./adv.) -- allowed by post

1471 -- exogamy (n.) -- inter-caste marriage || related word: **exogamous (adj.)**

1472 -- exonerate (v.) -- to officially free sb from blame || related word: **exoneration (n.)**

1473 -- exorbitant (adj.) -- excessive || related word: **exorbitantly (adv.)**

1474 -- exorcize (v.) -- to make evil spirit leave a particular body or place || related words: **exorcism (n.), exorcist (n.)**

1475 -- exotic (adj.) -- related to foreign; alien || related words: **exotically (adv.), exotica (n.)**

1476 -- expansionism (n.) -- belief of increasing power of your country, etc. || related word: **expansionist (adj./n.)**

1477 -- **expatriate (adj./n.)** -- not living in a country of your birth | emigrant

1478 -- **expedient (adj./n.)** -- useful or essential | useful or essential action || related words: **expediently (adv.), expediency (n.)**

1479 -- **expedite (v.)** -- to accelerate

1480 -- **expedition (n.)** -- trip or journey with a particular purpose

1481 -- **expeditious (adj.)** -- quick and well-organized || related word: **expeditiously (adv.)**

1482 -- **expiate (v.)** -- to apologize || related word: **expiation (n.)**

1483 -- **expletive (n.)** -- swear word

1484 -- **explicate (v.)** -- to fully explain sth

1485 -- **explicit (adj.)** -- very clear to understand || related words: **explicitly (adv.), explicitness (n.)**

1486 -- **exploit (n./v.)** -- adventurous action | to take full advantage of sb/sth; to treat sb unfairly || related word: **exploiter (n.)**

1487 -- **exponent (n.)** -- promoter

1488 -- **exponential (adj.)** -- getting faster

1489 -- **exposition (n.)** -- trade fair | explanation

1490 -- **expository (adj.)** -- intended to clarify or explain

1491 -- **expostulate (v.)** -- to complain or protest || related word: **expostulation (n.)**

1492 -- **expound (v.)** -- to give explanation

1493 -- **expropriate (v.)** -- to seize || related word: **expropriation (n.)**

1494 -- **expunge (v.)** -- to remove or erase memory, etc; to wipe out

1495 -- **expurgate (v.)** -- to edit content of written statement

1496 -- **exquisite (adj.)** -- delicate; beautiful || related word: **exquisitely (adv.)**

1497 -- **extant (adj.)** -- existing

1498 -- **extemporize (v.)** -- to speak without preparation || related word: **extempore (adj./adv.)**

1499 -- **extenuating (adj.)** -- explanatory

1500 -- **exterminate (v.)** -- to kill all people, animal, etc. from a particular group || related word: **extermination (n.)**

1501 -- **extern (n.)** -- a person who doesn't live in his/her working place

1502 -- **extirpate (v.)** -- to get rid of || related word: **extirpation (n.)**

1503 -- **extol (v.)** -- to praise

1504 -- **extort (v.)** -- to threaten sb into giving you sth || related word: **extortion (n.)**

1505 -- **extortionate (adj.)** -- overpriced || related word: **extortionately (adv.)**

1506 -- **extraneous (adj.)** -- irrelevant

1507 -- **extrapolate (v.)** -- to estimate || related word: **extrapolation (n.)**

1508 -- **extravaganza (n.)** -- entertainment

1509 -- **extricate (v.)** -- to escape

1510 -- **extrinsic (adj.)** -- existing outside

1511 -- **extrude (v.)** -- to push sth out of sth else || related word: **extrusion (n.)**

1512 -- **exuberant (adj.)** -- excited || related words: **exuberantly (adv.), exuberance (n.)**

1513 -- **exude (v.)** -- to show an emotion, etc.

1514 -- **exult (v.)** -- to delight || related words: **exultant (adj.), exultation (n.)**

Difficult English Words -- F

1515 -- **fabled (adj.)** -- mythical

1516 -- **fabricate (v.)** -- to manufacture | to trick || related word: **fabrication (n.)**

1517 -- **fabulist (n.)** -- story teller

1518 -- **fabulous (adj.)** -- wonderful || related word: **fabulously (adv.)**

1519 -- **facade (n.)** -- front part

1520 -- **facelift (n.)** -- change or modification to a building | plastic surgery to make sb look younger

1521 -- **face-off (n.)** -- fierce argument

1522 -- **facetious (adj.)** -- amusing (when you need to be serious) || related words: **facetiously (adv.), facetiousness (n.)**

1523 -- **facsimile (n.)** -- copy

1524 -- **factotum (n.)** -- sb who does many jobs

1525 -- **faddy (adj.)** -- crazy (particularly in regard with food) | related word: **fad (n.)**

1526 -- **fag (n.)** -- boring or tiring task

1527 -- **fag-end (n.)** -- last part

1528 -- **fagged (adj.)** -- completely tired

1529 -- **failing (n.)** -- weakness

1530 -- **fallacy (n.)** -- myth

1531 -- **fallout (n.)** -- unpleasant result of an action

1532 -- **fallow (adj.)** -- uncultivated | ineffective

1533 -- **falter (v.)** -- to become weaker; to speak in unclear voice || related word: **faltering (adj.)**

1534 -- **famished (adj.)** -- very hungry

1535 -- **fanatic (n.)** -- extremist or enthusiastic || related words: **fanatical (adj.), fanatically (adv.), fanaticism (n.)**

1536 -- **fanfare (n.)** -- enormous activity

1537 -- **farce (n.)** -- ridiculous situation || related word: **farcical (adj.)**

1538 -- **far-fetched (adj.)** -- unbelievable

1539 -- **fascinate (v.)** -- to attract very much || related words: **fascinated (adj.), fascinating (adj.), fascination (n.)**

1540 -- **fastidious (adj.)** -- being too careful about sth || related words: **fastidiously (adv.), fastidiousness (n.)**

1541 -- **fatal (adj.)** -- causing death or failure || related words: **fatally (adv.), fatality (n.)**

1542 -- **fatalism (n.)** -- extreme belief in fate || related words: **fatalistic (adj.), fatalistically (adv.), fatalist (n.)**

1543 -- **fathom (v.)** -- to understand

1544 -- **fatuous (adj.)** -- silly || related word: **fatuously (adv.)**

1545 -- **faux pas (n.)** -- embarrassing remark

1546 -- **fawn (v.)** -- to try to please sb

1547 -- **faze (v.)** -- to confuse sb very much

1548 -- **feasible (adj.)** -- that can be done; possible or practicable || related word: **feasibility (n.)**

1549 -- **feat (n.)** -- achievement

1550 -- **febrile (adj.)** -- excited

1551 -- **feckless (adj.)** -- incompetent; irresponsible || related word: **fecklessness (n.)**

1552 -- **fecund (adj.)** -- productive || related word: **fecundity (n.)**

1553 -- **feeble (adj.)** -- weak; ineffective || related words: **feebly (adv.), feebleness (n.)**

1554 -- **feign (v.)** -- to pretend

1555 -- **feint (v.)** -- to confuse sb by tricking them

1556 -- **feisty (adj.)** -- determined

1557 -- **felicity (n.)** -- delight

1558 -- feline (adj.) -- graceful; like a cat

1559 -- felony (n.) -- serious crime

1560 -- feral (adj.) -- living wild

1561 -- ferment (n./v.) -- political confusion | to have chemical change

1562 -- ferocious (adj.) -- cruel and violent || related words: **ferociously (adv.), ferocity (n.)**

1563 -- ferret (v.) -- to search

1564 -- ferry (v.) -- to carry sb/sth in a boat

1565 -- fervent (adj.) -- passionate || related word: **fervently (adv.)**

1566 -- fervid (adj.) -- fill with emotions || related word: **fervidly (adv.)**

1567 -- fervor (fervour) (n.) -- enthusiasm or great excitement

1568 -- fester (v.) -- to worsen; to be severely infected

1569 -- festive (adj.) -- joyful || related word: **festivity (n.)**

1570 -- festoon (v.) -- to decorate

1571 -- fetch (v.) -- to bring sth back

1572 -- fete (v.) -- to praise sb openly

1573 -- fetid (adj.) -- smelling too bad

1574 -- fetish (n.) -- obsession || related words: **fetishistic (adj.), fetishist (n.), fetishism (n.)**

1575 -- feud (n./v.) -- dispute | to have a dispute with sb || related word: **feuding (n.)**

1576 -- feverish (adj.) -- agitated || related word: **feverishly (adv.)**

1577 -- fey (adj.) -- too sentimental

1578 -- fiasco (n.) -- complete failure

1579 -- fiat (n.) -- official order

1580 -- fib (n./v.) -- lie | to tell a lie || related word: **fibber (n.)**

1581 -- fickle (adj.) -- changing in an unreasonable or sudden way || related word: **fickleness (n.)**

1582 -- fictionalize (v.) -- to tell a true story with some changes

1583 -- **fictitious (adj.)** -- invented; untrue

1584 -- **fiddle (v.)** -- to change the accounts in order to commit fraud | to anxiously move sth

1585 -- **fiddling (adj.)** -- annoying

1586 -- **fiddly (adj.)** -- small and complex

1587 -- **fidelity (n.)** -- loyalty

1588 -- **fidget (v.)** -- to anxiously keep on moving your body parts || related word: **fidgety (adj.)**

1589 -- **fiduciary (adj.)** -- involving trust

1590 -- **fief (n.)** -- an area of your control

1591 -- **fiend (n.)** -- violent person || related word: **fiendish (adj.)**

1592 -- **fiendishly (adv.)** -- extremely

1593 -- **fierce (adj.)** -- violent || related words: **fiercely (adv.), fierceness (n.)**

1594 -- **fig-leaf (n.)** -- a thing used to hide sth embarrassing

1595 -- **figurine (n.)** -- small statue

1596 -- **filch (v.)** -- to steal

1597 -- **filial (adj.)** -- related to the behavior of children towards their parents

1598 -- **fillip (n.)** -- boost

1599 -- **filth (n.)** -- very unpleasant substance

1600 -- **filthy (adj.)** -- unpleasant; angry; offensive || related words: **filthily (adv.), filthiness (n.)**

1601 -- **finagle (v.)** -- to behave in a deceitful manner

1602 -- **finery (n.)** -- clothes and jewelry that sb wears in an important event

1603 -- **finesse (n./v.)** -- great skill | to do sth skillfully

1604 -- **fine-tune (v.)** -- to make minor but useful improvements || related word: **fine-tuning (n.)**

1605 -- finicky (adj.) -- choosy

1606 -- firmament (n.) -- sky

1607 -- fisticuffs (n.) -- fight with fists

1608 -- fitful (adj.) -- irregular || related word: **fitfully (adv.)**

1609 -- fixture (n.) -- a pre-arranged sports event

1610 -- fizz (n./v.) -- bubbles | (of liquid) to make bubbles || related word: **fizzy (adj.)**

1611 -- fizzer (n.) -- failure

1612 -- fizzle (v.) -- to make a sound like 's'

1613 -- flab (n.) -- loose flesh, especially on stomach || related word: **flabby (adj.)**

1614 -- flabbergasted (adj.) -- shocked

1615 -- flaccid (adj.) -- loose; not tight

1616 -- flagellate (v.) -- to hit sb/yourself with whips as a religious punishment || related word: **flagellation (n.)**

1617 -- flagrant (adj.) -- shocking || related word: **flagrantly (adv.)**

1618 -- flagship (n.) -- the most important product of a company

1619 -- flail (v.) -- to move around uncontrollably

1620 -- flair (n.) -- talent

1621 -- flak (n.) -- criticism

1622 -- flamboyant (adj.) -- colorful; confident || related words: **flamboyantly (adv.), flamboyance (n.)**

1623 -- flaming (adj.) -- full of anger | burning

1624 -- flank (v.) -- to have sth on both sides

1625 -- flare (v.) -- to burn for a short period of time | to lose your temper

1626 -- flare-up (n.) -- expression of strong feeling

1627 -- flashy (adj.) -- showy || related word: **flashily (adv.)**

1628 -- flatulent (adj.) -- too impressive

1629 -- flaunt (v.) -- to openly show your qualities

1630 -- flawed (adj.) -- damaged || related words: **flawlessly (adv.), flaw (n.), flawless (n.)**

1631 -- flay (v.) -- to strongly criticize sb

1632 -- fleck (v.) -- to cover sth with small pieces or spots of sth

1633 -- fledgling (n.) -- inexperienced person, organization, etc.

1634 -- flee (v.) -- to run away

1635 -- fleece (v.) -- to charge unreasonable amount

1636 -- fleeting (adj.) -- short-lived || related word: **fleetingly (adv.)**

1637 -- flex (v.) -- to move your muscles

1638 -- flick (n./v.) -- sudden hit | to hit or move sth with quick sudden movements

1639 -- flicker (n./v.) -- unsteady shining, movement, or feelings | to shine, move or show unsteadily

1640 -- flimsy (adj.) -- weak | unbelievable || related words: **flimsily (adv.), flimsiness (n.)**

1641 -- flinch (v.) -- to make strange facial expressions

1642 -- flippant (adj.) -- superficial || related words: **flippantly (adv.), flippancy (n.)**

1643 -- flirtatious (adj.) -- playful || related words: **flirtatiously (adv.), flirtatiousness (n.)**

1644 -- flit (v.) -- to make a quick movement

1645 -- flock (n./v.) -- group of herds, etc. | to move in a group

1646 -- flog (v.) -- to hit sb with whips, especially as a punishment || related word: **flogging (n.)**

1647 -- flop (v.) -- to move, fall, sit or lie awkwardly

1648 -- florid (adj.) -- extremely decorated || related word: **floridly (adv.)**

1649 -- flotilla (n.) -- fleet

1650 -- flounder (v.) -- to struggle

1651 -- flout (v.) -- to disobey

1652 -- flub (n./v.) -- blunder | to make a big mistake

1653 -- fluff (v.) -- to fail at sth

1654 -- fluffy (adj.) -- very soft

1655 -- fluid (adj.) -- changeable

1656 -- fluke (n.) -- unusual things || related word: **fluky (adj.)**

1657 -- flummery (n.) -- insincere admiration

1658 -- flummox (v.) -- to confuse || related word: **flummoxed (adj.)**

1659 -- flunk (v.) -- to fail

1660 -- flurry (n.) -- short period of intense activities

1661 -- flushed (adj.) -- with a red or rosy face

1662 -- fluster (n./v.) -- confusion | to confuse sb || related word: **flustered (adj.)**

1663 -- flutter (n./v.) -- confusion; light and fast movement | to move lightly but quickly

1664 -- flux (n.) -- instability

1665 -- fogey (n.) -- old-fashioned person

1666 -- foible (n.) -- weak point in sb's character

1667 -- folly (n.) -- foolishness

1668 -- foment (v.) -- to provoke

1669 -- fondle (v.) -- to touch sb in loving way || related word: **fondly (adv.)**

1670 -- foolhardy (adj.) -- unwise || related word: **foolhardiness (n.)**

1671 -- footfall (n.) -- sound of your steps

1672 -- forage (n./v.) -- sth that cows, etc. eats | to search

1673 -- foray (n.) -- short journey | sudden attack or activity

1674 -- forbearance (n.) -- tolerance || related word: **forbearing (adj.)**

1675 -- **forbidding (adj.)** -- unfriendly || related word: **forbiddingly (adv.)**

1676 -- **ford (v.)** -- to drive across a river

1677 -- **foreboding (adj./n.)** -- threatening | an unpleasant sign for future

1678 -- **foreclose (v.)** -- to exclude; to seize property of defaulters

1679 -- **forestall (v.)** -- to prevent upcoming events, etc.

1680 -- **forfeit (v.)** -- to have to lose your belongings, etc.

1681 -- **forge (v.)** -- to build

1682 -- **forgo (v.)** -- to give up

1683 -- **forlorn (adj.)** -- unhappy; failed; lonely || related word: **forlornly (adv.)**

1684 -- **formidable (adj.)** -- impressive; awesome || related word: **formidably (adv.)**

1685 -- **fornicate (v.)** -- to make physical relationship with the person who is not the spouse || related words: **fornication (n.), fornicator (n.)**

1686 -- **forsake (v.)** -- to disown

1687 -- **forte (n.)** -- specialty

1688 -- **forthright (adj.)** -- frank || related words: **forthrightly (adv.), forthrightness (n.)**

1689 -- **forthwith (adv.)** -- immediately

1690 -- **fortify (v.)** -- to strengthen | to make sth safe from attack

1691 -- **fortitude (n.)** -- courage

1692 -- **fortuitous (adj.)** -- accidental || related words: **fortuitously (adv.), fortuitousness (n.)**

1693 -- **foster (v.)** -- to encourage | to take care of sb's child in your home for short period

1694 -- **fount (n.)** -- source for important thing

1695 -- **foxy (adj.)** -- cunning; crafty

1696 -- **foyer (n.)** -- lobby

1697 -- **fracas (n.)** -- fight among many people

1698 -- **fractious (adj.)** -- bad-tempered

1699 -- **fragile (adj.)** -- delicate; easily broken || related word: **fragility (n.)**

1700 -- **fragrance (n.)** -- pleasant smell || related words: **fragrant (adj.), fragrantly (adv.)**

1701 -- **frail (n.)** -- weak || related word: **frailty (n.)**

1702 -- **frantic (adj.)** -- quick but disorganized || related word: **frantically (adv.)**

1703 -- **fraternal (adj.)** -- relationship between closely-knit group || related word: **fraternally (adv.)**

1704 -- **fraternity (n.)** -- alliance; friendship

1705 -- **fraternize (v.)** -- to be friendly with your enemy, etc. || related word: **fraternization (n.)**

1706 -- **fraught (adj.)** -- filled with unpleasant thing | worried

1707 -- **fray (n./v.)** -- contest | to unravel; to get annoyed || related word: **frayed (adj.)**

1708 -- **frazzled (adj.)** -- exhausted; irritated

1709 -- **freak (adj./n./v.)** -- odd, shocking, etc. | odd person | to behave shockingly || related words: **freakish (adj.), freakishly (adv.)**

1710 -- **frenzied (adj.)** -- hysterical or mad | related word: **frenziedly (adv.)**

1711 -- **frenzy (n.)** -- too much emotions

1712 -- **fret (v.)** -- to be worried or restless || related words: **fretful (adj.), fretfully (adv.)**

1713 -- **Freudian slip (n.)** -- a truth that you say unknowingly

1714 -- **frigid (adj.)** -- having no feelings || related word: **frigidly (adv.)**

1715 -- **frill (n.)** -- a type of decoration

1716 -- **fringe (v.)** -- to create a border || related word: **fringed (adj.)**

1717 -- **frisk (v.)** -- to search weapons, etc. by passing your hands over sb | to behave in a lively way || related word: **frisky (adj.)**

1718 -- **frisson (n.)** -- thrill

1719 -- **frivolity (n.)** -- liveliness; amusement || related word: **frivolous (adj.)**

1720 -- **frizz (n./v.)** -- tightly curled hair | to curl

1721 -- **frizzle (v.)** -- to heat sth in order to make curls on it.

1722 -- **frolic (n./v.)** -- amusement | to play in a lively way

1723 -- **froth (n./v.)** -- bubbles | to form mass of bubbles || related word: **frothy (adj.)**

1724 -- **frowsty (adj.)** -- having unpleasant smell because of a lack of fresh air

1725 -- **frugal (adj.)** -- thrifty or economical || related words: **frugally (adv.), frugality (n.)**

1726 -- **fruitcake (n.)** -- crazy person

1727 -- **fruition (n.)** -- success; accomplishment

1728 -- **fuddled (adj.)** -- getting confused because of old age

1729 -- **fudge (v.)** -- to avoid giving clarification

1730 -- **fulcrum (n.)** -- central point

1731 -- **fulminate (v.)** -- to criticize; to rage || related word: **fulmination (n.)**

1732 -- **fulsome (adj.)** -- excessive || related word: **fulsomely (adv.)**

1733 -- **fumble (v.)** -- to move your hands awkwardly || related word: **fumbling (adj.)**

1734 -- **fume (n./v.)** -- great anger | to rage

1735 -- **fumigate (v.)** -- to disinfect || related word: **fumigation (n.)**

1736 -- **funk (n./v.)** -- anxiety | to avoid fearful actions

1737 -- **funky (adj.)** -- unusual

1738 -- furl (v.) -- to fold up

1739 -- furor (furore) (n.) -- public anger

1740 -- furtherance (n.) -- advancement

1741 -- furtive (adj.) -- secretive || related words: **furtively (adv.), furtiveness (n.)**

1742 -- fury (n.) -- great anger

1743 -- fusillade (n.) -- a large number of shots, objects, etc.

1744 -- fuss (n./v.) -- anxiety | to worry

1745 -- fussy (adj.) -- choosy || related words: **fussily (adv.), fussiness (n.)**

1746 -- fusty (adj.) -- damp

1747 -- fuzz (n.) -- unclear shape; confusion || related words: **fuzzy (adj.), fuzzily (adv.), fuzziness (n.)**

Difficult English Words -- G

1748 -- gabble (n./v.) -- confused talk | to talk nonsense

1749 -- gabfest (n.) -- informal meeting

1750 -- gaffe (n.) -- embarrassing mistake

1751 -- gaffer (n.) -- in charge of a particular group

1752 -- gag (n./v.) -- trick or joke; a piece of cloth that is used to shut sb's mouth in order to prevent them from speaking | to prevent sb from speaking or expressing their opinions

1753 -- gaga (adj.) -- confused or crazy

1754 -- gaggle (n.) -- flock of geese | group of noisy people

1755 -- gaiety (adj.) -- liveliness; joy

1756 -- gaily (adv.) -- cheerfully or brightly

1757 -- gainsay (v.) -- to deny; to disprove

1758 -- gait (n.) -- a way of walking

1759 -- gale (n.) -- strong wind; storm

1760 -- gall (n./v.) -- rude behavior; hatred | to annoy sb by not treating them in fair way || related word: **galling (adj.)**

1761 -- gallant (adj./n.) -- brave | polite and fashionable young man || related word: **gallantly (adv.)**

1762 -- gallop (n./v.) -- superfast speed | to run very fast

1763 -- galloping (adj.) -- increasing

1764 -- galore (adj.) -- plentiful

1765 -- galvanize (v.) -- to stimulate sb to do sth

1766 -- gambol (v.) -- to leap cheerfully

1767 -- gamesmanship (n.) -- an art to win games

1768 -- gamut (n.) -- collection or range of a particular type of things

1769 -- gangling (adj.) -- tall and awkward

1770 -- gape (v.) -- to stare shockingly | to be wide open

1771 -- garb (n.) -- dress

1772 -- garbled (adj.) -- confused

1773 -- gargantuan (adj.) -- very large

1774 -- garish (adj.) -- too bright || related word: **garishly (adv.)**

1775 -- garnish (v.) -- to add condiments, dry fruits, etc. to decorate a dish of food

1776 -- garrison (v.) -- to deploy military personnel in order to defend a place

1777 -- garrote (garrotte) (v.) -- to put wire around sb's neck and press it tightly to kill them

1778 -- garrulous (adj.) -- talkative || related word: **garrulously (adv.)**

1779 -- gash (n./v.) -- deep cut | to cut deeply

1780 -- gasp (n./v.) -- deep breath | to struggle for breath

1781 -- gatecrash (v.) -- to attend a party without being invited || related word: **gatecrasher (n.)**

1782 -- gaudy (adj.) -- too bright || related words: **gaudily (adv.), gaudiness (n.)**

1783 -- gauge (v.) -- to measure; to judge

1784 -- gaunt (adj.) -- thin | unattractive || related word: **gauntness (n.)**

1785 -- gawk (v.) -- to stare at sb rudely

1786 -- gawky (adj.) -- moving awkwardly || related words: **gawkily (adv.), gawkiness (n.)**

1787 -- gawp (v.) -- to keep on looking at sb/sth in an annoying way

1788 -- geek (n.) -- stupid or boring person || related word: **geeky (adj.)**

1789 -- genesis (n.) -- origin

1790 -- genial (adj.) -- cheerful || related words: **genially (adv.), geniality (n.)**

1791 -- genteel (adj.) -- courteous || related word: **genteelly (adv.)**

1792 -- genuflect (v.) -- to bow to sb in order to show respect || related word: **genuflection (n.)**

1793 -- geriatric (adj./n.) -- connected with old people or things | old and unhealthy person || related word: **geriatrician (n.)**

1794 -- gerontocracy (n.) -- government by old people || related words: **gerontocratic (adj.), gerontologist (n.), gerontology (n.)**

1795 -- gesticulate (v.) -- to make gesture || related word: **gesticulation (n.)**

1796 -- getaway (n.) -- escape | holiday for a few days

1797 -- ghastly (adj.) -- frightening or very bad

1798 -- ghoul (n.) -- ghost || related word: **ghoulish (adj.)**

1799 -- gibber (v.) -- to say sth in quick and fearful manner || related word: **gibberish (adj.)**

1800 -- giggle (n./v.) -- silly laugh | to laugh nervously or amusingly || related word: **giggly (adv.)**

1801 -- gild (v.) -- to cover sth with gold or gold paint || related words: **gilded (adj.), gilding (n.)**

1802 -- gimmick (n.) -- trick || related words: **gimmicky (adj.), gimmickry (n.)**

1803 -- gingerly (adv.) -- cautiously

1804 -- gird (v.) -- to surround

1805 -- girth (n.) -- the measurement around waist, tree, etc.

1806 -- glacial (adj.) -- icy

1807 -- glad rags (n.) -- sb's best dress

1808 -- gladiator (n.) -- fighter for entertainment

1809 -- glare (n./v.) -- bright light; angry look | to look angrily; to shine too brightly

1810 -- glaring (adj.) -- noticeable | aggressive || related word: **glaringly (adv.)**

1811 -- glaze (v.) -- to varnish | to appear to be tired || related word: **glazed (adj.)**

1812 -- **gleam (n./v.)** -- bright light | to shine || related word: **gleaming (adj.)**

1813 -- **glean (v.)** -- to collect information || related word: **gleanings (n.)**

1814 -- **glee (n.)** -- great happiness

1815 -- **glib (adj.)** -- convincing but insincere || related word: **glibly (adv.)**

1816 -- **glimmer (n./v.)** -- unsteady light | to shine unsteadily

1817 -- **glint (n./v.)** -- flash or shine; strong emotion shown in your eyes | to flash light; to show strong emotion through your eyes

1818 -- **glisten (v.)** -- to sparkle

1819 -- **glister (v.)** -- to shine with manly little flashes

1820 -- **glitch (n.)** -- small problem or fault

1821 -- **glitter (v.)** -- to shine with many little flashes | to show an emotion through your eyes || related word: **glittery (n.)**

1822 -- **glitterati (n.)** -- famous and stylish people

1823 -- **glittering (adj.)** -- impressive; splendid | sparkling

1824 -- **glitz (n.)** -- too impressive || related word: **glitzy (adj.)**

1825 -- **gloaming (n.)** -- faint light that is seen after sun sets

1826 -- **gloat (v.)** -- to boast || related word: **gloating (adj.)**

1827 -- **glom (v.)** -- to steal

1828 -- **gloom (n.)** -- darkness | hopelessness || related words: **gloomy (adj.), gloomily (adv.), gloominess (n.)**

1829 -- **gloop (n.)** -- thick and unpleasant substance || related word: **gloopy (adj.)**

1830 -- **gloss (n./v.)** -- shine; a comment added to explain a piece of writing | to explain a piece of writing by adding a comment to it

1831 -- **glower (v.)** -- to look angrily

1832 -- **glowing (adj.)** -- shining | admiring || related word: **glowingly (adv.)**

1833 -- glum (adj.) -- depressed || related word: **glumly (adv.)**

1834 -- glut (n./v.) -- surplus | to be in excess

1835 -- gluttony (n.) -- greediness

1836 -- gnaw (v.) -- to bite

1837 -- gnawing (adj.) -- worrying

1838 -- goad (n./v.) -- provocation | to irritate sb too much; to provoke

1839 -- gobble (v.) -- to eat too fast

1840 -- gooey (adj.) -- soft, thick and sticky

1841 -- goof (v.) -- to mess up | to make stupid mistake

1842 -- gore (n./v.) -- blood that oozes out from wound | to be injured with horn, tusk, etc.

1843 -- gorge (n./v.) -- deep valley | to eat too much

1844 -- gorgeous (adj.) -- extremely beautiful || related word: **gorgeously (adv.)**

1845 -- gory (adj.) -- violent | bloody

1846 -- gospel (n.) -- set of beliefs

1847 -- gouge (n./v.) -- deep cut | to cut sharply; to raise prices unreasonably

1848 -- gracious (adj.) -- kind and generous || related words: **graciously (adv.), graciousness (n.)**

1849 -- gradient (n.) -- slope | rate of rise and fall of temperature, etc.

1850 -- graffiti (n.) -- drawing on a wall

1851 -- grail (n.) -- sth that is impossible to get

1852 -- grandeur (n.) -- grand and impressive; awesome

1853 -- grandiloquent (adj.) -- using lengthy words || related word: **grandiloquence (n.)**

1854 -- grandiose (adj.) -- impressive but impractical

1855 -- grapple (v.) -- to struggle to solve the problem | to struggle to hold sb/sth

1856 -- grasping (adj.) -- greedy

1857 -- grate (v.) -- to irritate | to rub food in order to cut it into small pieces

1858 -- gratify (v.) -- to fulfill sb's wish; to please or satisfy || related words: **gratified (adj.), gratifying (adj.), gratifyingly (adv.)**

1859 -- grating (adj.) -- hoarse; rough

1860 -- gratitude (n.) -- thankfulness

1861 -- gratuitous (adj.) -- unnecessary || related word: **gratuitously (adv.)**

1862 -- greenback (n.) -- Dollar note from America

1863 -- greenhorn (n.) -- inexperienced person

1864 -- gregarious (adj.) -- social; outgoing || related words: **gregariously (adv.), gregariousness (n.)**

1865 -- gridlock (n.) -- traffic jam | deadlock || related word: **gridlocked (adj.)**

1866 -- grim (adj.) -- depressing | serious || related words: **grimly (adv.), grimness (n.)**

1867 -- grimace (n./v.) -- ugly expression in face | to make an ugly expression with your face

1868 -- grime (n.) -- dirt || related word: **grimy (adj.)**

1869 -- grin (v.) -- to smile

1870 -- grinding (adj.) -- not showing any possibility of improvement

1871 -- gripe (n./v.) -- complaint | to make a complaint

1872 -- gripping (adj.) -- attention-grabbing

1873 -- grisly (adj.) -- extremely violent; horrific

1874 -- grit (n.) -- small pieces of stone

1875 -- gritty (adj.) -- determined | rough || related words: **grittily (adv.), grittiness (n.)**

1876 -- grizzle (v.) -- to complain annoyingly

1877 -- groan (n./v.) -- loud cry | to cry out loudly

1878 -- groggy (adj.) -- weak and tired

1879 -- **groom (v.)** -- to clean up | to train sb

1880 -- **groovy (adj.)** -- marvelous

1881 -- **grope (v.)** -- to try to find sth using your hands

1882 -- **grossly (adv.)** -- disgustingly

1883 -- **grotesque (adj.)** -- strange and ugly; frightening || related word: **grotesquely (adv.)**

1884 -- **grotto (n.)** -- artificial cave

1885 -- **grotty (adj.)** -- unpleasant

1886 -- **grouch (n./v.)** -- unimportant complaint; complainant | to complain about insignificant things || related word: **grouchy (adj.)**

1887 -- **groundswell (n.)** -- increase of a feeling

1888 -- **grouse (v.)** -- to complain annoyingly

1889 -- **grove (n.)** -- group of trees

1890 -- **grovel (v.)** -- to beg

1891 -- **growl (v.)** -- to say sth in an angry way

1892 -- **grub (n./v.)** -- food | to dig

1893 -- **grubby (adj.)** -- dirty | immoral || related word: **grubbiness (n.)**

1894 -- **grudge (n./v.)** -- bitterness | to unwillingly do sth

1895 -- **grudging (adj.)** -- done unwillingly || related word: **grudgingly (adv.)**

1896 -- **grueling (gruelling) (adj.)** -- tough and tiring

1897 -- **gruesome (adj.)** -- horrible; horrific || related word: **gruesomely (adv.)**

1898 -- **gruff (adj.)** -- bad-tempered || related word: **gruffly (adv.)**

1899 -- **grumble (v.)** -- to complain rudely | to roar || related words: **grumbler (n.), grumbling (n.)**

1900 -- **grump (n.)** -- impolite person || related words: **grumpy (adj.), grumpily (adv.), grumpiness (n.)**

1901 -- **grunge (n.)** -- dirt || related word: **grungy (adj.)**

1902 -- **grunt (n./v.)** -- low sound | to murmur

1903 -- **guff (n.)** -- stupid ideas or talks

1904 -- **guffaw (n./v.)** -- noisy laugh | to laugh in a noisy way

1905 -- **guild (n.)** -- association; union

1906 -- **guile (n.)** -- deceit or trick || related words: **guileless (adj.), guilelessly (adv.)**

1907 -- **gullible (adj.)** -- inexperienced; immature || related word: **gullibility (n.)**

1908 -- **gulp (v.)** -- to swallow or breath quickly

1909 -- **gumption (n.)** -- courage

1910 -- **gung-ho (adj.)** -- enthusiastic about war

1911 -- **gunk (gunge) (n.)** -- unpleasant and sticky substance || related word: **gunky (adj.)**

1912 -- **gush (n./v.)** -- to flow liquid in large amounts; to express your feelings in an exaggerated way || related words: **gushing (adj.), gushingly (adv.)**

1913 -- **gust (n./v.)** -- strong wind; strong emotion | to blow strongly

1914 -- **gusto (n.)** -- enthusiasm; passion

1915 -- **gutsy (adj.)** -- brave

1916 -- **guzzle (v.)** -- to swallow sth in large amounts

1917 -- **gyp (n./v.)** -- cheating | to cheat

1918 -- **gyrate (v.)** -- to move around in circles || related word: **gyration (n.)**

Difficult English Words -- H

1919 -- **hack (v.)** -- to cut or kick

1920 -- **hackneyed (adj.)** -- frequently repeated and boring

1921 -- **hag (n.)** -- ugly woman

1922 -- **haggard (adj.)** -- tired

1923 -- **haggle (v.)** -- to bargain; to praise

1924 -- **hail (n./v.)** -- big amount | to summon

1925 -- **hairy (adj.)** -- terrifying but interesting || related word: **hairiness (n.)**

1926 -- **halcyon (adj.)** -- quiet and happy

1927 -- **hallowed (adj.)** -- sacred

1928 -- **hallucination (n.)** -- illusion || related word: **hallucinatory (adj.)**

1929 -- **halo (n.)** -- circle of light around sb's head; aura

1930 -- **halting (adj.)** -- hesitant || related word: **haltingly (adv.)**

1931 -- **ham-fisted (adj.)** -- awkward

1932 -- **hammering (n.)** -- severe defeat or criticism

1933 -- **hamper (v.)** -- to obstruct

1934 -- **hamstring (v.)** -- to restrict

1935 -- **handout (n.)** -- items that are given to poor person

1936 -- **hands-on (adj.)** -- realistic; practical

1937 -- **handy (adj.)** -- useful | skillful || related word: **handiness (n.)**

1938 -- **hanger-on (n.)** -- follower

1939 -- **hangover (n.)** -- old feelings | headache

1940 -- **hang-up (n.)** -- problem, especially about your emotions

1941 -- **hanker (v.)** -- to desire strongly || related word: **hankering (n.)**

1942 -- **hanky-panky (n.)** -- immoral or dishonest behavior

1943 -- **haphazard (adj.)** -- unorganized || related word: **haphazardly (adv.)**

1944 -- **hapless (adj.)** -- unlucky

1945 -- happenstance (n.) -- chance

1946 -- harangue (n./v.) -- strong criticism | to criticize

1947 -- harbinger (n.) -- forewarning about sth bad; omen

1948 -- harbor (harbour) (v.) -- to suppress your feelings | to give protection to a criminal | to let sth develop

1949 -- hardball (n.) -- determined behavior in politics

1950 -- hard-nosed (adj.) -- fanatical

1951 -- hare (v.) -- to move fast

1952 -- harlot (n.) -- a woman who behaves in very immoral way

1953 -- harmony (n.) -- agreement

1954 -- harness (v.) -- to attach | to exploit

1955 -- harrowing (adj.) -- shocking and disturbing

1956 -- harry (v.) -- to harass

1957 -- has-been (n.) -- former winner, etc.

1958 -- hassle (n./v.) -- complicated or annoying situation | to annoy

1959 -- hasten (v.) -- to make haste

1960 -- hatch (v.) -- to emerge

1961 -- haughty (adj.) -- too proud || related words: **haughtily (adv.), haughtiness (n.)**

1962 -- haul (n./v.) -- illegal or stolen items | to drag with effort; to forcefully bring sb to a particular place

1963 -- haulage (n.) -- shipping

1964 -- haunt (n./v.) -- most visited place by a lot of people | to bother; to come in a form of ghost || related word: **haunted (adj.)**

1965 -- haunting (adj.) -- impressive and unforgettable || related word: **hauntingly (adv.)**

1966 -- haute couture (n.) -- a business related to fashionable clothes for women

1967 -- havoc (n.) -- disaster

1968 -- hawk (n./v.) -- a politician who supports war | to sell sth door to door

1969 -- hazard (n./v.) -- dangerous or harmful thing | to put sth in danger || related word: **hazardous (adj.)**

1970 -- hazy (adj.) -- misty | confused or unclear || related word: **hazily (adv.)**

1971 -- headstrong (adj.) -- stubborn

1972 -- heave (n./v.) -- pull | to pull or drag

1973 -- heckle (v.) -- to interfere sb during their speech || related words: **heckler (n.), heckling (n.)**

1974 -- hedge (n./v.) -- protection against the loss | to avoid a question; to restrict

1975 -- heed (v.) -- to pay attention || related words: **heedful (adj.), heedless (adj.), heedlessly (adv.)**

1976 -- heft (n./v.) -- weight | to lift sth heavy

1977 -- hefty (adj.) -- large in amount or size || related word: **heftily (adv.)**

1978 -- hegemony (n.) -- dominion || related word: **hegemonic (adj.)**

1979 -- heinous (adj.) -- extremely shocking || related words: **heinously (adv.), heinousness (n.)**

1980 -- heirloom (n.) -- an object that is carried, generation after generation, in a family

1981 -- heist (n./v.) -- robbery | to rob

1982 -- henchman (n.) -- strong supporter of sb

1983 -- herald (n./v.) -- sign or hint for future event | to be a sign or hint

1984 -- herculean (adj.) -- that needs an extraordinary courage

1985 -- herd (n./v.) -- group | to move in a group

1986 -- heresy (n.) -- opposite opinion, especially in religious matters || related words: **heretic (n.), heretical (adv.)**

1987 -- hermit (n.) -- sb who stays alone; loner || related word: **hermitage (n.)**

1988 -- heterogeneous (adj.) -- mixed || related word: **heterogeneity (n.)**

1989 -- hew (v.) -- to cut sth into particular shape

1990 -- hex (v.) -- to harm sb through magic

1991 -- heyday (n.) -- past days of glory

1992 -- hick (n.) -- stupid person

1993 -- higgledy-piggledy (adj./adv.) -- untidy | disorderly

1994 -- high jinks (hi jinks) (n.) -- enjoyment

1995 -- hike (n./v.) -- long walk for pleasure; unexpected increase in price | to walk for pleasure; to increase price unexpectedly

1996 -- hilarious (adj.) -- funny; amusing || related words: **hilariously (adv.), hilarity (n.)**

1997 -- hinder (v.) -- to obstruct

1998 -- hindsight (n.) -- understanding of sth after it has occurred

1999 -- hinterland (n.) -- distant areas

2000 -- hireling (n.) -- sb who can do any sort of work for money

2001 -- hirsute (adj.) -- hairy

2002 -- hiss (v.) -- to say sth in quiet but angry way

2003 -- histrionic (adj.) -- showing too much emotions || related words: **histrionically (adv.), histrionics (n.)**

2004 -- hitchhike (v.) -- to get a free ride || related word: **hitchhiker (n.)**

2005 -- hither (adv.) -- to this place

2006 -- hoary (adj.) -- grey | old and well known

2007 -- hoax (n./v.) -- trick; prank | to trick || related word: **hoaxer (n.)**

2008 -- hobble (v.) -- to limp | to prevent

2009 -- hobnob (v.) -- to socialize with famous person

2010 -- hog (v.) -- to dominate or occupy

2011 -- **hogwash (n.)** -- nonsense

2012 -- **hoick (v.)** -- to pull or lift sth suddenly

2013 -- **hoist (v.)** -- to raise

2014 -- **holistic (adj.)** -- considering everything || related word: **holistically (adv.)**

2015 -- **holler (v.)** -- to shout

2016 -- **holocaust (n.)** -- disaster

2017 -- **homage (n.)** -- respect

2018 -- **hombre (n.)** -- a particular type of person

2019 -- **homily (n.)** -- speech on morality; discourse

2020 -- **honcho (n.)** -- in charge of sth

2021 -- **hone (v.)** -- to sharpen | to improve your skills

2022 -- **honk (v.)** -- to hoot

2023 -- **honorific (adj.)** -- showing respect

2024 -- **hoodlum (n.)** -- noisy and violent man

2025 -- **hoodoo (n.)** -- unlucky thing

2026 -- **hoodwink (v.)** -- to make fool of sb

2027 -- **hooligan (n.)** -- noisy and violent person

2028 -- **horde (n.)** -- mass or crowd

2029 -- **horizon (n.)** -- sphere

2030 -- **horrendous (adj.)** -- terrible or shocking || related word: **horrendously (adv.)**

2031 -- **horrid (adj.)** -- too unpleasant

2032 -- **horrify (v.)** -- to shock or frighten sb || related words: **horrified (adj.), horrific (adj.), horrifying (adj.), horrifically (adv.), horrifyingly (adv.)**

2033 -- **horseplay (n.)** -- noisy play for fun that includes pushing each other

2034 -- **hospice (n.)** -- hospital for dying people

2035 -- **hospitable (adj.)** -- generous | welcoming | favorable

2036 -- **hostile (adj.)** -- unfriendly | related word: **hostility (n.)**

2037 -- **hotly (adv.)** -- passionately

2038 -- **hotshot (n.)** -- very successful person

2039 -- **hovel (n.)** -- dirty or untidy room

2040 -- **hover (v.)** -- to stay

2041 -- **howl (n./v.)** -- loud cry | to cry; to say sth in a loud voice

2042 -- **howler (n.)** -- serious error

2043 -- **howling (adj.)** -- great or violent

2044 -- **hubris (n.)** -- pride

2045 -- **huddle (n./v.)** -- group | to form a group || related word: **huddled (adj.)**

2046 -- **hue (n.)** -- opinion | color

2047 -- **huff (v.)** -- to say sth irritatingly || related words: **huffy (adj.), huffily (adv.)**

2048 -- **hulk (n.)** -- large or heavy person or thing || related word: **hulking (adj.)**

2049 -- **hull (n./v.)** -- bottom part of a ship | to remove the skin of vegetables

2050 -- **humdrum (adj.)** -- routine and boring

2051 -- **humid (adj.)** -- warm and unpleasantly wet

2052 -- **humongous (adj.)** -- huge

2053 -- **hunch (n./v.)** -- guess | to bend upper part of your body || related word: **hunched (adj.)**

2054 -- **hunky-dory (adj.)** -- without any problem; perfect

2055 -- **hurl (v.)** -- to throw | to shout abusive words

2056 -- **hurly-burly (n.)** -- chaos

2057 -- **hurtle (v.)** -- to move with fast speed

2058 -- **husbandry (n.)** -- farming

2059 -- **hush (n./v.)** -- silence | to be quiet || related word: **hushed (adj.)**

2060 -- hush-hush (adj.) -- secret

2061 -- husk (n./v.) -- outer covering of nuts, grains, etc. | to remove husk

2062 -- husky (adj.) -- hoarse; rough || related words: **huskily (adv.), huskiness (n.)**

2063 -- hustle (n./v.) -- busy activity | to hurry up

2064 -- hydrate (v.) -- to make sth soak up water || related word: **hydration (n.)**

2065 -- hype (n./v.) -- exaggerated publicity | to publicize in an exaggerated way

2066 -- hyped up (adj.) -- too worried about future events

2067 -- hysteria (n.) -- unusual excitement or fear; madness || related words: **hysterical (adj.), hysterically (adv.), hysterics (n.)**

Difficult English Words -- I

2068 -- **idealize (v.)** -- to assume sb/sth as being perfect or faultless || related word: **idealization (n.)**

2069 -- **ideologue (n.)** -- believer of a particular ideology (set of rules or principles)

2070 -- **idiocy (n.)** -- very stupid or silly act or remark

2071 -- **idiolect (n.)** -- the way you use language

2072 -- **idiosyncrasy (n.)** -- an unusual way of behaving; eccentricity, peculiarity || related word: **idiosyncratic (adj.)**

2073 -- **idol (n.)** -- sb/sth that is liked by number of people

2074 -- **idolatry (n.)** -- worship of statues | great admiration || related word: **idolatrous (adj.)**

2075 -- **idyllic (adj.)** -- pleasant and peaceful || related words: **idyllically (adv.), idyll (n.)**

2076 -- **iffy (adj.)** -- uncertain or imperfect

2077 -- **ignite (v.)** -- to catch fire or to light || related word: **ignition (n.)**

2078 -- **ignoble (adj.)** -- shameful

2079 -- **ignominious (adj.)** -- disgraceful || related words: **ignominiously (adv.), ignominy (n.)**

2080 -- **ilk (n.)** -- type, kind or like

2081 -- **ill humor (ill humour) (n.)** -- bad mood || related word: **ill humored (ill humoured) (adj.)**

2082 -- **ill-advised (adj.)** -- unwise || related word: **ill-advisedly (adv.)**

2083 -- **ill-assorted (adj.)** -- unsuited

2084 -- **ill-bred (adj.)** -- impolite as a part of your nature

2085 -- **ill-concealed (adj.)** -- not hidden properly

2086 -- **ill-conceived (adj.)** -- not carefully planned

2087 -- **ill-disposed (adj.)** -- unfriendly

2088 -- **ill-founded (adj.)** -- baseless

2089 -- **ill-starred (adj.)** -- very unlucky

2090 -- **illuminate (v.)** -- to light | to clarify | to decorate with light || related words: **illuminated (adj.), illuminating (adj.), illumination (n.)**

2091 -- **illusion (n.)** -- false impression; unreal || related words: **illusive (adj.), illusory (adj.)**

2092 -- **illustrious (adj.)** -- memorable or admired

2093 -- **imbibe (v.)** -- to absorb or swallow

2094 -- **imbroglio (n.)** -- embarrassing situation

2095 -- **imbue (v.)** -- to instill strong feelings in sb/sth

2096 -- **imitate (v.)** -- to copy || related words: **imitative (adj.), imitation (n.), imitator (n.)**

2097 -- **immaculate (adj.)** -- without mistakes | very tidy || related word: **immaculately (adv.)**

2098 -- **immanent (adj.)** -- present in every place

2099 -- **immense (adj.)** -- huge or great; enormous || related words: **immensely (adv.), immensity (n.)**

2100 -- **immerse (v.)** -- to submerge || related word: **immersion (n.)**

2101 -- **imminent (adj.)** -- likely to happen very soon || related words: **imminently (adv.), imminence (n.)**

2102 -- **immiscible (adj.)** -- unmixable

2103 -- **immoderate (adj.)** -- too much; excessive || related word: **immoderately (adv.)**

2104 -- **immodest (adj.)** -- very proud or immoral

2105 -- **immolate (v.)** -- to burn sb to death || related word: **immolation (n.)**

2106 -- **immure (v.)** -- to put sth in jail or other enclosed space

2107 -- **immutable (adj.)** -- consistent; unchangeable || related word: **immutability (n.)**

2108 -- **impair (v.)** -- to damage or harm || related words: **impaired (adj.), impairment (n.)**

2109 -- **impale (v.)** -- to pierce or stab

2110 -- **impalpable (adj.)** -- unreal; imaginary

2111 -- **impart (v.)** -- to communicate; to convey

2112 -- **impassable (adj.)** -- blocked

2113 -- **impasse (n.)** -- deadlock or unsettlement

2114 -- **impassioned (adj.)** -- very excited

2115 -- **impassive (adj.)** -- without feelings or emotions; expressionless || related word: **impassively (adv.)**

2116 -- **impeach (v.)** -- to prosecute a very important person || related words: **impeachable (adj.), impeachment (n.)**

2117 -- **impeccable (adj.)** -- without any flaws; perfect || related word: **impeccably (adv.)**

2118 -- **impecunious (adj.)** -- without having money; very poor

2119 -- **impede (v.)** -- to obstruct || related word: **impediment (n.)**

2120 -- **impel (v.)** -- to force sb to do sth

2121 -- **impending (adj.)** -- likely to happen very soon

2122 -- **impenitent (adj.)** -- shameless

2123 -- **imperceptible (adj.)** -- unnoticeable or invisible because of being very small || related word: **imperceptibly (adv.)**

2124 -- **imperial (adj.)** -- related to empire

2125 -- **imperialism (n.)** -- rule of a country over other countries | influence of a powerful country || related word: **imperialist (adj./n.)**

2126 -- **imperil (v.)** -- to put sb/sth in danger or risk

2127 -- **imperious (adj.)** -- dominant || related word: **imperiously (adv.)**

2128 -- **imperishable (adj.)** -- everlasting

2129 -- **impertinent (adj.)** -- very impolite || related words: **impertinently (adj.), impertinence (n.)**

2130 -- **imperturbable (adj.)** -- very composed or calm || related words: **imperturbably (adv.), imperturbability (n.)**

2131 -- **impervious (adj.)** -- unaffected or not influenced by sth

2132 -- **impetuous (adj.)** -- hasty || related words: **impetuously (adv.), impetuosity (n.)**

2133 -- **impetus (n.)** -- force or stimulus

2134 -- **impinge (v.)** -- to have a bad effect on sth

2135 -- **impious (adj.)** -- having no faith in god; non-religious || related word: **impiety (n.)**

2136 -- **impish (adj.)** -- naughty || related word: **impishly (adv.)**

2137 -- **implacable (adj.)** -- unchangeable or unstoppable || related word: **implacably (adv.)**

2138 -- **implausible (adj.)** -- doubtful, unlikely or improbable || related word: **implausibly (adv.)**

2139 -- **implicate (v.)** -- to accuse or convict

2140 -- **implication (n.)** -- possible results of an activity, etc. | accusation

2141 -- **implicit (adj.)** -- indirectly expressed; understood || related word: **implicitly (adv.)**

2142 -- **implode (v.)** -- to explode | to completely fail || **related word: implosion (n.)**

2143 -- **implore (v.)** -- to ask for sth seriously or worriedly || related word: **imploring (adj.)**

2144 -- **impolitic (adj.)** -- unwise

2145 -- **imponderable (adj./n.)** -- immeasurable, incalculable, inestimable | something that is tough to be measured, calculated or estimated.

2146 -- **importune (v.)** -- to harass

2147 -- **impose (v.)** -- to enforce law, restrictions, opinions, etc. || related word: **imposition (n.)**

2148 -- **imposing (adj.)** -- impressive

2149 -- **impostor (n.)** -- pretender who tricks sb

2150 -- **impound (v.)** -- to take sth away; to confiscate

2151 -- **impoverish (v.)** -- to make poor or worse || related words: **impoverished (adj.), impoverishment (n.)**

2152 -- **imprecation (n.)** -- very rude words; curse

2153 -- **impregnable (adj.)** -- extremely strong

2154 -- **imprimatur (n.)** -- official approval or recognition

2155 -- **impromptu (adj.)** -- unprepared or unplanned

2156 -- **impropriety (n.)** -- very bad behavior; rudeness

2157 -- **improvident (n.)** -- careless and extravagant || related word: **improvidence (n.)**

2158 -- **improvise (v.)** -- to manage with whatever is available || related word: **improvisation (n.)**

2159 -- **imprudent (adj.)** -- insensible or unwise || related words: **imprudently (adv.), imprudence (n.)**

2160 -- **impudent (adj.)** -- impolite || related word: **impudence (n.)**

2161 -- **impugn (v.)** -- to be doubtful

2162 -- **impulsive (adj.)** -- reckless; irresponsible || related words: **impulsively (adv.), impulsiveness (n.)**

2163 -- **impunity (n.)** -- without suffering punishment for wrongdoing

2164 -- **inalienable (adj.)** -- not able to be taken away

2165 -- **inane (adj.)** -- meaningless and silly || related words: **inanely (adv.), inanity (n.)**

2166 -- **incandescent (adj.)** -- shining | having intense feelings || related word: **incandescence (n.)**

2167 -- **incapacitate (v.)** -- to prevent sb from making progress

2168 -- **incarcerate (v.)** -- to put sb in an enclosed space, especially in jail | related word: **incarceration (n.)**

2169 -- **incarnate (adj./v.)** -- personified | to personify

2170 -- **incarnation (n.)** -- life period in a particular form

2171 -- **incendiary (adj./n.)** -- that cause fire or feelings | firebomb

2172 -- **incense (v.)** -- to enrage sb || related word: **incensed (adj.)**

2173 -- **inception (n.)** -- inauguration; beginning

2174 -- **incessant (adj.)** -- never coming to an end || related word: **incessantly (adv.)**

2175 -- **incest (n.)** -- physical relationship between two very close relatives | related words: **incestuous (adj.), incestuously (adv.)**

2176 -- **inchoate (adj.)** -- undeveloped

2177 -- **incidental (adj./n.)** -- not much significant | natural effects

2178 -- **incidentally (adv.)** -- by the way

2179 -- **incinerate (v.)** -- to completely burn sth || related words: **incineration (n.), incinerator (n.)**

2180 -- **incipient (adj.)** -- in the early stage of development

2181 -- **incise (v.)** -- to cut a surface to make a design or words || related word: **incision (n.)**

2182 -- **incisive (adj.)** -- showing good judgment; insightful || related words: **incisively (adv.), incisiveness (n.)**

2183 -- **incite (v.)** -- to make sb angry in order to encourage them to do sth illegal or violent || related word: **incitement (n.)**

2184 -- **inclement (adj.)** -- cold, windy, stormy or unpleasant weather || related word: **inclemency (n.)**

2185 -- **incline (v.)** -- to be likely to behave in a particular way || related word: **inclination (n.)**

2186 -- **incognito (adj.)** -- secretly

2187 -- **incoherent (adj.)** -- illogical or unorganized || related words: **incoherently (adv.), incoherence (n.)**

2188 -- **incommode (v.)** -- to create problems for sb

2189 -- **incommunicado (adj.)** -- not talking with others

2190 -- **inconceivable (adj.)** -- unbelievable, unthinkable

2191 -- **incongruous (adj.)** -- inappropriate or inconsistent || related words: **incongruously (adv.), incongruity (n.)**

2192 -- **inconsiderate (adj.)** -- thoughtless; insensitive || related word: **inconsiderately (adv.)**

2193 -- **inconspicuous (adj.)** -- unnoticeable || related word: **inconspicuously (adv.)**

2194 -- **incorporeal (adj.)** -- formless; ghostly

2195 -- **incorrigible (adj.)** -- that can't be changed || related word: **incorrigibly (adv.)**

2196 -- **incredulous (adj.)** -- doubtful || related words: **incredulously (adv.), incredulity (n.)**

2197 -- **inculcate (v.)** -- to instill moral principles in sb || related word: **inculcation (n.)**

2198 -- **incumbency (n.)** -- a period of holding official position || related word: **incumbent (adj./n.)**

2199 -- **incur (v.)** -- to have to pay | to suffer

2200 -- **incursion (n.)** -- sudden attack or raid

2201 -- **indefatigable (adj.)** -- tireless or determined || related word: **indefatigably (adv.)**

2202 -- **indelible (adj.)** -- that cannot be removed || related word: **indelibly (adv.)**

2203 -- **indemnify (v.)** -- to insure or compensate || related word: **indemnity (n.)**

2204 -- **indenture (n.)** -- agreement to work for a certain period of time || related word: **indentured (adj.)**

2205 -- **indict (v.)** -- to charge for a crime || related words: **indictable (adj.), indictment (n.)**

2206 -- **indifference (n.)** -- lack of interest || related words: **indifferent (adj.), indifferently (adv.)**

2207 -- **indigenous (adj.)** -- connected with your original place

2208 -- **indigent (adj.)** -- very poor

2209 -- **indignant (adj.)** -- extremely angry or offended || related words: **indignantly (adv.), indignation (n.)**

2210 -- **indiscriminate (adj.)** -- random || related word: **indiscriminately (adv.)**

2211 -- **indispensable (adj.)** -- necessary

2212 -- **indisposed (adj.)** -- unwell or unwilling

2213 -- **indisposition (n.)** -- minor ailment

2214 -- **indoctrinate (v.)** -- to forcefully instill a particular set of beliefs in sb || related word: **indoctrination (n.)**

2215 -- **indolent (adj.)** -- lazy || related word: **indolence (n.)**

2216 -- **induce (v.)** -- to encourage sb to do sth; to persuade || related word: **inducement (n.)**

2217 -- **indulge (v.)** -- to be involved in doing sth bad || related words: **indulgent (adj.), indulgently (adv.), indulgence (n.)**

2218 -- **inebriated (adj.)** -- drunk || related word: **inebriation (n.)**

2219 -- **ineffable (adj.)** -- that cannot be described

2220 -- **ineluctable (adj.)** -- unavoidable || related word: **ineluctably (adv.)**

2221 -- **inert (adj.)** -- static or motionless

2222 -- **inertia (n.)** -- lack of energy

2223 -- **inevitable (adj.)** -- that cannot be avoided || related words: **inevitably (adv.), inevitability (n.)**

2224 -- **inexorable (adj.)** -- that cannot be stopped || related words: **inexorably (adv.), inexorability (n.)**

2225 -- **inexpedient (n.)** -- unfair action

2226 -- **inextricable (adj.)** -- that cannot be separated || related word: **inextricably (adv.)**

2227 -- **infallible (n.)** -- foolproof || related words: **infallibly (adv.), infallibility (n.)**

2228 -- **infantile (adj.)** -- babyish or childish || related words: **infantilism (n.), infantilize (v.)**

2229 -- **infatuated (adj.)** -- obsessed with sb

2230 -- **infer (v.)** -- to make a conclusion or an assumption || related word: **inference (n.)**

2231 -- **infernal (adj.)** -- very irritating || related word: **infernally (adv.)**

2232 -- **infest (v.)** -- to be completely filled with sth unpleasant || related word: **infestation (n.)**

2233 -- **infidel (n.)** -- nonbeliever

2234 -- **infidelity (n.)** -- disloyalty towards your spouse

2235 -- **infiltrate (v.)** -- to enter somewhere secretly | to pass || related words: **infiltration (n.), infiltrator (n.)**

2236 -- **infinitesimal (adj.)** -- extremely small || related word: **infinitesimally (adv.)**

2237 -- **infirm (adj.)** -- very weak; sick || related words: **infirmary (n.), infirmity (n.)**

2238 -- **inflamed (adj.)** -- swollen, irritated || related words: **inflammatory (adj.), inflammation (n.)**

2239 -- **inflatable (adj.)** -- filled with air

2240 -- **influx (n.)** -- arrival of numerous people, things, etc.

2241 -- **infraction (n.)** -- violation

2242 -- **infringe (v.)** -- to violate || related word: **infringement (n.)**

2243 -- **infuriate (v.)** -- to annoy sb very much || related words: **infuriating (adj.), infuriatingly (adv.)**

2244 -- **infuse (v.)** -- to instill

2245 -- **ingenious (adj.)** -- original || related word: **ingeniously (adv.)**

2246 -- **ingenuity (n.)** -- originality

2247 -- **ingenuous (adj.)** -- honest || related word: **ingenuously (adv.)**

2248 -- **ingrained (adj.)** -- well-established

2249 -- **ingratiate (v.)** -- to try to get favor from sb | related words: **ingratiating (adj.), ingratiatingly (adv.)**

2250 -- **ingress (n.)** -- entrance

2251 -- **inhibit (v.)** -- to prevent or restrain || related words: **inhibited (adj.), inhibition (n.), inhibitor (n.)**

2252 -- **inhospitable (adj.)** -- unwelcoming

2253 -- **inimical (adj.)** -- adverse

2254 -- **inimitable (adj.)** -- that cannot be copied

2255 -- **iniquitous (adj.)** -- very bad, immoral or unrighteous || related word: **iniquity (n.)**

2256 -- **injunction (n.)** -- official order or ruling

2257 -- **inkling (n.)** -- hint or clue

2258 -- **innards (n.)** -- internal organs, especially stomach and intestines

2259 -- **innate (adj.)** -- inherent or inborn || related word: **innately (adv.)**

2260 -- **innocuous (adj.)** -- not dangerous; harmless || related word: **innocuously (adv.)**

2261 -- **innovate (v.)** -- to introduce sth new || related words: **innovative (adj.), innovation (n.), innovator (n.)**

2262 -- **innuendo (n.)** -- indirect remark; allusion or insinuation

2263 -- **inoculate (v.)** -- to inject sb with mild form of a disease to make them immune to it || related word: **inoculation (n.)**

2264 -- **inordinate (adj.)** -- too much; excessive or unrestrained

2265 -- **inquest (n.)** -- inquiry || related words: **inquisitive (adj.), inquisitively (adv.), inquisitiveness (n.), inquisition (n.), inquisitor (n.)**

2266 -- **inscription (n.)** -- written words

2267 -- **inscrutable (adj.)** -- hard to make out || related words: **inscrutably (adv.), inscrutability (n.)**

2268 -- insidious (adj.) -- causing serious harm in gradual or unnoticeable way || related word: **insidiously (adv.)**

2269 -- insight (n.) -- understanding about sb/sth || related word: **insightful (adj.)**

2270 -- insignia (n.) -- a symbol to show your rank in an organization, etc.

2271 -- insinuate (v.) -- to indirectly suggest sth unpleasant || related word: **insinuation (n.)**

2272 -- insipid (adj.) -- ordinary; bland

2273 -- insolent (adj.) -- rude || related words: **insolence (adj.), insolently (adv.)**

2274 -- insouciance (n.) -- disinterest || related word: **insouciant (adj.)**

2275 -- instigate (v.) -- to cause sth unpleasant to happen | to officially start sth || related words: **instigation (n.), instigator (n.)**

2276 -- instinct (n.) -- natural tendency; impulse

2277 -- institute (v.) -- to initiate

2278 -- instrumental (adj.) -- significant || related word: **instrumentally (adv.)**

2279 -- insubordination (n.) -- disobedience || related word: **insubordinate (adj.)**

2280 -- insular (adj.) -- narrow-minded || related word: **insularity (n.)**

2281 -- insulate (v.) -- to protect from heat, electricity, or bad experience, etc. || related words: **insulated (adj.), insulating (adj.)**

2282 -- insurmountable (adj.) -- devastating

2283 -- insurrection (n.) -- rebellion || related word: **insurrectionary (adj.)**

2284 -- integration (n.) -- combination

2285 -- integrity (n.) -- honesty | unity

2286 -- intelligible (adj.) -- understandable || related words: **intelligibly (adv.), intelligibility (n.)**

2287 -- intemperate (adj.) -- quarrelsome, hot-headed || related word: **intemperance (n.)**

2288 -- intensify (v.) -- to strengthen; to increase || related word: **intensification (n.)**

2289 -- intercede (v.) -- to mediate || related word: **intercession (n.)**

2290 -- interlocutor (n.) -- a participant in a conversation

2291 -- interloper (n.) -- intruder

2292 -- interlude (n.) -- short period of time between two activities; interval

2293 -- intermediary (adj./n.) -- mediating | mediator

2294 -- interment (n.) -- burial or funeral

2295 -- interminable (adj.) -- everlasting || related word: **interminably (adv.)**

2296 -- intermingle (v.) -- to mix together

2297 -- intermission (n.) -- a break; interval

2298 -- intermittent (adj.) -- irregular || related word: **intermittently (adv.)**

2299 -- internalize (v.) -- to incorporate a particular set of beliefs in your behavior || related word: **internalization (n.)**

2300 -- internecine (adj.) -- happening within a group

2301 -- interpolate (v.) -- to insert or interrupt || related word: **interpolation (n.)**

2302 -- interregnum (n.) -- state of being without leadership

2303 -- intersperse (v.) -- to mix together

2304 -- intertwine (v.) -- to be twisted or connected together

2305 -- intimidate (v.) -- to frighten, threaten, or terrorize || related words: **intimidated (adj.), intimidating (adj.), intimidation (n.)**

2306 -- intonation (n.) -- tone

2307 -- intractable (adj.) -- that cannot be dealt with || related word: **intractability (n.)**

2308 -- **intransigent (adj.)** -- obstinate || related word: **intransigence (n.)**

2309 -- **intrepid (adj.)** -- bold and fearless

2310 -- **intricacy (n.)** -- complexity

2311 -- **intrigue (n./v.)** -- secret plan | to create interest in sth || related words: **intrigued (adj.), intriguing (adj.), intriguingly (adv.)**

2312 -- **intrinsic (adj.)** -- natural or essential || related word: **intrinsically (adv.)**

2313 -- **intrusive (adj.)** -- noticeable in an annoying way

2314 -- **intuit (v.)** -- to know sth through your feelings || related words: **intuitive (adj.), intuitively (adv.), intuition (n.)**

2315 -- **invade (v.)** -- to enter by force | to interfere || related words: **invader (n.), invasion (n.)**

2316 -- **invariable (adj.)** -- unchanging; constant || related word: **invariably (adv.)**

2317 -- **invective (n.)** -- very rude words

2318 -- **inveigle (v.)** -- to cheat

2319 -- **inveterate (adj.)** -- that cannot be stopped or changed

2320 -- **invidious (adj.)** -- offensive

2321 -- **invigorate (v.)** -- to energize || related word: **invigorating (adj.)**

2322 -- **invincible (adj.)** -- that cannot be defeated || related word: **invincibility (n.)**

2323 -- **invocation (n.)** -- chant or prayer

2324 -- **invoke (v.)** -- to mention

2325 -- **involuntary (adj.)** -- spontaneous || related word: **involuntarily (adv.)**

2326 -- **invulnerable (adj.)** -- safe; protected || related word: **invulnerability (n.)**

2327 -- **iota (n.)** -- very small amount

2328 -- **irascible (adj.)** -- bad-tempered || related word: **irascibility (adv.)**

2329 -- **irate (adj.)** -- extremely angry

2330 -- **irrefutable (adj.)** -- that cannot be proved wrong; certain || related word: **irrefutably (adv.)**

2331 -- **irretrievable (adj.)** -- that cannot be repaired || related word: **irretrievably (adv.)**

2332 -- **itinerant (adj./n.)** -- traveling | traveler

2333 -- **itinerary (n.)** -- journey plan

Difficult English Words -- J

2334 -- jab (n./v.) -- sudden push with pointed object | to push sth with a pointed object in a particular direction

2335 -- jabber (n./v.) -- confused talk | to talk in a confused way

2336 -- jack (v.) -- to steal sth that has not much value

2337 -- jaded (adj.) -- very tired; fed-up

2338 -- jagged (adj.) -- rough and sharp

2339 -- jangle (n./v.) -- sound of two metals hitting each other | to feel worried; to make a sound of two metals hitting each other

2340 -- jar (n./v.) -- sudden knock or hit | to have an unpleasant effect; to be unpleasantly different with sth; to hit suddenly

2341 -- jargon (n.) -- technical words

2342 -- jaunt (n.) -- a short and pleasing journey

2343 -- jaunty (adj.) -- lively, enthusiastic and cheerful || related words: **jauntily (adv.), jauntiness (n.)**

2344 -- jaywalk (v.) -- to carelessly walk in a street, etc. || related words: **jaywalker (n.), jaywalking (n.)**

2345 -- jeer (n./v.) -- an impolite remark to show your dislike about sb | to make an impolite remark to show your dislike; to boo or hoot

2346 -- jeopardize (v.) -- to put sb in a situation of danger; to endanger

2347 -- jerk (n./v.) -- a sharp pull, a silly person | to pull sth sharply; to yank or tug

2348 -- jest (n./v.) -- joke | to say sth in a way that Is not serious

2349 -- jetsam (n.) -- thrown-away things

2350 -- jettison (v.) -- to get rid of sth

2351 -- jetty (n.) -- a platform into the sea, etc.

2352 -- jib (v.) -- to not accept sth

2353 -- jibe (n.) -- taunt

2354 -- **jiffy (n.)** -- moment

2355 -- **jiggery-pokery (n.)** -- dishonest behavior

2356 -- **jiggle (v.)** -- to move making short movements

2357 -- **jilt (v.)** -- to suddenly end a love relationship with sb

2358 -- **jingle (n./v.)** -- tune | to make a tune

2359 -- **jingoism (n.)** -- unreasonable belief in the greatness of your own country

2360 -- **jink (v.)** -- to move in a zigzag motion

2361 -- **jinx (n.)** -- bad luck || related word: **jinxed (adj.)**

2362 -- **jitters (n.)** -- feeling nervous || related word: **jittery (adj.)**

2363 -- **jive (v.)** -- to tell sb sth that is not true in a way that seems to be true

2364 -- **jockey (n./v.)** -- horse rider | to try to gain advantage over others

2365 -- **jocularly (adj.)** -- humorous

2366 -- **jolt (n./v.)** -- sudden movement that is rough | to move roughly and suddenly

2367 -- **jostle (v.)** -- to push around

2368 -- **jotter (n.)** -- small notebook

2369 -- **jottings (n.)** -- short notes

2370 -- **joust (n./v.)** -- argument | to make an argument

2371 -- **jovial (adj.)** -- cheerful

2372 -- **jubilant (adj.)** -- delighted || related words: **jubilantly (adv.), jubilation (n.)**

2373 -- **Judas (n.)** -- traitor

2374 -- **judder (v.)** -- to shake in a violent manner

2375 -- **juggernaut (n.)** -- uncontrollable and powerful force

2376 -- **juggle (v.)** -- to manage to do more than one activities

2377 -- **juicy (adj.)** -- attractive

2378 -- jumble (n,/v.) -- mixture of different things | to mix many things || related word: **jumbled (adj.)**

2379 -- jumpstart (v.) -- to start an activity with great enthusiasm

2380 -- junket (n.) -- pleasure trip

2381 -- junkie (n.) -- an addict

2382 -- junta (n.) -- military government

2383 -- jut (v.) -- to stick out from a surface, etc.

2384 -- juxtapose (v.) -- to put together different things to compare them with each other || related word: **juxtaposition (n.)**

Difficult English Words -- K

2385 -- **keel (v.)** -- to fall over sideways

2386 -- **kerfuffle (n.)** -- needless excitement

2387 -- **kernel (n.)** -- inner or central part

2388 -- **kickback (n.)** -- bribe

2389 -- **killing (adj.)** -- making you tired

2390 -- **killjoy (n.)** -- enjoyment-spoiler

2391 -- **kindle (v.)** -- to inspire or encourage | to start burning

2392 -- **kindling (n.)** -- dry pieces of wood

2393 -- **kink (n./v.)** -- bend or twist | to twist sth

2394 -- **kinky (adj.)** -- unusual moral behavior that is unacceptable

2395 -- **kitsch (n.)** -- objects that seems to be too sentimental

2396 -- **knack (n.)** -- habit or skill

2397 -- **knave (n.)** -- dishonest person

2398 -- **knee-jerk (adj.)** -- unthinking; hurried

2399 -- **knock-on (adj.)** -- incidental

2400 -- **knoll (n.)** -- round hill

2401 -- **kosher (adj.)** -- legal

2402 -- **kowtow (v.)** -- to be too loyal to an authority

2403 -- **kudos (n.)** -- admiration

Difficult English Words -- L

2404 -- **laborious (adj.)** -- needing great effort || related word: **laboriously (adv.)**

2405 -- **labyrinth (n.)** -- complicated paths || related word: **labyrinthine (adj.)**

2406 -- **lacerate (v.)** -- to criticize | to slash || related word: **laceration (n.)**

2407 -- **lackadaisical (adj.)** -- careless; apathetic

2408 -- **lackey (n.)** -- assistant or servant

2409 -- **laconic (adj.)** -- brief || related word: **laconically (adv.)**

2410 -- **lacuna (n.)** -- gap

2411 -- **laddish (adj.)** -- in a manly way

2412 -- **lag (v.)** -- to trail

2413 -- **lager lout (n.)** -- a man who gets drunk and behaves in a noisy way

2414 -- **laggard (n.)** -- lazy person, authority, etc; idler

2415 -- **lagoon (n.)** -- pond or lake

2416 -- **laid-back (adj.)** -- negligent

2417 -- **lair (n.)** -- hiding place or den

2418 -- **lairy (adj.)** -- too confident

2419 -- **lambaste (v.)** -- to severely criticize sb/sth

2420 -- **lamely (adv.)** -- ineffectively

2421 -- **lament (v.)** -- to feel very sad; to grieve || related words: **lamentable (adj.), lamentably (adv.), lamentation (n.)**

2422 -- **lampoon (v.)** -- to make fun of sb/sth

2423 -- **languid (adj.)** -- not needing much energy or effort; unenergetic || related word: **languidly (adv.)**

2424 -- **languish (v.)** -- to suffer or to get weaker

2425 -- languor (n.) -- slowness || related words: **languorous (adj.), languorously (adv.)**

2426 -- lanky (adj.) -- long-limbed and awkward

2427 -- lapdog (n.) -- sb who is too submissive

2428 -- larceny (n.) -- theft

2429 -- largesse (n.) -- generosity

2430 -- largish (adj.) -- reasonably large

2431 -- lascivious (adj.) -- showing excessive immorality || related words: **lasciviously (adv.), lasciviousness (n.)**

2432 -- lash (v.) -- to hit forcefully; to criticize angrily

2433 -- lassitude (n.) -- tiredness

2434 -- last-ditch (adj.) -- final and desperate

2435 -- latent (adj.) -- suppressed || related word: **latency (n.)**

2436 -- latitude (n.) -- freedom

2437 -- laud (v.) -- to admire; to praise || related words: **laudable (adj.), laudatory (adj.), laudably (adv.)**

2438 -- lavish (adj.) -- luxurious || related word: **lavishly (adv.)**

2439 -- lax (adj.) -- careless || related word: **laxity (n.)**

2440 -- layabout (n.) -- lazy person

2441 -- lay-off (n.) -- dismissal from job

2442 -- leapfrog (v.) -- to suddenly reach at higher position

2443 -- lecher (n.) -- extremely immoral person || related words: **lecherous (adj.), lechery (n.)**

2444 -- leer (n./v.) -- unpleasant or immoral look or smile | to unpleasantly or immorally look or smile at sb

2445 -- leery (adj.) -- extremely cautious

2446 -- leeway (n.) -- freedom

2447 -- leftover (adj./n.) -- surplus | food that is left after having meal; historical object

2448 -- legacy (n.) -- inheritance

2449 -- **legalese (n.)** -- difficult language used in legal documents

2450 -- **legion (adj./n.)** -- numerous | crowd

2451 -- **leitmotif (n.)** -- repeated or typical phrase

2452 -- **leper (n.)** -- unacceptable person in society

2453 -- **lesion (n.)** -- damaged part of the body

2454 -- **lethal (adj.)** -- toxic; deadly || related word: **lethally (adv.)**

2455 -- **lethargy (n.)** -- unenergetic condition || related word: **lethargic (adj.)**

2456 -- **let-up (n.)** -- stillness; pause

2457 -- **leverage (n./v.)** -- influence | to take advantage of sth

2458 -- **lexicon (n.)** -- dictionary

2459 -- **liable (adj.)** -- responsible; likely

2460 -- **liaise (v.)** -- to mediate || related word: **liaison (n.)**

2461 -- **libel (v.)** -- to defame || related word: **libelous (libellous) (adj.)**

2462 -- **liberate (v.)** -- to set free; to release || related words: **liberated (adj.), liberation (n.), liberator (n.), liberty (n.)**

2463 -- **libido (n.)** -- desire to make physical relationship | **libidinous (adj.)**

2464 -- **licentious (adj.)** -- immoral and shameful || related word: **licentiousness (n.)**

2465 -- **lilt (n.)** -- rhythm || related word: **lilting (adj.)**

2466 -- **limbo (n.)** -- pause

2467 -- **limp (adj./v.)** -- not stiff; without energy | to move slowly because of injury in one leg || related word: **limply (adv.)**

2468 -- **limpid (adj.)** -- transparent

2469 -- **linchpin (n.)** -- central point

2470 -- **lineage (n.)** -- ancestry

2471 -- **line-up (n.)** -- arrangement; gathering

2472 -- **linger (v.)** -- to stay longer

2473 -- **lingering (adj.)** -- long-lasting || related word: **lingeringly (adv.)**

2474 -- **lingo (n.)** -- foreign language | jargon

2475 -- **link-up (n.)** -- connection

2476 -- **liquidate (v.)** -- to sell your business or pay your debt || related words: **liquidation (n.), liquidator (n.)**

2477 -- **liquidize (v.)** -- to mash fruits or vegetables

2478 -- **listless (adj.)** -- without energy || related words: **listlessly (adv,), listlessness (n.)**

2479 -- **litany (n.)** -- numerous events, reasons, etc.

2480 -- **literal (adj.)** -- factual || related words: **literally (adv.), literalness (n.)**

2481 -- **lithe (adj.)** -- flexible || related word: **lithely (adv.)**

2482 -- **litter (n./v.)** -- garbage or trash || to spread garbage or trash

2483 -- **livery (n.)** -- uniform

2484 -- **livid (adj.)** -- very angry; enraged

2485 -- **loath (adj.)** -- unwilling

2486 -- **loathe (v.)** -- to hate intensely || related words: **loathsome (adj.), loathing (n.)**

2487 -- **lob (v.)** -- to throw; to hurl

2488 -- **loft (v.)** -- to throw sth up in the air

2489 -- **lofty (adj.)** -- impressive || related words: **loftily (adv.), loftiness (n.)**

2490 -- **logging (n.)** -- cutting down of trees

2491 -- **logistic (adj.)** -- movement of goods or equipment || related words: **logistically (adv.), logistics (n.)**

2492 -- **logjam (n.)** -- blockage

2493 -- **loiter (v.)** -- to wait or stand somewhere unnecessarily

2494 -- **loll (v.)** -- to lie or stand in a lazy way

2495 -- **loom (v.)** -- to be going to happen in frightening way

2496 -- **loony (adj./n.)** -- very strange | odd person

2497 -- **loopy (adj.)** -- extremely angry | unusual

2498 -- **lop (v.)** -- to cut; to trim

2499 -- **lopsided (adj.)** -- uneven || related word: **lopsidedly (adv.)**

2500 -- **loquacious (adj.)** -- talkative

2501 -- **lore (n.)** -- knowledge or tradition

2502 -- **louche (adj.)** -- unacceptable but interesting

2503 -- **loudmouth (n.)** -- a person who is too talkative or say stupid things || related word: **loudmouthed (adj.)**

2504 -- **lounge (n./v.)** -- public or waiting room | to relax

2505 -- **lousy (adj.)** -- terrible

2506 -- **lout (n.)** -- aggressive person || related word: **loutish (adj.)**

2507 -- **low-down (adj./n.)** -- deceitful | important facts

2508 -- **low-end (n.)** -- cheaper products

2509 -- **lubricious (adj.)** -- extremely immoral

2510 -- **lucid (adj.)** -- clear || related words: **lucidly (adv.), lucidity (n.)**

2511 -- **Lucifer (n.)** -- evil spirit

2512 -- **lucre (n.)** -- money that is obtained deceitfully

2513 -- **luddite (n.)** -- sb who is too traditional in his views

2514 -- **ludicrous (adj.)** -- nonsensical || related words: **ludicrously (adv.), ludicrousness (n.)**

2515 -- **lug (v.)** -- to drag heavy things

2516 -- **lugubrious (adj.)** -- extremely depressed || related words: **lugubriously (adv.)**

2517 -- **lukewarm (adj.)** -- warm to some extent | unenthusiastic

2518 -- **lull (n./v.)** -- silence | to calm or to make sth less intense

2519 -- **lumber (v.)** -- to move heavily || related word: **lumbering (n.)**

2520 -- **luminary (n.)** -- expert

2521 -- **luminous (adj.)** -- very bright | glowing || related words: **luminously (adv.), luminosity (n.)**

2522 -- **lumpen (adj.)** -- looking awkward

2523 -- **lumpish (adj.)** -- clumsy

2524 -- **lunge (v.)** -- to move forward or attack suddenly

2525 -- **lurch (n./v.)** -- tilting movement | to tilt; to lose your balance

2526 -- **lure (n./v.)** -- bait or temptation | to tempt

2527 -- **lurid (adj.)** -- very shocking | extremely bright || related word: **luridly (adv.)**

2528 -- **lurk (v.)** -- to wait in order to do sth illegal or immoral

2529 -- **luscious (adj.)** -- very tasty; very attractive

2530 -- **lush (adj.)** -- flourishing | abundant | expensive

2531 -- **lust (n.)** -- strong desire, especially connected with immoral activity || related word: **lustful (n.)**

2532 -- **luster (lustre) (n.)** -- shine || related word: **lustrous (adj.)**

2533 -- **lusty (adj.)** -- healthy; robust || related word: **lustily (adv.)**

2534 -- **luxuriant (adj.)** -- attractive, abundant || related words: **luxuriantly (adv.), luxuriance (n.)**

2535 -- **lynch (v.)** -- to kill sb in the crowd by hanging || related words: **lynching (n.)**

Difficult English Words -- M

2536 -- **macabre (adj.)** -- deathly and frightening

2537 -- **machination (n.)** -- plot

2538 -- **maelstrom (n.)** -- confusing and frightening situation

2539 -- **magnanimous (adj.)** -- generous and noble; forgiving || related words: **magnanimously (adv.), magnanimity (n.)**

2540 -- **maiden (adj./n.)** -- first | young and unmarried woman

2541 -- **majesty (n.)** -- quality of being grand and impressive || related words: **majestic (adj.), majestically (adv.)**

2542 -- **makeover (n.)** -- big change or improvement

2543 -- **malaise (n.)** -- disappointment or dissatisfaction

2544 -- **malevolent (adj.)** -- harmful; wicked || related words: **malevolently (adv.), malevolence (n.)**

2545 -- **malice (adj.)** -- hatred

2546 -- **malign (adj./v.)** -- harmful | to damage reputation || related words: **malignant (adj.), malignancy (n.)**

2547 -- **malinger (v.)** -- to pretend to be ill || related word: **malingerer (n.)**

2548 -- **malleable (adj.)** -- flexible | changeable || related word: **malleability (n.)**

2549 -- **Mammon (n.)** -- enormous wealth

2550 -- **mammoth (adj.)** -- huge

2551 -- **mane (n.)** -- long hair

2552 -- **maneuver (manoeuvre) (n./v.)** -- careful action, movement or plan | to move or influence sth skillfully or dishonestly || related word: **maneuvering (manoeuvring) (n.)**

2553 -- **mangle (v.)** -- to twist, crush or spoil

2554 -- **mangy (adj.)** -- dirty

2555 -- manhandle (v.) -- to physically misbehave sb | to move heavy object

2556 -- manhunt (n.) -- intensive search for a criminal

2557 -- manifest (adj./v.) -- apparent | to clearly show sth; to be easily noticeable || related words: **manifestly (adv.), manifestation (n.)**

2558 -- manipulate (v.) -- to deceitfully or skillfully control or influence sth || related words: **manipulative (adj.), manipulation (n.), manipulator (n.)**

2559 -- mannequin (n.) -- human model

2560 -- manor (n.) -- large house

2561 -- marauding (adj.) -- waiting to loot sb || related word: **marauder (n.)**

2562 -- marginalize (v.) -- to make people powerless

2563 -- marginally (adv.) -- not enough

2564 -- maroon (v.) -- to leave sb in an island or other isolated place

2565 -- mascot (n.) -- an item that is believed to be lucky

2566 -- mason (n.) -- a worker who uses stones to build sth

2567 -- masonry (n.) -- building made of stone

2568 -- masquerade (n./v.) -- dishonest behavior | to pretend to be sth else; to impersonate

2569 -- matey (adj.) -- friendly but dishonest

2570 -- matriarch (n.) -- woman head of a family or group || related words: **matriarchal (adj.), matriarchy (n.)**

2571 -- matron (n.) -- nurse

2572 -- matronly (adj.) -- fat and aged

2573 -- matted (adj.) -- knotted

2574 -- maudlin (adj.) -- sentimental

2575 -- maul (v.) -- to attack or criticize severely || related word: **mauling (n.)**

2576 -- mausoleum (n.) -- place of burial; tomb

2577 -- **maven (n.)** -- specialist; expert

2578 -- **maverick (n.)** -- odd person

2579 -- **mayhem (n.)** -- violent disorder

2580 -- **maze (n.)** -- complicated system

2581 -- **meadow (n.)** -- grass field

2582 -- **meager (meagre) (adj.)** -- insufficient

2583 -- **meander (v.)** -- to walk | to be uncreative conversation | to keep on changing direction during movement || related word: **meanderings (n.)**

2584 -- **measly (adj.)** -- insufficient

2585 -- **measured (adj.)** -- well-controlled or very careful

2586 -- **meaty (adj.)** -- muscular

2587 -- **meddle (v.)** -- to interfere || related words: **meddling (n.), meddler (n.)**

2588 -- **mediocre (n.)** -- ordinary

2589 -- **mediocrity (n.)** -- not good enough | an average person

2590 -- **medley (n.)** -- mixture of various kinds of people or things

2591 -- **megalomania (n.)** -- feeling of too importance to yourself || related words: **megalomaniac (adv./n.)**

2592 -- **melancholy (adj./n.)** -- sorrowful | extreme feeling of sadness; depression

2593 -- **melee (n.)** -- confusing and violent crowd

2594 -- **mellifluous (adj.)** -- melodious

2595 -- **mellow (adj./v.)** -- pleasant | to become pleasant

2596 -- **memoir (n.)** -- written account about important person, thing, event, etc.

2597 -- **memorabilia (n.)** -- collection of different items related to important person, thing, event, etc.

2598 -- **menace (n./v.)** -- threat | to frighten, threaten or harm || related words: **menacing (adj.), menacingly (adv.)**

2599 -- **ménage (n.)** -- household

2600 -- **mendacious (adj.)** -- untruthful || related word: **mendacity (n.)**

2601 -- **menial (adj.)** -- unskilled and boring

2602 -- **mentor (n.)** -- tutor || related word: **mentoring (n.)**

2603 -- **mercurial (adj.)** -- lively

2604 -- **meritocracy (n.)** -- country ruled by intelligent people || related word: **meritocratic (adj.)**

2605 -- **meritorious (adj.)** -- admirable

2606 -- **merriment (n.)** -- happiness

2607 -- **mesmerize (v.)** -- to fascinate || related word: **mesmerizing (adj.)**

2608 -- **messianic (adj.)** -- involving tremendous changes in social or political system

2609 -- **messy (adj.)** -- untidy

2610 -- **mettle (n.)** -- determination

2611 -- **Midas touch (n.)** -- ability to succeed in all endeavor

2612 -- **midget (adj./n.)** -- very small | small person

2613 -- **miffed (adj.)** -- displeased

2614 -- **mightily (adv.)** -- forcefully | very

2615 -- **mighty (adj./adv.)** -- powerful; impressive | very

2616 -- **milieu (n.)** -- living or working background

2617 -- **mime (v.)** -- to express your thoughts without speaking

2618 -- **mimic (n./v.)** -- able to copy sb's way of behaving | to copy sb's way of behaving || related words: **mimetic (adj.), mimicry (n.)**

2619 -- **mince (v.)** -- to grind

2620 -- **mingle (v.)** -- to mix

2621 -- **mingy (adj.)** -- tightfisted

2622 -- **minion (n.)** -- servant

2623 -- **minnow (n.)** -- small or insignificant company or team

2624 -- **mint (n./v.)** -- money | to make coins

2625 -- **mired (adj.)** -- trapped in bog | trapped in difficult situation

2626 -- **mirth (n.)** -- laughter || related words: **mirthless (adj.), mirthlessly (adv.)**

2627 -- **misanthrope (n.)** -- sb who hates human beings || related words: **misanthropic (adj.), misanthropy (n.)**

2628 -- **misapprehension (n.)** -- misunderstanding

2629 -- **misappropriate (v.)** -- to cheat sb with their money || related word: **misappropriation (n.)**

2630 -- **misbegotten (adj.)** -- planned in a bad way

2631 -- **mischance (n.)** -- bad luck; misfortune

2632 -- **miscible (adj.)** -- easily mixable

2633 -- **misconceive (v.)** -- to misunderstand

2634 -- **misconceived (adj.)** -- planned in a bad way

2635 -- **misconception (n.)** -- mistaken belief

2636 -- **misconstruction (n.)** -- misunderstanding

2637 -- **misconstrue (v.)** -- to understand in a wrong way

2638 -- **miscreant (n.)** -- wrongdoer; criminal

2639 -- **misdemeanor (misdemeanour) (n.)** -- bad behavior

2640 -- **misfile (v.)** -- to place folder, files or other documents in wrong place

2641 -- **misgiving (n.)** -- doubt

2642 -- **misguided (adj.)** -- wrong; mistaken || related word: **misguidedly (adv.)**

2643 -- **mishandle (v.)** -- to misbehave sb physically | to manage in a wrong way || related word: **mishandling (n.)**

2644 -- **mishap (n.)** -- accident

2645 -- **mishmash (n.)** -- a big confusion because of mixing different things, etc.

2646 -- **mislay (v.)** -- to be unable to find sth

2647 -- **misname (v.)** -- to give wrong name to sth

2648 -- **misnomer (n.)** -- wrong or inappropriate name given to sth

2649 -- **misogynist (n.)** -- a man who detest women || related words: **misogynistic (adj.), misogyny (n.)**

2650 -- **missive (n.)** -- official letter

2651 -- **mitigate (v.)** -- to ease || related word: **mitigation (n.)**

2652 -- **moan (v.)** -- to sigh | to complain

2653 -- **modality (n.)** -- the way sth important is done

2654 -- **modicum (n.)** -- small amount

2655 -- **modulate (v.)** -- to change the pace or quality of sth || related word: **modulation (n.)**

2656 -- **molder (moulder) (v.)** -- to decay in a steady way

2657 -- **moll (n.)** -- female companion of a wrongdoer

2658 -- **mollify (v.)** -- to calm down

2659 -- **mollycoddle (v.)** -- to give too much protection to sb

2660 -- **momentous (adj.)** -- extraordinary; historic

2661 -- **monastic (adj.)** -- simple and severe; austere || related word: **monasticism (n.)**

2662 -- **monolith (n.)** -- large organization, institution, system etc. that does not give much importance to individuals | a large stone || related words: **monolithic (adj.)**

2663 -- **monologue (n.)** -- long speech or story

2664 -- **monster (adj./n.)** -- huge | cruel, evil, large or ugly person or thing || related words: **monstrous (adj.), monstrously (adv.), monstrosity (n.)**

2665 -- **mooch (v.)** -- to beg | to walk without good reason

2666 -- **moor (v.)** -- to fasten ship, etc. with a rope; to anchor

2667 -- **moot (adj./v.)** -- unlikely | to propose

2668 -- **mope (v.)** -- to waste your time in thinking about things that upset you

2669 -- **moppet (n.)** -- attractive girl child

2670 -- **moralize (v.)** -- to give lecture on morality

2671 -- **morass (n.)** -- bog | complicated situation that you cannot escape from

2672 -- **moratorium (n.)** -- official suspension of an activity

2673 -- **morbid (adj.)** -- depressing || related words: **morbidly (adv.), morbidity (n.)**

2674 -- **mordant (adj.)** -- unkind but amusing || related words: **mordantly (adv.)**

2675 -- **moribund (adj.)** -- in the last stage; ineffective or dying

2676 -- **moron (n.)** -- stupid person or thing || related word: **moronic (adj.)**

2677 -- **morose (adj.)** -- bad-tempered; irritating || related word: **morosely (adv.)**

2678 -- **morsel (n.)** -- small amount of food

2679 -- **mortify (v.)** -- to embarrass || related words: **mortifying (adj.), mortification (n.)**

2680 -- **mote (n.)** -- small piece of dirt or dust

2681 -- **mothball (v.)** -- to postpone a plan

2682 -- **moth-eaten (adj.)** -- in a bad state

2683 -- **motif (n.)** -- decoration in a form of pattern

2684 -- **motley (adj.)** -- mixed

2685 -- **motormouth (n.)** -- talkative

2686 -- **mourn (v.)** -- to grieve or lament || related words: **mournful (adj.), mournfully (adv.), mourner (n.), mourning (n.)**

2687 -- **mow (v.)** -- to cut grass; to trim || related word: **mower (n.)**

2688 -- **muck (n.)** -- manure | dirty or unpleasant thing || related word: **mucky (adj.)**

2689 -- **mucker (n.)** -- rude person

2690 -- **muddle (n./v.)** -- mess | to mess or confuse || related word: **muddled (adj.)**

2691 -- **muffle (v.)** -- to quiet | to wrap || related word: **muffled (adj.)**

2692 -- **mug (v.)** -- to attack and steal || related words: **mugger (n.),** **mugging (n.)**

2693 -- **muggy (adj.)** -- unpleasantly wet; humid

2694 -- **mulch (n./v.)** -- manure | to add manure on the soil

2695 -- **mumble (n./v.)** -- quiet and unclear words | to say sth quietly and unclearly

2696 -- **mumbo-jumbo (n.)** -- sth that is too complicated; rubbish

2697 -- **munch (v.)** -- to chew sth in a noisy way; to crunch

2698 -- **mundane (adj.)** -- boring

2699 -- **munificent (adj.)** -- generous; benevolent || related word: **munificence (n.)**

2700 -- **murk (n.)** -- darkness || related word: **murky (adj.)**

2701 -- **muse (n./v.)** -- inspiration | to consider || related word: **musing (n.)**

2702 -- **mush (n.)** -- thick mixture || related word: **mushy (adj.)**

2703 -- **muster (n./v.)** -- group of soldiers | to get together

2704 -- **musty (adj.)** -- unpleasantly wet and cold

2705 -- **muzzle (v.)** -- to silence sb; to gag

2706 -- **muzzy (adj.)** -- unclear

2707 -- **myriad (adj./n.)** -- countless | countless things, etc.

2708 -- **mystic (n.)** -- spiritualist || related words: **mystical (adj.),** **mystically (adv.), mysticism (n.)**

2709 -- **mystify (v.)** -- to completely confuse sb || related words: **mystifying (adj.), mystification (n.)**

2710 -- **mystique (n.)** -- fascination

Difficult English Words -- N

2711 -- **nag (v.)** -- to harass

2712 -- **nagging (adj.)** -- complaining | continuing

2713 -- **naïve (adj.)** -- without much experience || related words: **naively (adv.), naivety (n.)**

2714 -- **namby-pamby (adj.)** -- sentimental

2715 -- **nap (n./v.)** -- short sleep during the day | to take a short sleep

2716 -- **narcissism (n.)** -- self-importance || related word: **narcissistic (n.)**

2717 -- **nark (n.)** -- police-informer

2718 -- **narked (adj.)** -- annoyed || related word: **narky (adj.)**

2719 -- **nary (adj.)** -- no

2720 -- **nascent (adj.)** -- undeveloped

2721 -- **nasty (adj.)** -- very unpleasant || related words: **nastily (adv.), nastiness (n.)**

2722 -- **natter (n./v.)** -- chat | to make informal conversation

2723 -- **natty (adj.)** -- fashionable or well-designed || related word: **nattily (adv.)**

2724 -- **navigate (v.)** -- to find direction or position of the ship || related words: **navigational (adj.), navigation (n.), navigator (n.)**

2725 -- **nay (adv.)** -- no

2726 -- **nebula (n.)** -- a mass of dust in the night sky

2727 -- **nebulous (adj.)** -- unclear

2728 -- **nefarious (adj.)** -- immoral

2729 -- **negate (v.)** -- to nullify || related word: **negation (n.)**

2730 -- **nemesis (n.)** -- unavoidable punishment

2731 -- **neonatal (adj.)** -- related to newborn child

2732 -- **nerd (n.)** -- bore || related word: **nerdy (adj.)**

2733 -- **nerve (v.)** -- to encourage

2734 -- **nervy (adj.)** -- anxious

2735 -- **nest egg (n.)** -- future savings

2736 -- **nestle (v.)** -- to be in a safe position

2737 -- **nestling (n.)** -- a young bird that is unable to leave its nest

2738 -- **nettle (v.)** -- to annoy || related word: **nettlesome (adj.)**

2739 -- **nibble (n./v.)** -- small bite | to take small bites

2740 -- **nick (v.)** -- small cut | to arrest, cut or steal

2741 -- **nifty (adj.)** -- skillful or practical

2742 -- **niggardly (adj.)** -- not generous

2743 -- **niggle (n./v.)** -- complaint | to annoy

2744 -- **niggling (adj.)** -- unimportant

2745 -- **nihilism (n.)** -- used to show there is no value of anything || related words: **nihilistic (adj.), nihilist (n.)**

2746 -- **nimble (adj.)** -- quick and lively || related word: **nimbly (adv.)**

2747 -- **nip (v.)** -- to pinch

2748 -- **nit-picking (n.)** -- bad habit of finding small faults in others || related word: **nit-picker (n.)**

2749 -- **nitty-gritty (n.)** -- most important details

2750 -- **nitwit (n.)** -- stupid person

2751 -- **nix (n./v.)** -- nothing | to say 'no'

2752 -- **nob (n.)** -- member of upper-class

2753 -- **nomad (n.)** -- wanderer || related word: **nomadic (adj.)**

2754 -- **nominal (adj.)** -- in name only || related word: **nominally (adv.)**

2755 -- **nonchalant (adj.)** -- relaxed; indifference || related words: **nonchalantly (adv.), nonchalance (n.)**

2756 -- **nondescript (adj.)** -- ordinary

2757 -- **nonentity (n.)** -- unimportant person

2758 -- **nonplussed (adj.)** -- very confused

2759 -- **nonsensical (adj.)** -- meaningless

2760 -- **nook (n.)** -- corner

2761 -- nosy (adj.) -- interfering || related word: **nosily (adv.), nosiness (n.)**

2762 -- notch (n./v.) -- level | to win

2763 -- notion (n.) -- belief

2764 -- novelty (adj./n.) -- new | newness

2765 -- novice (n.) -- inexperienced person

2766 -- noxious (adj.) -- harmful

2767 -- nuance (n.) -- slight difference

2768 -- nubile (adj.) -- (of a girl/woman) having attractive figure

2769 -- nudge (n./v.) -- slight push with the elbow | to push gently with elbow

2770 -- nugatory (adj.) -- purposeless

2771 -- nugget (n.) -- small thing

2772 -- nuisance (n.) -- annoyance

2773 -- numismatist (n.) -- coin-collector

2774 -- nuptial (adj.) -- related to marriage

2775 -- nuts (adj.) -- crazy

2776 -- nymphet (n.) -- extremely attractive young girl

Difficult English Words -- O

2777 -- **oaf (n.)** -- a stupid man || related word: **oafish (adj.)**

2778 -- **oasis (n.)** -- place of water in desert | haven

2779 -- **obdurate (adj.)** -- stubborn || related words: **obdurately (adv.), obduracy (n.)**

2780 -- **obeisance (n.)** -- willingness to obey

2781 -- **obfuscate (v.)** -- to confuse or obscure || related word: **obfuscation (n.)**

2782 -- **obituary (n.)** -- advertisement in newspaper about sb's death

2783 -- **obliging (adj.)** -- helpful || related word: **obligingly (adv.)**

2784 -- **oblique (adj.)** -- indirect || related word: **obliquely (adv.)**

2785 -- **obliterate (v.)** -- to destroy completely || related word: **obliteration (n.)**

2786 -- **oblivion (n.)** -- forgetfulness | complete destruction || related words: **oblivious (adj.), obliviously (adv.)**

2787 -- **obnoxious (adj.)** -- extremely unpleasant; hateful || related word: **obnoxiously (adv.)**

2788 -- **obscene (adj.)** -- morally offensive || related word: **obscenity (n.)**

2789 -- **obscure (adj./v.)** -- unclear or unknown | to make sth unclear || related word: **obscurely (adv.), obscurity (n.)**

2790 -- **obsequies (n.)** -- funereal ceremonies

2791 -- **obsequious (adj.)** -- trying to impress powerful person || related words: **obsequiously (adv.}, obsequiousness (n.)**

2792 -- **obsess (v.)** -- to keep on thinking about a particular person or thing || related words: **obsessive (adj.), obsessively (adv.), obsession (n.)**

2793 -- **obsolescence (n.)** -- no longer useful || related word: **obsolescent (adj.)**

2794 -- obsolete (adj.) -- outdated

2795 -- obstinate (adj.) -- stubborn || related words: **obstinately (adv.), obstinacy (n.)**

2796 -- obstreperous (adj.) -- bad-tempered

2797 -- obtrude (v.) -- to make sth noticeable in an unpleasant way || related word: **obtrusive (adj.), obtrusively (adv.)**

2798 -- obtuse (adj.) -- unwilling to understand || related word: **obtuseness (n.)**

2799 -- obverse (n.) -- opposite

2800 -- obviate (v.) -- to prevent sth from happening

2801 -- occlude (v.) -- to block sth || related word: **occlusion (n.)**

2802 -- oddity (n.) -- strangeness

2803 -- odious (adj.) -- extremely bad or unpleasant

2804 -- odyssey (n.) -- long journey

2805 -- offbeat (adj.) -- unusual

2806 -- officiate (v.) -- to oversee or supervise

2807 -- officious (adj.) -- self-important || related words: **officiously (adv.), officiousness (n.)**

2808 -- offset (v.) -- to balance the situation

2809 -- offshoot (n.) -- subsidiary

2810 -- ogle (v.) -- to stare offensively or indecently

2811 -- ogre (n.) -- frightening person

2812 -- oligarch (n.) -- extremely rich person

2813 -- ombudsman (n.) -- government auditor

2814 -- omen (n.) -- warning; sign

2815 -- ominous (adj.) -- threatening || related word: **ominously (adv.)**

2816 -- omnibus (adj./n.) -- having many types of things | compilation of books in a form of a large book

2817 -- omniscient (adj.) -- having knowledge about everything || related word: **omniscience (n.)**

2818 -- **one-off (adj./n.)** -- occurring only once | sth that occurs only once

2819 -- **onerous (adj.)** -- requiring great effort

2820 -- **one-upmanship (n.)** -- advantage over others

2821 -- **on-off (adj.)** -- frequently interrupted

2822 -- **onset (n.)** -- beginning

2823 -- **onslaught (n.)** -- severe attack

2824 -- **onus (n.)** -- responsibility

2825 -- **oodles (n.)** -- large amount

2826 -- **oomph (n.)** -- liveliness

2827 -- **ooze (n./v.)** -- flow of thick liquid | (of thick liquid) to come out of sth || related word: **oozy (adj.)**

2828 -- **opaque (adj.)** -- not clear | transparent

2829 -- **open-ended (adj.)** -- unrestricted

2830 -- **oppress (v.)** -- to dominate and afflict || related words: **oppressed (adj.), oppression (n.)**

2831 -- **opprobrium (n.)** -- harsh criticism || related word: **opprobrious (adj.)**

2832 -- **opulent (adj.)** -- wealthy or lavish || related words: **opulently (adv.), opulence (n.)**

2833 -- **opus (n.)** -- literary work on a large scale

2834 -- **oration (n.)** -- formal speech in public

2835 -- **orator (n.)** -- a person who is good in public speaking || related word: **oratorical (adj.)**

2836 -- **orchestrate (v.)** -- to organize || related word: **orchestration (n.)**

2837 -- **ordeal (n.)** -- suffering

2838 -- **orderly (adj.)** -- well-arranged || related word: **orderliness (n.)**

2839 -- **ordnance (n.)** -- materials related to military

2840 -- organic (n.) -- produced from living beings || related word: **organically (adv.)**

2841 -- ornate (adj.) -- decorated || related word: **ornately (adv.)**

2842 -- oscillate (v.) -- to move back and forth; to keep changing || related word: **oscillation (n.)**

2843 -- ostensible (adj.) -- apparent or seeming || related word: **ostensibly (adv.)**

2844 -- ostentation (n.) -- display of your wealth, power, etc. || related words: **ostentatious (adj.), ostentatiously (adv.)**

2845 -- ostracize (v.) -- to get rid of sb; to exclude sb from your group

2846 -- otiose (adj.) -- useless

2847 -- outage (n.) -- a period of time without electricity

2848 -- out-and-out (adj.) -- absolute; complete

2849 -- outbreak (n.) -- sudden eruption of violence, virus, etc.

2850 -- outburst (n.) -- expression of a strong feeling

2851 -- outcry (n.) -- strong protest

2852 -- outdo (v.) -- to do better than sb; to surpass

2853 -- outface (v.) -- to defeat your enemy

2854 -- outgoing (adj.) -- friendly or sociable

2855 -- outgoings (n.) -- spending

2856 -- outlandish (adj.) -- strange || related word: **outlandishly (adv.)**

2857 -- outlay (n.) -- money that is needed to start a new project

2858 -- outlive (v.) -- to live longer than sb

2859 -- outlook (n.) -- attitude or prospect | view

2860 -- outmaneuver (outmanoeuvre) (v.) -- to be better than your opponent

2861 -- outmoded (adj.) -- old-fashioned

2862 -- outpouring (n.) -- sudden expression of emotions | a large amount

2863 -- **outrage (n./v.)** -- anger | to shock sb || related words: **outrageous (adj.), outrageously (adv.)**

2864 -- **outright (adj./adv.)** -- complete or direct | completely or directly

2865 -- **outsmart (v.)** -- to be cleverer than other

2866 -- **outwit (v.)** -- to be better than your opponent

2867 -- **ovation (n.)** -- prolonged applause

2868 -- **overarching (adj.)** -- extremely important

2869 -- **overbearing (adj.)** -- dominant

2870 -- **overcast (adj.)** -- cloudy

2871 -- **overdue (adj.)** -- unpaid or unsettled

2872 -- **overhear (v.)** -- to accidentally hear a conversation

2873 -- **overkill (n.)** -- too much of sth

2874 -- **overlay (n./v.)** -- cover | to cover

2875 -- **overlook (v.)** -- to miss or ignore

2876 -- **overly (adv.)** -- excessively

2877 -- **overreach (v.)** -- to exceed your limit

2878 -- **override (v.)** -- to be more important than sth else | to overrule || related word: **overriding (adj.)**

2879 -- **overshadow (v.)** -- to make sth less impressive

2880 -- **oversight (n.)** -- mistake | in charge of sth

2881 -- **overt (adj.)** -- obvious || related word: **overtly (adv.)**

2882 -- **overtax (v.)** -- to exceed your limit | to ask for unreasonable amount of tax

2883 -- **overture (n.)** -- proposal

2884 -- **overturn (v.)** -- to change the decision | to turn upside down

2885 -- **overwhelming (adj.)** -- very strong || related word: **overwhelmingly (adv.)**

Difficult English Words -- P

2886 -- pacify (v.) -- to bring peace | to calm || related word: **pacification (n.)**

2887 -- paean (n.) -- song of praise

2888 -- pageant (n.) -- a type of beauty competition to test beauty and skills of a woman | interesting events

2889 -- pageantry (n.) -- impressive public ceremonies in which people wear special costumes

2890 -- palatable (adj.) -- delicious or pleasant

2891 -- palatial (adj.) -- grand; impressive

2892 -- palimony (n.) -- regular payment to a former partner (not wife or husband)

2893 -- pall (v.) -- to seem to be less impressive over a period of time

2894 -- palliate (v.) -- to decrease the intensity of pain || related word: **palliative (adj./n.)**

2895 -- pallid (adj.) -- pale

2896 -- palpable (adj.) -- easily noticed by senses || related word: **palpably (adv.)**

2897 -- palpate (v.) -- to touch a part of body in order to examine || related word: **palpation (n.)**

2898 -- palpitate (v.) -- to beat quickly and irregularly; to throb || related word: **palpitations (n.)**

2899 -- paltry (adj.) -- worthless or meager

2900 -- panache (n.) -- attractive style

2901 -- pandemic (n.) -- a disease that spreads over a whole country

2902 -- pandemonium (n.) -- a situation of great confusion; chaos

2903 -- panegyric (n.) -- a speech that praises sb/sth

2904 -- pang (n.) -- sudden, strong pain

2905 -- pantheon (n.) -- group of a particular type of famous people

2906 -- paparazzo (n.) -- photographer who is interested in getting photos of famous people

2907 -- parable (n.) -- short story with moral or spiritual lesson

2908 -- paradigm (n.) -- typical example, model or pattern || related word: **paradigmatic (adj.)**

2909 -- paradigm shift (n.) -- very big change in the theory, policy, etc.

2910 -- paradox (n.) -- contradiction || related words: **paradoxical (adj.), paradoxically (adv.)**

2911 -- paragon (n.) -- role modal

2912 -- paramount (adj.) -- supreme; most important

2913 -- paramour (n.) -- lover

2914 -- paranoia (n.) -- unreasonable fear that you are being harmed by other people | related word: **paranoid (adj.)**

2915 -- paraphernalia (n.) -- equipments that are needed for a particular activity

2916 -- paraplegia (n.) -- paralysis in lower part of the body || related word: **paraplegic (adj./n.)**

2917 -- pare (v.) -- to remove skin of fruit | to decrease

2918 -- pariah (n.) -- a person who is unacceptable in society | outcast

2919 -- parish (n.) -- a particular area

2920 -- parity (n.) -- equality; uniformity

2921 -- parley (n./v.) -- discussion to resolve the disagreement | to discuss with this purpose

2922 -- parlous (adj.) -- dangerous, uncertain and risky

2923 -- parochial (adj.) -- narrow-minded || related word: **parochialism (n.)**

2924 -- paroxysm (n.) -- uncontrollable feeling

2925 -- parry (v.) -- to avoid answering a difficult question | to deflect

2926 -- partake (v.) -- to participate | to eat or drink

2927 -- **partisan (adj./n.)** -- biased | supporter || related word: **partisanship (n.)**

2928 -- **party-pooper (n.)** -- fun-spoiler

2929 -- **passable (adj.)** -- unblocked | reasonably good || related word: **passably (adv.)**

2930 -- **passé (adj.)** -- old-fashioned or outdated

2931 -- **passivity (n.)** -- submissiveness, meekness or compliance

2932 -- **pastoral (adj.)** -- relating to animals-farming or countryside || related words: **pastoralist (adj./n.), pastoralism (n.)**

2933 -- **patchwork (n.)** -- mess | needlework

2934 -- **patchy (adj.)** -- uneven or incomplete || related words: **patchily (adv.), patchiness (n.)**

2935 -- **patently (adv.)** -- clearly or obviously

2936 -- **paterfamilias (n.)** -- head of a family

2937 -- **pathetic (adj.)** -- very sad or weak || related word: **pathetically (adv.)**

2938 -- **patriarchal (adj.)** -- ruled by men || related words: **patriarch (n.), patriarchy (n.)**

2939 -- **patrician (adj.)** -- belonging to upper class

2940 -- **patrimony (n.)** -- inheritance

2941 -- **paucity (n.)** -- shortage

2942 -- **paunch (n.)** -- fat stomach on men's body

2943 -- **pay dirt (n.)** -- earth with valuable metals or minerals

2944 -- **payload (n.)** -- load carried by satellite, aircraft or vehicle, etc.

2945 -- **payola (n.)** -- bribery

2946 -- **payout (n.)** -- big amount of money

2947 -- **peacenik (n.)** -- strong supporter of non-violence

2948 -- **peaky (adj.)** -- ill and pale

2949 -- **peal (n./v.)** -- loud sound | to ring; to laugh

2950 -- **peasant (n.)** -- impolite person | a farmer who is owner of a small piece of land || related word: **peasantry (n.)**

2951 -- **peccadillo (n.)** -- minor wrongdoing

2952 -- **peculiar (adj.)** -- strange || related words: **peculiarly (adv.), peculiarity (n.)**

2953 -- **pecuniary (adj.)** -- financial

2954 -- **pedagogic (adj.)** -- relating to the methods of teaching; educational || related words: **pedagogue (n.), pedagogy (n.)**

2955 -- **pedantic (adj.)** -- very choosy || related words: **pedantically (adv.), pedantry (n.)**

2956 -- **peddle (v.)** -- to sell sth door to door | to spread your thoughts

2957 -- **peddler (n.)** -- seller of illegal drugs

2958 -- **pedestal (n.)** -- base of a statue, etc.

2959 -- **pedigree (n.)** -- family background | record of breeding history of animal

2960 -- **peek (n./v.)** -- quick look; peep | to have a quick look

2961 -- **peer (n./v.)** -- colleague | to look at sth in a careful way; to gaze

2962 -- **peeved (adj.)** -- very angry; irritated || related words: **peevish (adj.), peevishly (adv.)**

2963 -- **peg (v.)** -- to fasten | to fix prices

2964 -- **pejorative (adj.)** -- critical || related word: **pejoratively (adv.)**

2965 -- **pellet (n.)** -- small hard ball

2966 -- **pellucid (adj.)** -- crystal clear

2967 -- **penance (n.)** -- self-punishment; atonement

2968 -- **penchant (n.)** -- affection: fondness

2969 -- **penitent (adj./n.)** -- regretful | regretful person || related word: **penitential (adj.)**

2970 -- **penitentiary (n.)** -- prison

2971 -- **pensive (adj.)** -- thoughtful || related word: **pensively (adv.)**

2972 -- **penury (n.)** -- poverty || related word: **penurious (adj.)**

2973 -- **pep (n./v.)** -- liveliness | to make sb/sth lively || related word: **peppy (adj.)**

2974 -- **pep talk (n.)** -- inspirational talk

2975 -- **perambulate (v.)** -- to walk or travel for pleasure || related word: **perambulation (n.)**

2976 -- **perceptible (adj.)** -- noticeable || related word: **perceptibly (adv.)**

2977 -- **perceptive (adj.)** -- insightful; understanding || related words: **perceptively (adv.), perceptiveness (n.), perception (n.)**

2978 -- **perch (n./v.)** -- high seat | to land or sit on sth

2979 -- **percipient (adj.)** -- insightful; perceptive

2980 -- **percolate (v.)** -- to seep or spread; to permeate || related word: **percolation (n.)**

2981 -- **percussion (n.)** -- musical instruments that are played with a stick or hand

2982 -- **peremptorily (adv.)** -- unconditionally; firmly || related word: **peremptory (adj.)**

2983 -- **perennial (adj./n.)** -- repeated; continuing | plant that lives more than two years || related word: **perennially (adv.)**

2984 -- **perfidious (adj.)** -- that cannot be trusted; disloyal | **perfidy (n.)**

2985 -- **perforate (v.)** -- to pierce or tear sth to make hole || related word: **perforation (n.)**

2986 -- **perforce (adv.)** -- necessarily; inevitably

2987 -- **perfunctory (adj.)** -- automatic || related word: **perfunctorily (adv.)**

2988 -- **peril (n.)** -- serious threat or danger || related words: **perilous (adj.), perilously (adv.)**

2989 -- **perish (v.)** -- to die suddenly

2990 -- **perjure (v.)** -- to tell lie in a court || related words: **perjurer (n.), perjury (n.)**

2991 -- **permafrost (n.)** -- frozen layer of a soil

2992 -- **permeate (v.)** -- to seep or spread || related word: **permeation (n.)**

2993 -- **permissive (adj.)** -- allowing freedom for bad behavior || related word: **permissiveness (n.)**

2994 -- **permutation (n.)** -- different combinations or variations

2995 -- **pernicious (adj.)** -- very harmful

2996 -- **perpetrate (v.)** -- to do sth illegal, to commit crime || related words: **perpetration (n.), perpetrator (n.)**

2997 -- **perpetual (adj.)** -- everlasting || related word: **perpetually (adv.)**

2998 -- **perplex (v.)** -- to confuse || related words: **perplexed (adj.), perplexing (adj.), perplexity (n.), perplexedly (adv.)**

2999 -- **perquisite (n.)** -- special rights; privilege

3000 -- **persecute (v.)** -- to harass sb, especially because of their race, etc. || related word: **persecution (n.)**

3001 -- **persist (v.)** -- to continue || related word: **persistence (n.)**

3002 -- **persistent (adj.)** -- obstinate; continuing || related word: **persistently (adv.)**

3003 -- **persona (n.)** -- personality

3004 -- **personable (adj.)** -- with attractive personality

3005 -- **personage (n.)** -- very famous person

3006 -- **perspicacious (adj.)** -- very smart to understand sth; insightful || related word: **perspicacity (n.)**

3007 -- **perspire (v.)** -- to sweat

3008 -- **persuade (v.)** -- to convince || related words: **persuasive (adj.), persuasively (adv.), persuasion (n.), persuasiveness (n.)**

3009 -- **pertain (v.)** -- to relate

3010 -- **pertinacious (adj.)** -- determined; willful || related word: **pertinacity (n.)**

3011 -- **pertinent (adj.)** -- relevant || related words: **pertinently (adv.), pertinence (n.)**

3012 -- **perturb (v.)** -- to bother || related words: **perturbed (adj.), perturbation (n.)**

3013 -- **peruse (v.)** -- to read carefully || related word: **perusal (adj.)**

3014 -- **pervade (v.)** -- to spread or pass through sth || related words: **pervasively (adv.), pervasiveness (n.)**

3015 -- **perverse (adj.)** -- stubborn or wicked || related words: **perversely (adv.), perversity (n.)**

3016 -- **pervert (n./v.)** -- immoral person | to affect in a bad, immoral or unacceptable way; to distort the rule, law or system || related words: **perverted (adj.), perversion (n.)**

3017 -- **pesky (adj.)** -- irritating

3018 -- **pester (v.)** -- to irritate

3019 -- **pestilence (n.)** -- infectious and deadly disease || related word: **pestilential (adj.)**

3020 -- **petite (adj.)** -- having short, attractive stature

3021 -- **petrify (v.)** -- to frighten or horrify || related word: **petrified (adj.)**

3022 -- **pettifogging (adj.)** -- emphasizing insignificant details; trivial

3023 -- **petulant (adj.)** -- irritable || related words: **petulantly (adv.), petulance (n.)**

3024 -- **phalanx (n.)** -- a group of closely standing people or things

3025 -- **phantasm (n.)** -- fantasy

3026 -- **phenomenal (adj.)** -- very impressive || related word: **phenomenally (adv.)**

3027 -- **philanthropist (n.)** -- very generous towards poor people || related word: **philanthropic (adj.), philanthropically (adv.), philanthropy (n.)**

3028 -- **philistine (adj./n.)** -- showing no interest in art, music, etc. | sb who shows no interest in art, literature, etc. || related word: **philistinism (n.)**

3029 -- **phlegmatic (adj.)** -- indifferent or calm || related word: **phlegmatically (adv.)**

3030 -- **phonetics (n.)** -- scientific study of speech sounds || related word: **phonetician (n.)**

3031 -- **phony (phoney) (adj./n.)** -- fake | a fake person

3032 -- **picket (n.)** -- group of protestors outside factory, office, etc; group of soldiers | to protest in a group outside factory, office, etc || related words: **picketer (n.), picketing (n.)**

3033 -- **pickled (adj.)** -- drunk | preserved in vinegar, etc.

3034 -- **picky (adj.)** -- very choosy

3035 -- **piddling (adj.)** -- unimportant; petty

3036 -- **pidgin (n.)** -- a language in very simple form

3037 -- **piecemeal (adj./adv.)** -- done in a gradual way | gradually

3038 -- **piety (n.)** -- godliness || related words: **pious (adj.), piously (adv.)**

3039 -- **piffle (n.)** -- rubbish; nonsense

3040 -- **piffling (adj.)** -- having no significance

3041 -- **pile-up (n.)** -- accident of several vehicles

3042 -- **pilfer (v.)** -- to steal in small amounts || related words: **pilferage (n.), pilferer (n.), pilfering (n.)**

3043 -- **pillage (v.)** -- to steal things in war || related word: **pillager (n.)**

3044 -- **pillory (v.)** -- to publicly criticize or humiliate sb

3045 -- **pine (v.)** -- to become sad at sb's demise; to feel unhappy when sb has left you

3046 -- **pinion (v.)** -- to tie sb by their arms

3047 -- **pinprick (n.)** -- small hole | sth that irritates you in spite of its being very small

3048 -- **pip (v.)** -- to defeat sb with a very low margin

3049 -- **pipsqueak (n.)** -- insignificant young person

3050 -- **piquant (adj.)** -- spicy | interesting || related word: **piquancy (n.)**

3051 -- **pique (n./v.)** -- irritation | to irritate || related word: **piqued (adj.)**

3052 -- **pirouette (n./v.)** -- a spinning or turning movement that sb makes on one foot | to spin or turn on one foot

3053 -- **pitch-black (adj.)** -- completely dark || related word: **pitch-dark (adj.)**

3054 -- **pitched battle (n.)** -- a war or fight in which large number of people takes part

3055 -- **pitfall (n.)** -- danger

3056 -- **pith (n.)** -- the most significant part

3057 -- **pithy (adj.)** -- clearly expressed in a few words || related word: **pithily (adv.)**

3058 -- **pittance (n.)** -- meager amount for your livelihood

3059 -- **pivotal (adj.)** -- being the central part of sth; most important

3060 -- **placate (v.)** -- to make sb calm || related word: **placatory (adj.)**

3061 -- **placid (adj.)** -- peaceful || related words: **placidly (adv.), placidity (n.)**

3062 -- **plagiarize (v.)** -- to illegally copy sb's work || related word: **plagiarism (n.)**

3063 -- **plague (v.)** -- to annoy or bother sb

3064 -- **plaint (n.)** -- sad cry | complaint filed in court

3065 -- **plaintive (adj.)** -- sad || related word: **plaintively (adv.)**

3066 -- **plank (n.)** -- one of the most significant parts of a policy

3067 -- **plateau (n./v.)** -- stability | to remain stable

3068 -- **platitude (n.)** -- repeated and boring comment || related word: **platitudinous (adj.)**

3069 -- **platonic (adj.)** -- loving but not physical

3070 -- **plaudit (n.)** -- admiration

3071 -- **plausible (adj.)** -- believable and reasonable || related words: **plausibly (adv.), plausibility (n.)**

3072 -- **pleading (n.)** -- emotions || related word: **pleadingly (adv.)**

3073 -- **pleasantry (n.)** -- pleasant and friendly remark

3074 -- **plebeian (adj./n.)** -- ordinary | person who belongs to lower class

3075 -- **pledge (n./v.)** -- promise | to promise

3076 -- **plenary (adj.)** -- complete | attended by every member of a particular group

3077 -- **plenitude (n.)** -- plentiful

3078 -- **plethora (n.)** -- surplus

3079 -- **pliable (adj.)** -- flexible | controllable

3080 -- **pliant (adj.)** -- controllable | related words: **pliantly (adv.), pliancy (n.)**

3081 -- **plinth (n.)** -- base of a statue or column

3082 -- **plod (v.)** -- to walk in tiring way

3083 -- **plodding (adj.)** -- doing sth in slow, steady and boring way || related word: **plodder (n.)**

3084 -- **plop (n./v.)** -- sound of sth falling into water or other liquid | to drop sth into water or other liquid

3085 -- **ploy (n.)** -- careful efforts to achieve sth; tactic

3086 -- **plum (adj.)** -- exceptional

3087 -- **plume (n.)** -- cloud of sth

3088 -- **plummet (v.)** -- to fall from a high position

3089 -- **plump (n./v.)** -- soft, fat and round | to increase size or softness of sth

3090 -- **plunder (n./v.)** -- stolen things | to steal things in war || related word: **plunderer (n.)**

3091 -- plunge (n./v.) -- downward movement | to move downwards or forwards

3092 -- plunk (plonk) (n./v.) -- sound of sth falling | to noisily put sth down; to sit down in this way

3093 -- plush (adj.) -- lavish; luxurious

3094 -- plutocracy (n.) -- rule by the wealthy people || related word: **plutocrat (n.)**

3095 -- pneumatic (adj.) -- filled with or worked by air

3096 -- poach (v.) -- to simmer | to kill birds illegally || related word: **poacher (n.)**

3097 -- pocked (adj.) -- filled with holes

3098 -- pockmark (n.) -- scar on body || related word: **pockmarked (adj.)**

3099 -- pogrom (n.) -- mass killing of people who belongs to a particular race or religion

3100 -- poignant (adj.) -- upsetting || related words: **poignantly (adv.), poignancy (n.)**

3101 -- poise (n./v.) -- self-confidence; steadiness | to be steady || related word: **poised (adj.)**

3102 -- poker-faced (adj.) -- expressionless || related word: **poker-face (n.)**

3103 -- poky (adj.) -- without enough space | irritating because of being slow

3104 -- polemic (n.) -- strong argument || related words: **polemical (adv.), polemicist (n.)**

3105 -- polity (n.) -- the process of forming government

3106 -- pomp (n.) -- open display of decorations in a ceremony

3107 -- pompous (adj.) -- proud || related words: **pompously (adv.), pomposity (n.)**

3108 -- ponder (v.) -- to consider

3109 -- **pontificate (v.)** -- to express your opinion too confidently

3110 -- **poodle (n.)** -- sb who is too obedient

3111 -- **pooh-pooh (v.)** -- to reject a suggestion, etc.

3112 -- **poppycock (n.)** -- nonsense

3113 -- **populism (n.)** -- rule by ordinary people || related word: **populist (adj./n.)**

3114 -- **portend (v.)** -- to foretell sth bad || related word: **portent (n.)**

3115 -- **portentous (adj.)** -- foretelling sth bad | trying to impress in an unreasonable way || related words: **portentously (adv.), portentousness (n.)**

3116 -- **portly (adj.)** -- well-built

3117 -- **poser (n.)** -- complicated problem

3118 -- **posit (v.)** -- to hypothesize

3119 -- **posse (n.)** -- group

3120 -- **posterity (n.)** -- future generations

3121 -- **posthumous (adj.)** -- happening after sb's death || related word: **posthumously (adv.)**

3122 -- **postnatal (adj.)** -- related to the time after birth

3123 -- **postprandial (adj.)** -- occurring after a meal

3124 -- **postulate (n./v.)** -- hypothesis or suggestion | to hypothesize or suggest

3125 -- **potentate (n.)** -- emperor

3126 -- **potter (v.)** -- to do unimportant but enjoyable things

3127 -- **pounce (v.)** -- to attack suddenly

3128 -- **pound (v.)** -- to hit many times

3129 -- **powwow (n.)** -- meeting

3130 -- **pragmatic (adj.)** -- practical and sensible || related words: **pragmatically (adv.), pragmatics (n.), pragmatism (n.), pragmatist (n.)**

3131 -- **prance (v.)** -- to move fast in order to attract other people attention

3132 -- **prank (n.)** -- trick or joke | related word: **prankster (n.)**

3133 -- **prattle (n./v.)** -- gossip | to gossip

3134 -- **preach (v.)** -- to talk about religious or moral things || related words: **preachy (adj.), preacher (n.)**

3135 -- **preamble (n.)** -- introduction

3136 -- **precarious (adj.)** -- unstable and dangerous || related words: **precariously (adv.), precariousness (n.)**

3137 -- **precept (n.)** -- principle

3138 -- **precipice (n.)** -- cliff

3139 -- **precipitate (adj./n./v.)** -- happening suddenly | a chemical substance | to make sth bad happen in a sudden way

3140 -- **precipitation (n.)** -- rainfall or snowfall

3141 -- **precipitous (adj.)** -- steep | quick || related word: **precipitously (adv.)**

3142 -- **preclude (v.)** -- to prevent

3143 -- **precocious (adj.)** -- talented || related words: **precociously (adv.), precocity (n.), precociousness (n.)**

3144 -- **precursor (n.)** -- predecessor or forerunner

3145 -- **predicament (n.)** -- complicated situation

3146 -- **predilection (n.)** -- preference

3147 -- **predispose (v.)** -- to incline or influence || related word: **predisposition (n.)**

3148 -- **preemie (n.)** -- premature baby

3149 -- **pre-eminent (adj.)** -- exceptional || related words: **pre-eminently (adv.), pre-eminence (n.)**

3150 -- **pre-empt (v.)** -- to prevent or obstruct

3151 -- **preen (v.)** -- to clean up; to groom or spruce

3152 -- **prelude (n.)** -- introduction or preface

3153 -- **premeditated (adj.)** -- pre-planned || related word: **premeditation (n.)**

3154 -- **premonition (n.)** -- forewarning || related word: **premonitory (adj.)**

3155 -- **preponderance (n.)** -- dominance || related words: **preponderantly (adv.), preponderant (adj.)**

3156 -- **prepossessing (adj.)** -- good-looking

3157 -- **preposterous (adj.)** -- shocking || related word: **preposterously (adv.)**

3158 -- **preprandial (adj.)** -- that occurs just before meal

3159 -- **prerequisite (adj./n.)** -- precondition

3160 -- **prerogative (n.)** -- special right

3161 -- **presage (n./v.)** -- sign | to be forewarned

3162 -- **preside (v.)** -- to be in charge of a meeting, etc.

3163 -- **presumptive (adj.)** -- possibly true

3164 -- **presumptuous (adj.)** -- proud

3165 -- **presuppose (v.)** -- to guess | related word: **presupposition (n.)**

3166 -- **prettify (v.)** -- to unsuccessfully try to improve sth

3167 -- **prevaricate (v.)** -- to evade || related word: **prevarication (n.)**

3168 -- **prim (adj.)** -- formal || related word: **primly (adv.)**

3169 -- **primeval (adj.)** -- ancient

3170 -- **primordial (adj.)** -- primitive

3171 -- **princely (adj.)** -- generous | like a prince

3172 -- **prissy (adj.)** -- easily shocked

3173 -- **pristine (adj.)** -- new; perfect

3174 -- **privation (n.)** -- hardship

3175 -- **privileged (adj.)** -- enjoying special rights; advantaged

3176 -- **proactive (adj.)** -- realistic || related word: **proactively (adv.)**

3177 -- **probity (n.)** -- honesty

3178 -- **proceeds (n.)** -- profits

3179 -- **proclaim (v.)** -- to officially declare sth || related word: **proclamation (n.)**

3180 -- **proclivity (n.)** -- tendency

3181 -- **procrastinate (v.)** -- to postpone || related word: **procrastination (n.)**

3182 -- **procreate (v.)** -- to reproduce

3183 -- **prod (n./v.)** -- encouragement; push | to encourage; to push sb/sth with pointed object

3184 -- **prodigal (adj.)** -- reckless || related word: **prodigality (n.)**

3185 -- **prodigious (adj.)** -- extraordinary || related word: **prodigiously (adv.)**

3186 -- **profane (adj./v.)** -- blasphemous or secular | to insult holy things || related word: **profanity (n.)**

3187 -- **profess (v.)** -- to openly express your beliefs || related word: **professed (adj.)**

3188 -- **proffer (v.)** -- to offer

3189 -- **profligate (adj.)** -- extravagant || related word: **profligacy (n.)**

3190 -- **profound (adj.)** -- intense | needing or showing great understanding | related word: **profoundly (adv.)**

3191 -- **profundity (n.)** -- depth or greatness

3192 -- **profuse (adj.)** -- plentiful || related word: **profusely (adv.)**

3193 -- **progenitor (n.)** -- ancestor

3194 -- **progeny (n.)** -- children; offspring

3195 -- **prognosis (n.)** -- medical opinion about an illness | to make a guess || related words: **prognostic (adj.), prognostication (n.)**

3196 -- **progressive (adj./n.)** -- supporting new ideas; developing gradually | supporter of new ideas || related word: **progressivism (n.)**

3197 -- **proletarian (adj.)** -- related to ordinary people; blue-collar || related word: **proletariat (n.)**

3198 -- **proliferate (v.)** -- to multiply || related word: **proliferation (n.)**

3199 -- **prolific (adj.)** -- fruitful | plentiful || related word: **prolifically (adv.)**

3200 -- **prolong (v.)** -- to extend for long time || related words: **prolonged (adj.), prolongation (n.)**

3201 -- **promenade (n./v.)** -- walk for pleasure | to walk for pleasure

3202 -- **promiscuous (adj.)** -- immoral || related words: **promiscuously (adv.), promiscuity (n.)**

3203 -- **prompting (n.)** -- opinion

3204 -- **promulgate (v.)** -- to publicize || related word: **promulgation (n.)**

3205 -- **pronto (adv.)** -- instantly

3206 -- **propagate (v.)** -- to publicize | to grow plants || related word: **propagation (n.)**

3207 -- **propensity (n.)** -- tendency

3208 -- **prophesy (v.)** -- to forecast || related word: **prophecy (n.)**

3209 -- **prophylactic (adj.)** -- preventing disease

3210 -- **propitiate (v.)** -- to make sb calm || related words: **propitiatory (adj.), propitiation (n.)**

3211 -- **propitious (adj.)** -- favorable or promising

3212 -- **proponent (n.)** -- supporter

3213 -- **proposition (n.)** -- proposal

3214 -- **propound (v.)** -- to propose publicly

3215 -- **propriety (n.)** -- acceptable behavior; decorum

3216 -- **propulsion (n.)** -- driving force || related word: **propulsive (adj.)**

3217 -- **prosaic (adj.)** -- ordinary or dull || related word: **prosaically (adv.)**

3218 -- **proscribe (adj.)** -- to ban || related word: **proscription (n.)**

3219 -- **prosecute (v.)** -- to put sb on trial || related word: **prosecution (n.)**

3220 -- **proselytize (v.)** -- to spread your religious or political beliefs

3221 -- **prosthesis (n.)** -- artificial leg, arm or other body part || related word: **prosthetics (n.)**

3222 -- **prostrate (adj./v.)** -- lying face downward; shocked | to lie with face downward: to shock

3223 -- **prostration (n.)** -- physical weakness | state of lying face downward during worship

3224 -- **protagonist (n.)** -- leading or central character

3225 -- **protean (adj.)** -- changeable

3226 -- **pro-tem (adv.)** -- temporarily

3227 -- **protracted (adj.)** -- lasting too longer

3228 -- **protrude (v.)** -- to stick out; to obtrude || related word: **protrusion (n.)**

3229 -- **provenance (n.)** -- origin

3230 -- **proverbial (adj.)** -- well-known || related word: **proverbially (adv.)**

3231 -- **providence (n.)** -- destiny

3232 -- **provident (adj.)** -- wise

3233 -- **providential (adj.)** -- that happens in a timely manner || related word: **providentially (adv.)**

3234 -- **provoke (v.)** -- to cause a particular feeling | to irritate || related words: **provocative (adj.), provocatively (adv.), provocation (n.)**

3235 -- **prowl (v.)** -- to stalk (chase) in order to hunt or commit crime || related word: **prowler (n.)**

3236 -- **proximity (n.)** -- closeness

3237 -- **prudish (adj.)** -- easily shocked || related word: **prudishly (adv.)**

3238 -- **prune (v.)** -- to trim || related word: **pruning (n.)**

3239 -- **prurient (adj.)** -- immoral || related word: **prurience (n.)**

3240 -- **pry (v.)** -- to be curious about sb's private life in an irritating way

3241 -- **pucker (v.)** -- to crease

3242 -- **puckish (adj.)** -- naughty

3243 -- **puddle (n.)** -- water collected in the small place on the ground

3244 -- **pudgy (adj.)** -- fat

3245 -- **puerile (adj.)** -- childish

3246 -- **pugilist (n.)** -- boxer || related words: **pugilistic (adj.), pugilism (n.)**

3247 -- **pugnacious (adj.)** -- aggressive || related words: **pugnaciously (adv.), pugnacity (n.)**

3248 -- **pulchritude (n.)** -- beauty

3249 -- **pulsate (v.)** -- to throb | to be very exciting || related word: **pulsation (n.)**

3250 -- **pulverize (v.)** -- to crush | to defeat

3251 -- **pummel (v.)** -- to hit with fists

3252 -- **pungent (adj.)** -- having strong taste, smell or effect || related words: **pungently (adv.), pungency (n.)**

3253 -- **punitive (adj.)** -- penalizing || related word: **punitively (adv.)**

3254 -- **punk (adj.)** -- impolite or violent person

3255 -- **punter (n.)** -- client

3256 -- **puny (adj.)** -- weak

3257 -- **purge (n./v.)** -- removal of unacceptable people from an organization | to remove unacceptable people from an organization

3258 -- **purist (adj.)** -- traditionalist || related word: **purism (n.)**

3259 -- **puritan (n.)** -- sb who has unreasonably strict moral attitudes || related words: **puritanical (adj.), puritanism (n.)**

3260 -- **purloin (v.)** -- **to** steal

3261 -- **purport (n./v.)** -- general meaning | to claim || related words: **purported (adj.), purportedly (adv.)**

3262 -- **purser (n.)** -- an officer who takes care of the passengers on a ship

3263 -- **pursuant (adj.)** -- according to a rule

3264 -- **pursue (v.)** -- to follow || related word: **pursuer (n.)**

3265 -- **pursuit (n.)** -- hobby | chase or search

3266 -- **purvey (v.)** -- to provide or supply || related word: **purveyor (n.)**

3267 -- **pushover (n.)** -- easy target

3268 -- **pushy (adj.)** -- forceful || related word: **pushiness (n.)**

3269 -- **pusillanimous (adj.)** -- cowardly

3270 -- **pussyfoot (v.)** -- to be too careful to express your thoughts

3271 -- **putative (adj.)** -- assumed

3272 -- **put-down (n.)** -- insulting remark

3273 -- **putrefy (v.)** -- to rot || related word: **putrefaction (n.)**

3274 -- **putrid (adj.)** -- rotting; very bad

3275 -- **putsch (n.)** -- sudden removal of government

3276 -- **put-upon (adj.)** -- harassed

3277 -- **pygmy (n.)** -- person or thing that is too small

3278 -- **pyrrhic victory (n.)** -- victory in which winner suffers heavily

Difficult English Words -- Q

3279 -- **qua (prep.)** -- as sth

3280 -- **quadriplegic (n.)** -- a person who can't use their arms and legs || related word: **quadriplegia (n.)**

3281 -- **quaff (v.)** -- to drink quickly and in a large amount

3282 -- **quagmire (n.)** -- marsh | complicated situation

3283 -- **quaint (adj.)** -- unusually attractive || related words: **quaintly (adv.), quaintness (n.)**

3284 -- **qualm (n.)** -- doubt on yourself

3285 -- **quandary (n.)** -- complicated and difficult situation

3286 -- **quash (v.)** -- to nullify or restrain

3287 -- **quatrain (n.)** -- a poem that has four lines

3288 -- **queasy (adj.)** -- nauseous; worried || related words: **queasily (adv.), queasiness (n.)**

3289 -- **queer (adj.)** -- strange

3290 -- **quell (v.)** -- to control or suppress unpleasant feelings

3291 -- **quench (v.)** -- to satisfy your thirst | to extinguish a fire

3292 -- **quibble (n./v.)** -- unnecessary argument | to argue unnecessarily

3293 -- **quid pro quo (n.)** -- a thing that is given in return for sth else

3294 -- **quiescent (adj.)** -- quiet | undeveloped || related word: **quiescence (n.)**

3295 -- **quintessence (n.)** -- ideal example || related words: **quintessential (adj.), quintessentially (adv.)**

3296 -- **quip (n./v.)** -- quick remark | to make a quick remark in a clever way

3297 -- **quirk (n.)** -- oddness in somebody's behavior || related word: **quirky (adj.)**

3298 -- **quisling (n.)** -- traitor

3299 -- **quiver (v.)** -- to shake a little

3300 -- **quotidian (adj.)** -- ordinary

Difficult English Words -- R

3301 -- **rabble (n.)** -- mob

3302 -- **rabid (adj.)** -- radical; violent || related word: **rabidly (adv.)**

3303 -- **racket (n.)** -- unpleasant noise

3304 -- **raconteur (n.)** -- story teller

3305 -- **radiant (adj.)** -- happy; bright || related words: **radiantly (adv.), radiance (n.)**

3306 -- **radical (adj.)** -- fundamental and effective || related word: **radically (adv.)**

3307 -- **raffish (adj.)** -- odd

3308 -- **raft (n.)** -- large amount or quantity

3309 -- **rag (v.)** -- to trick

3310 -- **rage (n./v.)** -- extreme anger | to be very angry about sth; to be violent; to spread fast

3311 -- **ragged (adj.)** -- tattered; extremely tired || related words: **raggedly (adv.), raggedness (n.)**

3312 -- **ragtag (adj.)** -- disorganized

3313 -- **rake-off (n.)** -- profit that sb gets from illegal activity

3314 -- **rakish (adj.)** -- immoral || related word: **rakishly (adv.)**

3315 -- **ramble (n./v.)** -- ambiguous talk; walk for enjoyment | to talk ambiguously; to walk for enjoyment

3316 -- **rambling (adj.)** -- confused | sprawling

3317 -- **Rambo (n.)** -- strong and agressive man

3318 -- **rambunctious (rumbustious) (adj.)** -- lively and cheerful

3319 -- **ramification (n.)** -- consequence

3320 -- **rampage (n./v.)** -- violent and destructive behavior | to behave in a violent and destructive way

3321 -- **rampant (adj.)** -- widespread || related word: **rampantly (adv.)**

3322 -- **rampart (n.)** -- very high wall

3323 -- **ramshackle (adj.)** -- broken down; disorganized

3324 -- **rancid (adj.)** -- stale

3325 -- **rancor (rancour) (n.)** -- hatred; enmity || related words: **rancorous (rancourous) (adj.)**

3326 -- **rangy (adj.)** -- tall and thin

3327 -- **rankle (v.)** -- to upset you

3328 -- **ransack (v.)** -- to search in an untidy way

3329 -- **rant (n./v.)** -- loud complaint | to complain angrily

3330 -- **rap (n./v.)** -- hit; conviction | to hit; to criticize; to say sth angrily

3331 -- **rapacious (adj.)** -- greedy || related words: **rapaciously (adv.), rapacity (n.)**

3332 -- **rapport (n.)** -- friendly relationship

3333 -- **rapprochement (n.)** -- improvement in relationship between two countries or groups

3334 -- **rapt (adj.)** -- extremely interested in sth || related word: **raptly (adv.)**

3335 -- **raptor (n.)** -- bird of prey

3336 -- **rapture (n.)** -- delight || related words: **rapturous (adj.), rapturously (adv.)**

3337 -- **rarefied (adj.)** -- mysterious

3338 -- **raring (n.)** -- enthusiastic

3339 -- **raspy (adj.)** -- harsh, croaky

3340 -- **ratify (v.)** -- to give official approval; to sanction || related word: **ratification (n.)**

3341 -- **ratiocination (n.)** -- process of logical argument

3342 -- **rational (adj.)** -- based on reason || related words: **rationally (adv.), rationality (n.)**

3343 -- **rationale (n.)** -- basis, justification

3344 -- **rattle (n./v.)** -- a series of sounds | to make series of sounds; to frighten

3345 -- **ratty (adj.)** -- bad-tempered | in bad state

3346 -- **raucous (adj.)** -- harsh || related words: **raucously (adv.), raucousness (n.)**

3347 -- **raunchy (adj.)** -- vulgar | untidy

3348 -- **ravage (v.)** -- to destroy || related word: **ravages (n.)**

3349 -- **rave (v.)** -- to talk or shout enthusiastically or insensibly

3350 -- **ravel (v.)** -- to worsen the situation

3351 -- **ravenous (adj.)** -- very hungry || related word: **ravenously (adv.)**

3352 -- **rave-up (n.)** -- celebration

3353 -- **ravine (n.)** -- narrow valley

3354 -- **raving (adj.)** -- crazy || related word: **ravings (n.)**

3355 -- **ravish (v.)** -- to delight sb

3356 -- **ravishing (adj.)** -- gorgeous || related word: **ravishingly (adv.)**

3357 -- **raze (v.)** -- to completely destroy a building, etc.

3358 -- **razor-sharp (adj.)** -- extremely intelligent and smart

3359 -- **readily (adv.)** -- willingly | without restraint

3360 -- **realm (n.)** -- empire

3361 -- **ream (v.)** -- to cheat or deceive

3362 -- **reap (v.)** -- to harvest | to obtain

3363 -- **rearguard action (n.)** -- unsuccessful struggle

3364 -- **rearing (n.)** -- childhood | breeding of animals and birds

3365 -- **reassert (v.)** -- to make sth happen again || related word: **reassertion (n.)**

3366 -- **reassure (v.)** -- to console || related words: **reassuring (adj.), reassuringly (adv.)**

3367 -- **reawaken (v.)** -- to stir up

3368 -- **rebarbative (adj.)** -- unattractive; unpleasant

3369 -- **rebate (n.)** -- discount

3370 -- **rebuff (n./v.)** -- rejection | to reject

3371 -- **rebuke (v.)** -- to say sth in severe or critical way; to scold

3372 -- **rebut (v.)** -- to deny || related word: **rebuttal (n.)**

3373 -- **recalcitrant (adj.)** -- stubborn || related word: **recalcitrance (n.)**

3374 -- **recant (v.)** -- to give up your beliefs | to renounce || related word: **recantation (n.)**

3375 -- **recapitulate (v.)** -- to review or summarize || related word: **recapitulation (n.)**

3376 -- **recast (v.)** -- to put sth in different way

3377 -- **recede (v.)** -- to withdraw, to decrease

3378 -- **recess (n./v.)** -- break; vacation | to take or give vacation

3379 -- **recession (n.)** -- a period of time when economy of a country is in decline

3380 -- **reciprocate (v.)** -- to give back || related word: **reciprocation (n.)**

3381 -- **reckless (adj.)** -- irresponsible || related words: **recklessly (adv.), recklessness (n.)**

3382 -- **reclaim (v.)** -- to regain or recover; to rescue || related word: **reclamation (n.)**

3383 -- **recline (v.)** -- to lie down; to relax

3384 -- **recluse (n.)** -- loner || related word: **reclusive (adj.)**

3385 -- **recoil (v.)** -- to suddenly move back

3386 -- **recompense (v.)** -- to compensate

3387 -- **reconcile (v.)** -- to resolve the issue; to patch up || related words: **reconcilable (adj.), reconciliation (n.)**

3388 -- **recondite (adj.)** -- difficult to understand

3389 -- **reconnaissance (n.)** -- inspection

3390 -- **reconnoiter (reconnoitre) (v.)** -- to try to find military-related information

3391 -- **recoup (v.)** -- to recover your money

3392 -- **recourse (n.)** -- alternative or option

3393 -- **recreant (adj.)** -- cowardly

3394 -- **recreation (n.)** -- hobby || related word: **recreational (adj.)**

3395 -- **recrimination (n.)** -- angry criticism or accusation || related word: **recriminatory (adj.)**

3396 -- **recrudesce (v.)** -- to occur again || related word: **recrudescent (adj.), recrudescence (n.)**

3397 -- **rectify (v.)** -- to set sth right; to correct || related words: **rectifiable (adj.), rectification (n.)**

3398 -- **rectitude (n.)** -- correctness; honesty

3399 -- **recumbent (adj.)** -- lying down

3400 -- **recuperate (v.)** -- to recover from an illness; to recover your money || related words: **recuperative (adj.), recuperation (n.)**

3401 -- **recur (v.)** -- to happen again || related words: **recurrent (adj.), recurrence (n.)**

3402 -- **redact (v.)** -- to remove information from documents and files || related word: **redaction (n.)**

3403 -- **redeem (v.)** -- to compensate | to exchange | to buy back || related word: **redeemable (adj.)**

3404 -- **redemption (n.)** -- rescue | exchange

3405 -- **redemptive (adj.)** -- saving your from sth evil

3406 -- **redolent (adj.)** -- scented || related word: **redolence (n.)**

3407 -- **redress (n./v.)** -- compensation | to put sth right; to restore

3408 -- **redundant (adj.)** -- unnecessary || related word: **redundantly (adv.)**

3409 -- **reeducate (v.)** -- to make sb change their way of thinking or behaving

3410 -- **reek (n./v.)** -- very unpleasant smell | to stink

3411 -- **referendum (n.)** -- voting by all the people on matter of a national interest

3412 -- **refine (v.)** -- to make improvement

3413 -- **refit (v.)** -- to repair

3414 -- **reflex (n.)** -- uncontrollable movement of sb's body

3415 -- **reformist (n.)** -- sb who brings big changes to political or social system

3416 -- **refract (v.)** -- to change direction of light || related word: **refraction (n.)**

3417 -- **refractory (n.)** -- stubborn

3418 -- **refrain (n./v.)** -- repeated comment, line, etc. | to desist from sth

3419 -- **refreshing (adj.)** -- stimulating || related word: **refreshingly (adv.)**

3420 -- **refulgent (adj.)** -- bright; shining

3421 -- **refurbish (v.)** -- to decorate your home, etc. || related word: **refurbishment (n.)**

3422 -- **refute (v.)** -- to prove that sth is false; to deny || related words: **refutable (adj.), refutation (n.)**

3423 -- **regal (adj.)** -- majestic; royal || related word: **regally (adv.)**

3424 -- **regalia (n.)** -- special dress

3425 -- **regicide (n.)** -- killing of king or queen

3426 -- **regime (n.)** -- government or management

3427 -- **regress (v.)** -- to be less advanced || related words: **regression (n.), regressive (adj.)**

3428 -- **regurgitate (v.)** -- to repeat || related word: **regurgitation (n.)**

3429 -- **reimburse (v.)** -- to pay back || related word: **reimbursement (n.)**

3430 -- **reincarnate (v.)** -- to take birth in new form || related word: **reincarnation (n.)**

3431 -- **reinforce (v.)** -- to strengthen || related word: **reinforcement (n.)**

3432 -- **reinstate (v.)** -- to restore || related word: **reinstatement (n.)**

3433 -- **reiterate (v.)** -- to repeat || related word: **reiteration (n.)**

3434 -- **rejig (v.)** -- to rearrange

3435 -- **rejoice (v.)** -- to show openly that you are delighted; to celebrate || related word: **rejoicing (n.)**

3436 -- **rejoinder (n.)** -- a particular type of reply

3437 -- **rejuvenate (v.)** -- to make younger; to invigorate

3438 -- **rekindle (v.)** -- to revive

3439 -- **relapse (n./v.)** -- setback | to go back to the earlier state of illness

3440 -- **relegate (v.)** -- to downgrade || related word: **relegation (n.)**

3441 -- **relent (v.)** -- to become less strict || related words: **relentless (adj.), relentlessly (adv.)**

3442 -- **relic (n.)** -- historical object

3443 -- **relinquish (v.)** -- to give up sth unwillingly

3444 -- **relish (n./v.)** -- delight | to enjoy greatly

3445 -- **relive (v.)** -- to remember

3446 -- **reluctant (adj.)** -- hesitant; unwilling || related words: **reluctantly (adv.), reluctance (n.)**

3447 -- **reminisce (v.)** -- to recall you past || related words: **reminiscent (adj.), reminiscence (n.)**

3448 -- **remiss (adj.)** -- careless

3449 -- **remission (n.)** -- reduction | improvement in illness

3450 -- **remit (v.)** -- to make payment | to cancel a fine, etc. || related word: **remittance (n.)**

3451 -- **remnant (n.)** -- remains

3452 -- **remonstrate (v.)** -- to object, protest, argue or complain || related word: **remonstrance (n.)**

3453 -- **remorse (n.)** -- regret || related words: **remorseful (adj.), remorsefully (adv.)**

3454 -- **remorseless (n.)** -- cruel | continuing || related word: **remorselessly (adv.)**

3455 -- **remount (v.)** -- to begin again

3456 -- **remunerate (v.)** -- to make payment to the worker || related words: **remunerative (adj.), remuneration (n.)**

3457 -- **renaissance (n.)** -- revival

3458 -- **rend (v.)** -- to split or slit

3459 -- **render (v.)** -- to give | to perform | to put sb/sth in a particular situation

3460 -- **rendezvous (n./v.)** -- arranged meeting | to meet in a planned way

3461 -- **rendition (n.)** -- performance of songs, etc.

3462 -- **renegade (n.)** -- deserter

3463 -- **renege (v.)** -- to break your promise, etc.

3464 -- **renounce (v.)** -- to reject or disown || related word: **renunciation (n.)**

3465 -- **renovate (v.)** -- to repair a building, etc. || related word: **renovation (n.)**

3466 -- **renowned (adj.)** -- well-known

3467 -- **reorient (v.)** -- to change the direction || related word: **reorientation (n.)**

3468 -- **reparation (n.)** -- compensation

3469 -- **repartee (n.)** -- quick comments

3470 -- **repast (n.)** -- a meal

3471 -- **repatriate (v.)** -- to send sb back to their own country || related word: **repatriation (n.)**

3472 -- **repeal (v.)** -- to cancel a law

3473 -- **repel (v.)** -- to drive sth away or back

3474 -- **repellent (adj.)** -- disgusting; horrible

3475 -- **repertoire (n.)** -- range or collection

3476 -- **replenish (v.)** -- to refill || related word: **replenishment (n.)**

3477 -- **replete (adj.)** -- completely filled

3478 -- **replicate (v.)** -- to make exact copy of sth || related word: **replication (n.)**

3479 -- **repose (n./v.)** -- rest | to relax

3480 -- **repository (n.)** -- storeroom; warehouse

3481 -- **reprehensible (adj.)** -- shocking and unacceptable

3482 -- **repress (v.)** -- to control your feelings | to forcefully suppress freedom of a particular group || related words: **repressive (adj.), repressed (adj.), repressively (adv.), repression (n.), repressiveness (n.)**

3483 -- **reprieve (n./v.)** -- official pardon | to pardon officially

3484 -- **reprimand (v.)** -- to scold; to rebuke

3485 -- **reprisal (n.)** -- retaliation

3486 -- **reproach (n./v.)** -- criticism, dishonor | to criticize; to blame || related words: **reproachful (adj.), reproachfully (adv.)**

3487 -- **reprobate (adj./n.)** -- immoral | immoral person

3488 -- **reprove (v.)** -- to criticize || related words: **reproving (adj.), reprovingly (adv.)**

3489 -- **repudiate (v.)** -- to reject or deny || related word: **repudiation (n.)**

3490 -- **repugnance (n.)** -- strong hatred || related word: **repugnant (n.)**

3491 -- **repulse (v.)** -- to resist or reject | to drive back || related words: **repulsive (adj.), repulsion (n.)**

3492 -- **requisite (adj./n.)** -- essential | essential thing

3493 -- **requisition (n./v.)** -- official demand | to demand sth officially

3494 -- **requite (v.)** -- to give sth in return

3495 -- **rerun (v.)** -- to repeat

3496 -- **rescind (v.)** -- to officially cancel a law, etc. || related word: **rescission (n.)**

3497 -- **resent (v.)** -- to get angry at sth unfair || related words: **resentful (adj.), resentfully (adv.), resentment (n.)**

3498 -- **reshuffle (n./v.)** -- rearrangement | to reorganize the group of people by changing their jobs and responsibilities

3499 -- **residuary (adj.)** -- remaining

3500 -- **resilience (n.)** -- flexibility || related word: **resilient (adj.)**

3501 -- **resolute (adj.)** -- firm || related words: **resolutely (adv.), resoluteness (n.)**

3502 -- **resolution (n.)** -- declaration

3503 -- **resonate (v.)** -- to reverberate || related word: **resonation (n.)**

3504 -- **resounding (adj.)** -- very great or loud || related word: **resoundingly (adv.)**

3505 -- **resourceful (adj.)** -- creative || related words: **resourcefully (adv.), resourcefulness (n.)**

3506 -- **resplendent (adj.)** -- bright and impressive; dazzling || related word: **resplendently (adv.)**

3507 -- **restive (adj.)** -- restless || related word: **restiveness (n.)**

3508 -- **restrain (v.)** -- to control || related word: **restrained (adj.)**

3509 -- **resurgence (n.)** -- revival, recovery || related word: **resurgent (adj.)**

3510 -- **resurrect (v.)** -- to revive || related word: **resurrection (n.)**

3511 -- **resuscitate (v.)** -- to revive || related word: **resuscitation (n.)**

3512 -- **retard (v.)** -- to delay || related words: **retarded (adj.), retardation (n.)**

3513 -- **reticent (adj.)** -- quiet or reserved || related word: **reticence (n.)**

3514 -- **retort (n./v.)** -- angry or quick reply | to reply quickly or angrily

3515 -- **retract (v.)** -- to withdraw your statement || to move back into main part || related words: **retractable (adj.), retraction (n.)**

3516 -- **retreat (v.)** -- to move back

3517 -- **retrench (v.)** -- to save money in business || related word: **retrenchment (n.)**

3518 -- **retribution (n.)** -- severe punishment || related word: **retributive (adj.)**

3519 -- **retrieve (v.)** -- to get sth back || related words: **retrievable (adj.), retrieval (n.)**

3520 -- **retrogressive (adj.)** -- to becoming old-fashioned in your ideas, beliefs, etc.

3521 -- **retrospection (n.)** -- observing past events || related words: **retrospective (adj.), retrospectively (adv.)**

3522 -- **revamp (n./v.)** -- improvement | to improve appearance of sth

3523 -- **revel (n./v.)** -- great enjoyment | to enjoy greatly

3524 -- **revelry (n.)** -- noisy celebration

3525 -- **reverberate (v.)** -- echo || related word: **reverberation (n.)**

3526 -- **revere (v.)** -- to respect or admire || related words: **reverent (adj.), reverential (adj.), reverently (adv.), reverentially (adv.), reverence (n.)**

3527 -- **reverie (n.)** -- daydream

3528 -- **revile (v.)** -- to criticize or condemn sb too much

3529 -- **revisit (v.)** -- to repeat

3530 -- **revivify (v.)** -- to refresh; to revive

3531 -- **revoke (v.)** -- to officially cancel a rule, etc. || related word: **revocation (n.)**

3532 -- **revulsion (n.)** -- strong hatred

3533 -- **rhapsodize (v.)** -- to express sth enthusiastically || related words: **rhapsodic (adj.), rhapsody (n.)**

3534 -- **rhetoric (n.)** -- influential but insincere speech or writing || related words: **rhetorical (adj.), rhetorically (adv.)**

3535 -- **ribald (adj.)** -- slightly vulgar || related word: **ribaldry (n.)**

3536 -- **rib-tickler (n.)** -- amusing story || related word: **rib-tickling (adj.)**

3537 -- **rickety (adj.)** -- not strong enough

3538 -- **ricochet (v.)** -- to rebound

3539 -- **ridicule (n./v.)** -- mockery | to mock

3540 -- **rife (adj.)** -- full of unpleasant things

3541 -- **rift (n.)** -- disagreement | crack

3542 -- **rigid (adj.)** -- inflexible || related words: **rigidly (adv.), rigidity (n.)**

3543 -- **rigmarole (n.)** -- irritating and unnecessary process

3544 -- **rigorous (adj.)** -- strict | precise || related words: **rigorously (adv.), rigor (rigour) (n.)**

3545 -- **rile (v.)** -- to irritate sb

3546 -- **rip-off (n.)** -- too expensive | cheap copy of sth

3547 -- **riposte (n.)** -- quick reply to a criticism

3548 -- **ripple (n./v.)** -- small waves on water | to move like a wave

3549 -- **risible (adj.)** -- mocking

3550 -- **rising (n.)** -- rebellion; revolt

3551 -- **rival (adj./n.)** -- belonging to opposite party | opponent || related word: **rivalry (n.)**

3552 -- **riven (adj.)** -- divided

3553 -- **rivet (v.)** -- to be strongly fascinated with sth || related word: **riveting (adj.)**

3554 -- **rivulet (n.)** -- small river

3555 -- **robust (adj.)** -- strong || related words: **robustly (adv.), robustness (n.)**

3556 -- **rogue (n.)** -- rude but harmless person | immoral person

3557 -- **roguish (adj.)** -- naughty || related word: **roguishly (adv.)**

3558 -- **rollicking (adj.)** -- carefree; joyful

3559 -- **roll-out (n.)** -- launching of a new product

3560 -- **romp (n./v.)** -- easy victory; exciting book, movie, etc. | to play noisily

3561 -- **rookie (n.)** -- inexperienced person

3562 -- **roost (n./v.)** -- a place that is used by birds to sleep | (of birds) to sleep

3563 -- **roster (n.)** -- list of names

3564 -- **rote (n.)** -- repetition of sth in order to learn it by heart

3565 -- **rotten (adj./adv.)** -- decayed, terrible | very much || related word: **rottenness (n.)**

3566 -- **rotund (adj.)** -- having fat body || related word: **rotundity (n.)**

3567 -- **roué (n.)** -- an old person who is involved in immoral and illegal activities

3568 -- **rough and tumble (n.)** -- aggressive or noisy activity

3569 -- **roughage (n.)** -- fiber (fibre)

3570 -- **roundabout (adj.)** -- done in a long and complicated way

3571 -- **roundup (n.)** -- summary | a situation when people are gathered together

3572 -- **rouse (v.)** -- to awaken or enthuse || related word: **rousing (adj.)**

3573 -- **roust (v.)** -- to disturb

3574 -- **rout (n./v.)** -- huge defeat | to defeat severely

3575 -- **rove (v.)** -- to wander || related word: **roving (adj.)**

3576 -- **rowdy (adj.)** -- disorderly; unruly || related words: **rowdily (adv.), rowdiness (n.), rowdyism (n.)**

3577 -- **rubble (n.)** -- debris

3578 -- **rubric (n.)** -- instructions given in exam papers, etc.

3579 -- **ruckus (n.)** -- noisy confusion

3580 -- **ructions (n.)** -- strong protest; uproar

3581 -- **ruddy (adj.)** -- reddish

3582 -- **rudimentary (adj.)** -- basic

3583 -- **rudiments (n.)** -- essentials

3584 -- **rue (v.)** -- to feel sorry; to regret || related words: **rueful (adj.), ruefully (adv.)**

3585 -- **ruffian (n.)** -- criminal

3586 -- **ruffle (v.)** -- to mess up; to upset

3587 -- **rugged (adj.)** -- rough | determined || related words: **ruggedly (adv.), ruggedness (n.)**

3588 -- **rumble (n./v.)** -- series of sounds | to make a series of sounds

3589 -- **ruminate (v.)** -- to think about sth in a serious way || related words: **ruminative (adj.), ruminatively (adv.), rumination (n.)**

3590 -- **rummage (v.)** -- to search frantically

3591 -- **rumpus (n.)** -- public disturbance

3592 -- **runaway (adj./n.)** -- having left; easy and quick | escapee

3593 -- **run-down (adj.)** -- neglected

3594 -- **rundown (n.)** -- reduction | explanation

3595 -- **run-in (n.)** -- disagreement or quarrel

3596 -- **runny (adj.)** -- soft

3597 -- **run-up (n.)** -- preparation for upcoming event

3598 -- **ruse (n.)** -- a trick to cheat sb

3599 -- **rustic (adj.)** -- made of wood

3600 -- **rustle (n./v.)** -- crunching sound | to crunch || related word: **rustling (adj.)**

3601 -- **rusty (adj.)** -- out of practice || related word: **rustiness (n.)**

3602 -- **rut (n.)** -- a way of life that is monotonous and boring

3603 -- **ruthless (adj.)** -- cruel

Difficult English Words -- S

3604 -- **sabbatical (n.)** -- vacation given to teacher in order to study

3605 -- **saber-rattling (sabre-rattling) (n.)** -- action of terrifying sb

3606 -- **sabotage (n./v.)** -- destruction | to destruct or spoil || related word: **saboteur (n.)**

3607 -- **saccharine (adj.)** -- sentimental

3608 -- **sacerdotal (adj.)** -- related to priests

3609 -- **sacrilege (n.)** -- disrespect to holy things || related word: **sacrilegious (adj.)**

3610 -- **sacrosanct (adj.)** -- holy or extremely revered

3611 -- **sadden (v.)** -- to make sb sad

3612 -- **sadism (n.)** -- entertainment from others' suffering

3613 -- **sadist (n.)** -- sb who hurts other people in order to get pleasure || related words: **sadistic (adj.), sadistically (adv.)**

3614 -- **safe haven (n.)** -- perfectly safe place

3615 -- **sag (v.)** -- to drop || to be reduced

3616 -- **saga (n.)** -- long or historical story

3617 -- **sagacious (adj.)** -- wise || related word: **sagacity (n.)**

3618 -- **saggy (adj.)** -- loose

3619 -- **salivate (v.)** -- to produce saliva || related word: **salivation (n.)**

3620 -- **sallow (n.)** -- pale and unhealthy

3621 -- **sally (n.)** -- amusing remark | unexpected attack

3622 -- **salubrious (adj.)** -- hygienic and pleasant

3623 -- **salutary (adj.)** -- affecting in positive way

3624 -- **salvage (n./v.)** -- things that have been saved | to save or recover sth from destruction

3625 -- **salvation (n.)** -- rescue

3626 -- **salve (v.)** -- to ease

3627 -- **salvo (n.)** -- sudden attack

3628 -- **sanctify (v.)** -- to bless | to legalize || related word: **sanctification (n.)**

3629 -- **sanctimonious (adj.)** -- proud; arrogant || related words: **sanctimoniously (adv.), sanctimoniousness (n.)**

3630 -- **sanctity (n.)** -- purity; holiness

3631 -- **sanctum (n.)** -- holy place

3632 -- **sangfroid (n.)** -- self-control

3633 -- **sanguinary (adj.)** -- related to killing

3634 -- **sanguine (adj.)** -- hopeful || related word: **sanguinely (adv.)**

3635 -- **sanitize (v.)** -- to disinfect

3636 -- **sanity (n.)** -- common sense

3637 -- **sans (prep.)** -- without

3638 -- **sap (n./v.)** -- silly person | to weaken

3639 -- **sapient (adj.)** -- having deep knowledge of sth || related words: **sapiently (adv.), sapience (n.)**

3640 -- **sapling (n.)** -- a very small tree

3641 -- **sapper (n.)** -- soldier who has been assigned a job related to buildings, bridges, etc.

3642 -- **sarcasm (n.)** -- mockery || related words: **sarcastic (adj.), sarcastically (adv.)**

3643 -- **sardonic (adj.)** -- mocking; arrogant || related word: **sardonically (adv.)**

3644 -- **sartorial (adj.)** -- connected with men's clothes || related word: **sartorially (adv.)**

3645 -- **sashay (v.)** -- to walk confidently

3646 -- **sass (n./v.)** -- impolite talk or behavior | to talk or behave impolitely

3647 -- **sassy (adj.)** -- too confident

3648 -- **satanic (adj.)** -- evil, wicked || related word: **satanically (adv.)**

3649 -- **sated (adj.)** -- completely satisfied

3650 -- **satiate (v.)** -- to satisfy || related words: **satiation (n.), satiety (n.)**

3651 -- **satirize (v.)** -- to criticize sb in humorous way; to mock || related words: **satirical (adj.), satirically (adv.), satire (n.), satirist (n.)**

3652 -- **saturnalian (adj.)** -- that involves wild celebrations

3653 -- **saucy (adj.)** -- slightly rude but amusing

3654 -- **saunter (n./v.)** -- slow walk | to walk slowly

3655 -- **savage (adj./n./v.)** -- cruel and violent | very cruel person; critical | to attack violently; to criticize || related word: **savagery (n.)**

3656 -- **savant (n.)** -- a person with great knowledge or abilities

3657 -- **savor (n.)** -- pleasant taste or smell | to enjoy taste/smell or feeling || related word: **savory (savoury) (adj./n.)**

3658 -- **savvy (adj./n.)** -- having good knowledge of sth | understanding

3659 -- **scabbard (n.)** -- cover of a sword

3660 -- **scabrous (adj.)** -- not decent | rough

3661 -- **scads (adj.)** -- sth in large quantity or amount

3662 -- **scalawag (scallywag) (n.)** -- slightly bad-tempered child

3663 -- **scald (n./v.)** -- injury with hot liquid | to burn body parts with hot liquid || related word: **scalding (adj./adv.)**

3664 -- **scamp (n.)** -- troublemaker child

3665 -- **scamper (v.)** -- to walk with short steps

3666 -- **scant (adj.)** -- little || related words: **scanty (adj.), scantily (adv.)**

3667 -- **scapegoat (n.)** -- sb who is blamed for the mistakes done by sb else

3668 -- **scaremonger (n.)** -- sb who spreads horrifying stories

3669 -- **scarify (v.)** -- to cut grass or skin

3670 -- **scarlet (n.)** -- bright red

3671 -- **scarp (n.)** -- steep slope

3672 -- **scarper (v.)** -- to leave

3673 -- **scary (adj.)** -- horrifying; frightening

3674 -- **scathing (adj.)** -- criticizing severely || related word: **scathingly (adv.)**

3675 -- **scatter (v.)** -- to disperse or spread in an untidy way

3676 -- **scatterbrain (n.)** -- sb who can't do any work in sensible or organized way || related word: **scatterbrained (adj.)**

3677 -- **scavenge (v.)** -- to search food items through waste, etc. || related word: **scavenger (n.)**

3678 -- **schadenfreude (adj.)** -- pleasure that sb gets from grief of other person

3679 -- **schematize (v.)** -- to organize

3680 -- **scheming (adj.)** -- tricky

3681 -- **schism (n.)** -- severe disagreement among people of a religious group || related word: **schismatic (adj.)**

3682 -- **schizophrenia (n.)** -- a serious mental illness related to abnormal behavior || related word: **schizophrenic (adj./n.)**

3683 -- **schlock (n.)** -- low-quality or cheap things

3684 -- **schmaltz (n.)** -- too sentimental || related word: **schmaltzy (adv.)**

3685 -- **schmo (adj.)** -- foolish and irritating

3686 -- **schmooze (v.)** -- to talk to sb in order to get sth || related word: **schmoozer (n.)**

3687 -- **schmuck (n.)** -- stupid person

3688 -- **schnook (n.)** -- worthless person

3689 -- **scintilla (n.)** -- too small amount

3690 -- **scintillating (adj.)** -- amusing and exciting

3691 -- **scion (n.)** -- young person from reputed family

3692 -- **scoff (v.)** -- to make fun of sb

3693 -- **scofflaw (n.)** -- sb who indulges in minor illegal activities

3694 -- **scoot (v.)** -- to leave at once

3695 -- **scorch (v.)** -- to burn slightly

3696 -- **scorcher (n.)** -- very hot day

3697 -- **scorching (adj.)** -- too hot or strong

3698 -- **scorn (n./v.)** -- disrespect | to disrespect; to mock | related words: **scornful (adj.), scornfully (adv.)**

3699 -- **scotch (v.)** -- to stop an activity

3700 -- **scot-free (adv.)** -- blameless

3701 -- **scour (v.)** -- to search a place | to rub

3702 -- **scourge (n./v.)** -- troublemaker | to cause trouble; to afflict

3703 -- **scout (v.)** -- to search a place

3704 -- **scowl (n./v.)** -- angry look | to look angrily

3705 -- **scrabble (v.)** -- to do sth with your hands hurriedly

3706 -- **scraggly (adj.)** -- thin and uneven

3707 -- **scraggy (adj.)** -- seeming unhealthy

3708 -- **scram (v.)** -- to leave a place immediately

3709 -- **scramble (n./v.)** -- action of walking or climbing with the help of your hands | to mix up; to confuse; to rush; to cook an egg

3710 -- **scrap (n./v.)** -- piece of paper, etc; fragment | to get rid of sth; to fight

3711 -- **scrappy (adj.)** -- untidy

3712 -- **scrawl (n./v.)** -- careless writing | to write in a careless way

3713 -- **scrawny (adj.)** -- thin and unattractive

3714 -- **scream (n./v.)** -- loud shout | to shout loudly

3715 -- **screamingly (adj.)** -- extremely

3716 -- **screech (n./v.)** -- very loud shout or noise | to make loud shout or noise

3717 -- **screed (n.)** -- uninteresting piece of writing

3718 -- **scribble (n./v.)** -- untidy writing | to write quickly

3719 -- **scrimmage (n.)** -- fight or dispute

3720 -- **scrimp (v.)** -- to spend your money very carefully

3721 -- **scrip (n.)** -- a share in business

3722 -- **Scrooge (n.)** -- miser

3723 -- **scrounge (v.)** -- to beg || related word: **scrounger (n.)**

3724 -- **scrub (n./v.)** -- action of rubbing | to rub || related word: **scrubber (n.)**

3725 -- **scruffy (adj.)** -- very untidy || related words: **scruffily (adv.), scruffiness (n.)**

3726 -- **scrummy (adj.)** -- delicious

3727 -- **scrumptious (adj.)** -- delicious

3728 -- **scrunch (v.)** -- to crush or crunch

3729 -- **scruple (n.)** -- doubt

3730 -- **scrupulous (adj.)** -- very careful; perfect || related word: **scrupulously (adv.), scrupulousness (n.)**

3731 -- **scud (v.)** -- (of clouds) to move across the sky

3732 -- **scuff (v.)** -- to scratch or rub || related word: **scuffed (adj.)**

3733 -- **scuffle (n./v.)** -- fight between two or more people | to fight in this way; to move fast

3734 -- **scum (n.)** -- foam || related word: **scummy (adj.)**

3735 -- **scupper (v.)** -- to foil; to thwart

3736 -- **scurrilous (adj.)** -- defamatory; insulting | related word: **scurrilously (adv.)**

3737 -- **scurry (n./v.)** -- sb's movement with short steps | to run with short steps

3738 -- scuttle (v.) -- to foil | to run with short steps

3739 -- seam (n.) -- a thin or deep line or layer || related word: seamy (adj.)

3740 -- seamless (adj.) -- without any fault or pause || related word: seamlessly (adv.)

3741 -- sear (v.) -- to burn strongly | to feel a feeling of pain suddenly

3742 -- searing (adj.) -- burning | critical || related word: searingly (adv.)

3743 -- seasoned (adj.) -- experienced

3744 -- secession (n.) -- independence from a particular group or country || related word: secessionist (adj./n.)

3745 -- seclude (v.) -- to be reserved and alone || related words: secluded (adj.), seclusion (n.)

3746 -- sedate (adj./v.) -- relaxed | to tranquilize (to give drugs to sb in order to make them unconscious) || related words: sedation (n.), sedative (n.)

3747 -- sedentary (adj.) -- deskbound

3748 -- sedition (n.) -- treason || related word: seditious (adj.)

3749 -- seduce (v.) -- to entice | to persuade sb to make physical relationship with sb else || related words: seductive (adj.), seductively (adv.), seducer (n.), seduction (n.), seductiveness (n.), seductress (n.)

3750 -- sedulous (adj.) -- hard-working || related word: sedulously (adv.)

3751 -- seedy (adj.) -- immoral or illegal || related word: seediness (n.)

3752 -- seeming (adj.) -- apparent || related word: seemingly (adv.)

3753 -- seemly (adj.) -- suitable

3754 -- seethe (v.) -- to be very angry; to fume

3755 -- segregate (v.) -- to separate || related word: segregation (n.)

3756 -- **segue (v.)** -- to change the subject, etc. smoothly

3757 -- **seismic (adj.)** -- related to earthquakes | very powerful; great

3758 -- **seizure (n.)** -- attack

3759 -- **self-contained (adj.)** -- independent

3760 -- **self-delusion (n.)** -- action of intentionally making yourself believe in untrue things

3761 -- **self-deprecating (adj.)** -- reducing the value of your own achievements || related word: **self-deprecation (n.)**

3762 -- **self-effacing (adj.)** -- shy || related word: **self-effacement (n.)**

3763 -- **self-induced (adj.)** -- caused by yourself

3764 -- **self-perpetuating (adj.)** -- continuing on itself

3765 -- **self-reliant (adj.)** -- independent

3766 -- **self-righteous (adj.)** -- showing that you can never be morally wrong || related words: **self-righteously (adv.), self-righteousness (n.)**

3767 -- **selfsame (adj.)** -- identical

3768 -- **semantic (adj.)** -- related to the meanings of words || related word: **semantically (adv.)**

3769 -- **semblance (n.)** -- resemblance

3770 -- **seminal (adj.)** -- influential

3771 -- **sendoff (n.)** -- farewell

3772 -- **senescent (adj.)** -- related to getting old || related word: **senescence (n.)**

3773 -- **senile (adj.)** -- behaving in a confused way because of old age || related word: **senility (n.)**

3774 -- **sententious (adj.)** -- behaving as if you are very intelligent || related word: **sententiously (adv.)**

3775 -- **sentient (adj.)** -- conscious

3776 -- **sepulchral (adj.)** -- very sad; similar to death

3777 -- **sequester (v.)** -- to seize sb's property, etc. | to not allow jury members to talk other people

3778 -- **sequestrate (v.)** -- to seize sb's property or other assets || related word: **sequestration (n.)**

3779 -- **seraphic (adj.)** -- very happy | like an angel

3780 -- **serenade (v.)** -- to sing a song to sb

3781 -- **serendipity (n.)** -- coincidence, fortune || related word: **serendipitous (adj.)**

3782 -- **serene (n.)** -- quiet and peaceful || related words: **serenely (adv.), serenity (n.)**

3783 -- **serf (n.)** -- a worker of landlord (in past)

3784 -- **sermonize (v.)** -- to give moral advice || related word: **sermon (n.)**

3785 -- **serrated (adj.)** -- saw-toothed

3786 -- **serviette (n.)** -- napkin

3787 -- **servile (adj.)** -- praising excessively || related word: **servility (n.)**

3788 -- **servitor (n.)** -- male servant

3789 -- **servitude (n.)** -- slavery

3790 -- **sever (v.)** -- to cut | to end a relationship with sb

3791 -- **shabby (adj.)** -- untidy || related word: **shabbily (adv.)**

3792 -- **shack (n.)** -- hut

3793 -- **shackle (v.)** -- to restrict sb from expressing their views || related word: **shackles (n.)**

3794 -- **shady (adj.)** -- appearing to be illegal

3795 -- **shakedown (n.)** -- action of obtaining sth by threat | intensive search

3796 -- **shake-up (n.)** -- too many changes

3797 -- **sham (adj./n./v.)** -- unreal | deception | to pretend

3798 -- **shamble (v.)** -- to drag your feet

3799 -- **shambles (n.)** -- big confusion; chaos | untidy place | related word: **shambolic (adj.)**

3800 -- **shanty (n.)** -- hut

3801 -- **shard (n.)** -- piece of sth broken

3802 -- **sheaf (n.)** -- bundle of papers, etc.

3803 -- **shear (v.)** -- to cut off; to shave

3804 -- **sheathe (v.)** -- to cover sth to protect it

3805 -- **shed (v.)** -- to drop | to get rid of sth

3806 -- **sheer (adj.)** -- complete

3807 -- **shelve (v.)** -- to cancel your plan

3808 -- **shenanigans (n.)** -- mischievous activities

3809 -- **Sherlock (n.)** -- an inquisitive person

3810 -- **shilly-shally (v.)** -- to hesitate to make a decision

3811 -- **shimmer (n./v.)** -- shining light | to shine

3812 -- **shingle (n.)** -- small stones, especially at river bank or on beach || related words: **shingled (adj.), shingly (adj.)**

3813 -- **shoal (n.)** -- group of fish

3814 -- **shoddy (adj.)** -- substandard || related words: **shoddily (adv.), shoddiness (n.)**

3815 -- **shoo (v.)** -- to gesture sb to go away

3816 -- **shoo-in (n.)** -- sb who can win with a little effort

3817 -- **shove (n./v.)** -- rough push | to push roughly

3818 -- **showdown (n.)** -- final argument

3819 -- **show-stopper (n.)** -- impressive performance || related word: **show-stopping (adj.)**

3820 -- **shred (n./v.)** -- small pieces | to cut

3821 -- **shrewd (adj.)** -- clever; wise; sharp || related words: **shrewdly (adv.), shrewdness (n.)**

3822 -- **shrewish (n.)** -- (of a woman) very bad tempered

3823 -- **shriek (n./v.)** -- loud shout | to shout loudly

3824 -- **shrill (n./v.)** -- unpleasant loud sound | to make an unpleasant loud sound; to say sth in this way || related words: **shrilly (adv.), shrillness (n.)**

3825 -- **shrivel (v.)** -- to shrink or wrinkle || related word: **shriveled (shrivelled) (adj.)**

3826 -- **shroud (n./v.)** -- covering | to cover or hide

3827 -- **shrug (n./v.)** -- up and down movement of your shoulder | to move your shoulders up and down

3828 -- **shtick (n.)** -- a special ability

3829 -- **shudder (n./v.)** -- shaking movement | to shake

3830 -- **shun (v.)** -- to avoid

3831 -- **shush (v.)** -- to shut up sb

3832 -- **shutterbug (n.)** -- a person who is extremely fond of taking photographs

3833 -- **shuttle (v.)** -- to travel or transport

3834 -- **sicken (v.)** -- to shock or disappoint sb too much || related words: **sickening (adj.), sickeningly (adv.), sickener (n.)**

3835 -- **sickly (adj.)** -- unhealthy and weak

3836 -- **sideswipe (v.)** -- to make indirect and critical comment on sb | to hit from the side

3837 -- **sift (v.)** -- to examine; to sort or separate

3838 -- **signatory (n.)** -- a party in an official agreement

3839 -- **silage (n.)** -- fodder

3840 -- **similitude (n.)** -- similarity

3841 -- **simmer (n./v.)** -- a period of sth boiling | to cook sth at high temperature; (of protest, disagreement, etc.) to continue to develop

3842 -- **simper (v.)** -- to smile annoyingly || related words: **simpering (adj.), simperingly (adv.)**

3843 -- **simulate (v.)** -- to copy; to imitate | to pretend

3844 -- **simulated (adj.)** -- unreal

3845 -- **simultaneous (adj.)** -- (of two or more activities, etc.) occurring at the same time; concurrent || related words: **simultaneously (adv.), simultaneity (n.)**

3846 -- **sine die (adv.)** -- till indefinite time in future

3847 -- **sinecure (n.)** -- easy job

3848 -- **sinewy (adj.)** -- very thin

3849 -- **singe (v.)** -- to burn slightly

3850 -- **sinister (adj.)** -- threatening

3851 -- **sinuous (adj.)** -- having curves [during movement] || related word: **sinuously (adv.)**

3852 -- **siphon (v.)** -- to transfer money illegally

3853 -- **sire (v.)** -- to become the male parent of a horse

3854 -- **siren (n.)** -- attractive but dangerous women

3855 -- **sissy (adj./n.)** -- stupid | stupid boy

3856 -- **sizeable (adj.)** -- large or substantial; plentiful

3857 -- **sizzle (v.)** -- to make hissing sound like sth is being cooked in frying oil

3858 -- **sizzling (adj.)** -- too hot | exciting

3859 -- **skank (n.)** -- unpleasant person || related word: **skanky (adj.)**

3860 -- **skeptical (adj.)** -- doubtful || related words: **skeptically (adv.), skepticism (n.)**

3861 -- **sketchy (adj.)** -- without details | rough || related words: **sketchily (adv.), sketchiness (n.)**

3862 -- **skew (v.)** -- to distort; to tilt | to negatively influence sth || related word: **skewed (adj.)**

3863 -- skid (n./v.) -- uncontrollable movement towards one side | to slide uncontrollably

3864 -- skim (v.) -- to remove cream from milk, etc | to move or read quickly

3865 -- skimp (v.) -- to be overcautious to use your money, time, etc.

3866 -- skimpy (adj.) -- insufficient

3867 -- skin-deep (adj.) -- superficial

3868 -- skinflint (n.) -- miser

3869 -- skinhead (n.) -- violent person with short hair

3870 -- skint (adj.) -- without money

3871 -- skirmish (n./v.) -- short argument or fight | to take part in a short argument or fight || related words: **skirmisher (n.), skirmishing (n.)**

3872 -- skirt (v.) -- to go around sth; to evade | to avoid embarrassing issue

3873 -- skit (n.) -- parody

3874 -- skivvy (n./v.) -- boring activities | to do boring activities

3875 -- skulk (v.) -- to move secretly in order to harm sb or do sth bad

3876 -- skullduggery (skulduggery) (n.) -- deceitful behavior

3877 -- slack (adj./v.) -- loose; careless | to work in a careless way || related words: **slackly (adv.), slackness (n.)**

3878 -- slacken (v.) -- to loosen | to slow down

3879 -- slacker (n.) -- lazy person

3880 -- slag (n.) -- a type of waste material from rock

3881 -- slam (n./v.) -- action of hard hitting | to shut; to bang; to criticize severely

3882 -- slammer (n.) -- jail

3883 -- slander (n./v.) -- rude and false remark about sb | to make rude and false remarks about sb || related word: **slanderous (adj.)**

3884 -- **slant (n./v.)** -- slope | to lean or slope || related words: **slanted (adj.), slanting (adj.)**

3885 -- **slapdash (adj.)** -- hasty

3886 -- **slap-happy (adj.)** -- joyful but careless; insincere

3887 -- **slapstick (n.)** -- humorous action

3888 -- **slash (n./v.)** -- sharp cut | to cut sharply

3889 -- **slash-and-burn (n.)** -- aggressive and violent

3890 -- **slate (n.)** -- to severely criticize sb | to schedule

3891 -- **slattern (n.)** -- untidy woman || related word: **slatternly (adv.)**

3892 -- **slaughter (n./v.)** -- butchery | to kill an animal for its meat; to kill many peoples, animals in violent way

3893 -- **slave-driver (n.)** -- oppressor, tormentor

3894 -- **slavish (adj.)** -- unoriginal || related word: **slavishly (adv.)**

3895 -- **slay (v.)** -- to kill || related word: **slaying (n.)**

3896 -- **sleaze (n.)** -- unpleasant, deceitful, illegal or immoral behavior || related words: **sleazy (adj.), sleaziness (n.)**

3897 -- **sleek (n./v.)** -- silky and smooth | to make your hair silky and smooth || related words: **sleekly (adj.), sleekness (n.)**

3898 -- **sleet (n./v.)** -- mixture of rain and hail or snow | to fall in this way from sky

3899 -- **sleight of hand (n.)** -- clever movement of your hands; dexterity

3900 -- **slender (adj.)** -- thin; slim | insufficient || related word: **slenderness (n.)**

3901 -- **sleuthing (n.)** -- investigation of a crime, etc.

3902 -- **slew (n./v.)** -- large quantity or amount | to turn direction

3903 -- **slick (adj./v.)** -- skillful; slippery; convincing | to sleek || related words: **slickly (adv.), slickness (n.)**

3904 -- **slime (n.)** -- substance that is thick and unpleasant

3905 -- **sling (v.)** -- to throw

3906 -- **slink (v.)** -- to move slowly and quietly

3907 -- **slinky (adj.)** -- graceful; attractive

3908 -- **slippage (n.)** -- incompetency | reduction

3909 -- **slipshod (adj.)** -- careless

3910 -- **slip-up (n.)** -- mistake; blunder

3911 -- **slit (n./v.)** -- narrow cut | to make narrow cut

3912 -- **slither (v.)** -- to move smoothly; to slide or glide || related word: **slithery (adj.)**

3913 -- **slob (n.)** -- sb who is lazy and untidy

3914 -- **slobber (v.)** -- to salivate

3915 -- **slog (n./v.)** -- period of making great effort | to make great effort

3916 -- **slop (n./v.)** -- waste product | to spill

3917 -- **sloppy (adj.)** -- careless; loose || related words: **sloppily (adv.), sloppiness (n.)**

3918 -- **slosh (v.)** -- to make noisy movement

3919 -- **sloshed (adj.)** -- drunk

3920 -- **slot (n./v.)** -- position or period | to fit sth into particular space

3921 -- **sloth (n.)** -- laziness || related word: **slothful (adj.)**

3922 -- **slouch (v.)** -- to bend lazily || related word: **slouchy (adj.)**

3923 -- **slough (n./v.)** -- wet land; marsh | to drop dead skin

3924 -- **slough of despond (n.)** -- state of great depression or hopelessness

3925 -- **sludge (n.)** -- wet mud

3926 -- **slug (v.)** -- to hit sb/sth hard

3927 -- **slugfest (n.)** -- insulting remarks made to each other

3928 -- **sluggard (n.)** -- lazy person || related word: **sluggardly (adj.)**

3929 -- **sluggish (adj.)** -- lazy | related words: **sluggishly (adv.), sluggishness (n.)**

3930 -- **sluice (v.)** -- to flow enormously

3931 -- **slumber (n./v.)** -- sleep | to sleep

3932 -- **slump (n./v.)** -- decline | to fall down

3933 -- **slumped (adj.)** -- unconscious or sleepy and leaning

3934 -- **slur (n./v.)** -- insult | to insult sb

3935 -- **slurp (n./v.)** -- noise that you make when your are sipping or drinking sth | to sip or drink nosily

3936 -- **slush (n.)** -- dirty snow | sentimental movies, stories, etc. || related word: **slushy (adj.)**

3937 -- **slut (n.)** -- dirty or characterless woman || related word: **sluttish (adj.)**

3938 -- **sly (adj.)** -- clever or tricky; cunning || related words: **slyly (adv.), slyness (n.)**

3939 -- **smack (adv./n./v.)** -- suddenly or exactly | slap | to slap

3940 -- **smacking (n.)** -- hitting with open hands

3941 -- **smarmy (adj.)** -- insincere; too courteous

3942 -- **smash (n./v.)** -- action of breaking, hitting, defeating sb; popular song or movie | to break; to hit; to defeat

3943 -- **smashing (adj.)** -- excellent

3944 -- **smash-up (n.)** -- horrific accident

3945 -- **smattering (n.)** -- slight knowledge of a language

3946 -- **smear (n./v.)** -- oily, muddy or dirty mark | to spread oily or muddy substance; to make insulting remark about sb

3947 -- **smelly (adj.)** -- having foul smell

3948 -- **smidgen (n.)** -- small amount

3949 -- **smirk (n./v.)** -- silly smile | to smile in a silly way

3950 -- **smite (v.)** -- to hit with full force

3951 -- **smitten (adj.)** -- deeply affected by a particular feeling, etc.

3952 -- **smolder (smoulder) (v.)** -- to burn | to have very strong feelings

3953 -- **smoothie (n.)** -- sb who is too polite

3954 -- **smother (v.)** -- to suffocate; to suppress

3955 -- **smudge (n./v.)** -- dirty or oily mark | to spread oily or muddy substance || related word: **smudgy (adj.)**

3956 -- **smug (adj.)** -- completely satisfied with your achievement || related words: **smugly (adv.), smugness (n.)**

3957 -- **smutty (adj.)** -- indecent

3958 -- **snaffle (v.)** -- to grab sth before sb else

3959 -- **snag (n./v.)** -- difficulty | to tear; to succeed

3960 -- **snaggle (n./v.)** -- disordered collection | to become disordered or confused

3961 -- **snappy (adj.)** -- attractive, lively, clever or impatient || related words: **snappily (adv.), snappiness (n.)**

3962 -- **snare (n./v.)** -- trap | to trap

3963 -- **snarky (adj.)** -- unkind or unfair criticism

3964 -- **snarl (n./v.)** -- roaring voice | to roar

3965 -- **snarl-up (n.)** -- traffic jam

3966 -- **snatch (v.)** -- to steal suddenly | to grab

3967 -- **snazzy (adj.)** -- smart and attractive

3968 -- **sneak (adj./v.)** -- done suddenly | to act in a mysterious way; to complain about a child

3969 -- **sneer (n./v.)** -- insult | to mock

3970 -- **snicker (v.)** -- to laugh quietly at sb's problems; to mock

3971 -- **snide (adj.)** -- criticizing sb/sth cruelly and indirectly || related word: **snidely (adv.)**

3972 -- **sniff (n./v.)** -- hint | to inhale; to complain

3973 -- **snigger (n./v.)** -- quiet laugh | to laugh slowly

3974 -- **snip (n.)** -- a cut made with scissors | to cut with scissors

3975 -- **snipe (v.)** -- to shoot secretly; to criticize || related word: **snipper (n.)**

3976 -- **snippet (n.)** -- a piece of information

3977 -- **snippy (adj.)** -- impolite

3978 -- **snitch (n./v.)** -- a complaint about a child | to complain about a child

3979 -- **snivel (v.)** -- to cry in an irritating way || related word: **sniveling (snivelling) (adj.)**

3980 -- **snob (n.)** -- a person who is too proud; a person who is unreasonably fond of people who belong to higher class || related words: **snobbish (adj.), snobbery (n.), snobbishness (n.)**

3981 -- **snog (n./v.)** -- kiss | to keep on kissing each other

3982 -- **snoop (n./v.)** -- spy; action of looking at sb/sth secretly | to spy

3983 -- **snooty (adj.)** -- too proud || related words: **snootily (adv.), snootiness (n.)**

3984 -- **snooze (n./v.)** -- short sleep during daytime; nap | to sleep during daytime; to nap

3985 -- **snub (v.)** -- to insult; to ignore || related word: **snub-nosed (adj.)**

3986 -- **snuff (v.)** -- to smell | to extinguish a fire

3987 -- **snuffle (v.)** -- to breath noisily || related word: **snuffling (n.)**

3988 -- **snug (adj.)** -- warm || related words: **snuggly (adv.), snugness (n.)**

3989 -- **snuggle (v.)** -- to get into warm place to avoid cold

3990 -- **soak (v.)** -- to put sth into liquid; to immerse || related words: **soaked (adj.), soaking (adj.)**

3991 -- **soar (v.)** -- to rise

3992 -- **sob (n./v.)** -- cry | to cry or weep

3993 -- **sobriety (n.)** -- seriousness || related word: **sobering (adj.)**

3994 -- **sobriquet (n.)** -- nickname

3995 -- **socialite (n.)** -- a partygoer who is also a famous personality

3996 -- **sociopath (n.)** -- mentally ill person

3997 -- **sodden (adj.)** -- completely wet

3998 -- **soggy (adj.)** -- unpleasantly moist

3999 -- **sojourn (n./v.)** -- break in your journey; stopover | to take break in your journey

4000 -- **solace (n./v.)** -- consolation | to console

4001 -- **soldier of fortune (n.)** -- mercenary

4002 -- **soldiery (n.)** -- a group of a particular kind of soldiers

4003 -- **solecism (n.)** -- mistake

4004 -- **solely (adv.)** -- exclusively

4005 -- **solemn (adj.)** -- serious; sincere || related words: **solemnly (adv.), solemnity (n.)**

4006 -- **solemnize (v.)** -- to perform marriage in a religious manner

4007 -- **solicit (v.)** -- to ask for support, etc; to beg || related word: **solicitation (n.)**

4008 -- **solicitous (adj.)** -- caring || related word: **solicitously (adv.)**

4009 -- **solicitude (n.)** -- kindness

4010 -- **solidarity (n.)** -- unity

4011 -- **soliloquy (n.)** -- self-talking || related word: **soliloquize (v.)**

4012 -- **solitary (adj./n.)** -- done alone | introvert person related word: **solitariness (n.)**

4013 -- **solitude (n.)** -- privacy; state of being alone but not lonely

4014 -- **solstice (n.)** -- longest/shortest day of the year

4015 -- **somber (sombre) (adj.)** -- very sad and serious || related words: **somberly (sombrely) (adv.), somberness (sombreness) (n.)**

4016 -- **somersault (n./v.)** -- action of turning over | to turn over in a way that your heels are above your head

4017 -- **somnambulist (n.)** -- sleepwalker || related word: **somnambulism (n.)**

4018 -- **somnolent (adj.)** -- sleepy or tiring || related word: **somnolence (n.)**

4019 -- **sonorous (adj.)** -- having loud and pleasant voice || related words: **sonorously (adv.), sonority (n.)**

4020 -- **soot (n.)** -- black dust generated from burnt wood

4021 -- **soothe (v.)** -- to calm sb || related words: **soothing (adj.), soothingly (adv.)**

4022 -- **sop (n.)** -- offering

4023 -- **sophist (n.)** -- sb who makes clever but wrong arguments || related word: **sophistry (n.)**

4024 -- **sophisticated (adj.)** -- experienced and stylish | complicated || related words: **sophisticate (v.), sophistication (n.)**

4025 -- **soporific (adj.)** -- sleep-inducing

4026 -- **sopping (adj.)** -- completely wet

4027 -- **soppy (adj.)** -- too sentimental

4028 -- **sorcery (n.)** -- black magic

4029 -- **sordid (adj.)** -- extremely unpleasant, deceitful or immoral

4030 -- **sore (adj./n.)** -- irritated; painful | a painful swelling || related word: **soreness (n.)**

4031 -- **sorely (adv.)** -- greatly

4032 -- **sortie (n.)** -- a short journey | raid | an effort

4033 -- **sough (v.)** -- to blow with whistling sound

4034 -- **sought after (adj.)** -- most desired

4035 -- **souvenir (n.)** -- memento

4036 -- **sovereign (adj./n.)** -- independent | king or queen

4037 -- spadework (adj.) -- hard work

4038 -- spangle (v.) -- to decorate sth with shiny pieces of sth else

4039 -- spank (n./v.) -- hit | to hit; to smack

4040 -- spanking (adj./adv./n.) -- excellent | new | a series of hits

4041 -- spar (v.) -- to make arguments in friendly way

4042 -- sparing (adj.) -- careful and thrifty || related word: **sparingly (adv.)**

4043 -- sparkling (adj.) -- bright | exciting or excellent

4044 -- sparky (adj.) -- lively

4045 -- sparse (adj.) -- meager; spread far and wide in small amount or quantity || related words: **sparsely (adv.), sparseness (n.)**

4046 -- spartan (adj.) -- simple; not much promising

4047 -- spasm (n.) -- sudden feeling | sudden contracting of a muscle

4048 -- spasmodic (adj.) -- sudden and occasional || related word: **spasmodically (adv.)**

4049 -- spat (n.) -- unimportant argument or quarrel

4050 -- spate (n.) -- sudden increase of sth unpleasant

4051 -- spatial (adj.) -- connected with size, shape, etc. of space || related word: **spatially (adv.)**

4052 -- spatter (n./v.) -- drops of liquid | to spray; to fall nosily

4053 -- spawn (v.) -- to produce | to lay eggs

4054 -- spearhead (n./v.) -- leader or head | to lead

4055 -- spec (n./v.) -- description of design and materials used in particular product | to standardize

4056 -- specimen (n.) -- sample or example

4057 -- specious (adj.) -- misleading; false

4058 -- speck (n.) -- spot

4059 -- speckle (n.) -- mark or spot || related word: **speckled (adj.)**

4060 -- **specter (spectre) (n.)** -- ghost | sth unpleasant that is probable to happen in near future

4061 -- **spectrum (n.)** -- range of related facts, etc.

4062 -- **speculate (v.)** -- to guess || related words: **speculative (adj.), speculatively (adv.), speculation (n.)**

4063 -- **spellbinding (adj.)** -- fascinating || related word: **spellbound (adj.)**

4064 -- **spew (v.)** -- to suddenly come or flow out

4065 -- **spiel (n.)** -- repeated and long speech that is used by salesperson

4066 -- **spiffy (adj.)** -- stylish

4067 -- **spike (n./v.)** -- sharp object | to push a pointed object into sb/sth; to rise quickly in value

4068 -- **spill (v.)** -- to drop or fall

4069 -- **spillover (n.)** -- overflow, spread

4070 -- **spindly (adj.)** -- long, think and weak

4071 -- **spin-off (n.)** -- positive side-effect

4072 -- **spinster (n.)** -- old and unmarried woman || related word: **spinsterhood (n.)**

4073 -- **spiteful (adj.)** -- mean, unkind or hurtful || related words: **spitefully (adv.), spitefulness (n.)**

4074 -- **splash (v.)** -- to spray nosily; to spatter

4075 -- **splashy (adj.)** -- bright and noticeable

4076 -- **splat (n.)** -- a sound that is generated when wet thing falls on a surface

4077 -- **splatter (v.)** -- to noisily fall in the form of large drops

4078 -- **splay (v.)** -- (of fingers, legs, etc.) to be spread out

4079 -- **splendor (splendour) (n.)** -- magnificence; grand

4080 -- **splenetic (adj.)** -- rude

4081 -- splice (v.) -- to join two things by sticking or twisting them together

4082 -- splinter (n./v.) -- a thin piece of sth | to fall apart

4083 -- splodge (n.) -- spot or mark

4084 -- splosh (v.) -- to move through water in a noisy way

4085 -- splurge (adj./v.) -- overspending; wastage of money | to overspend

4086 -- splutter (n./v.) -- a sound that is similar to an minor explosion | to make a series of explosive sounds; to say sth quickly and unclearly

4087 -- spoof (n./v.) -- humorous copy | to make humorous copy || related word: **spoofing (n.)**

4088 -- spook (n./v.) -- ghost | to frighten || related word: **spooky (adj.)**

4089 -- sporadic (adj.) -- infrequent || related word: **sporadically (adv.)**

4090 -- spout (v.) -- to flow out liquid

4091 -- sprawl (v.) -- to spread disorderly | to sit or lie in a lazy way with spreading out your arms or legs || related words: **sprawled (adj.), sprawling (adj.)**

4092 -- spread-eagle (spreadeagle) (v.) -- to spread out your arms and legs || related word: **spread-eagled (adj.)**

4093 -- spree (n.) -- period of enjoyable activity | period of criminal activity

4094 -- sprightly (adj.) -- energetic || related word: **sprightliness (n.)**

4095 -- springboard (v.) -- to help in starting a particular activity

4096 -- sprinkle (n./v.) -- spray; light rain | to spray; to rain lightly

4097 -- sprint (n./v.) -- fast race | to run or swim fast || related word: **sprinter (n.)**

4098 -- spritz (v.) -- to spray

4099 -- sprout (v.) -- to produce buds

4100 -- **spruce (adj.)** -- neat and tidy

4101 -- **spud (n.)** -- potato

4102 -- **spunk (n.)** -- bravery; determination || related word: **spunky (adj.)**

4103 -- **spur (v.)** -- to encourage

4104 -- **spurious (adj.)** -- fake || related word: **spuriously (adv.)**

4105 -- **spurn (v.)** -- to reject

4106 -- **spurt (n./v.)** -- sudden increase | to increase; to burst

4107 -- **squabble (n./v.)** -- noisy and unnecessary argument | to argue nosily and unnecessarily

4108 -- **squalid (adj.)** -- dirty | immoral

4109 -- **squall (n./v.)** -- storm | to cry loudly || related word: **squally (adj.)**

4110 -- **squalor (n.)** -- unpleasantness

4111 -- **squander (v.)** -- to waste money, etc.

4112 -- **squarely (adv.)** -- exactly

4113 -- **squash (v.)** -- to press or crush | to destroy

4114 -- **squat (adj./v.)** -- unpleasantly wide | to sit on your heels; to live somewhere without permission || related word: **squatter (n.)**

4115 -- **squawk (n./v.)** -- loud cry | to cry loudly

4116 -- **squeak (n./v.)** -- short sound | to make short sound || related word: **squeaky (adj.)**

4117 -- **squeaker (n.)** -- very tough competition

4118 -- **squeal (n./v.)** -- long sound | to make long cry; to shriek; to say sth in this way

4119 -- **squeamish (adj.)** -- easily offended | avoiding immoral activities || related word: **squeamishness (n.)**

4120 -- **squelch (v.)** -- to make a sound like that of walking on mud; to suppress || related word: **squelchy (adj.)**

4121 -- **squidgy (adj.)** -- that can be easily crushed

4122 -- **squiffy (adj.)** -- slightly drunk

4123 -- **squiggle (n.)** -- careless writing || related word: **squiggly (adj.)**

4124 -- **squint (n./v.)** -- quick look | to look sideways

4125 -- **squirm (v.)** -- to turn and twist while moving | to be embarrassed

4126 -- **squirrelly (adj.)** -- crazy | restless

4127 -- **squirt (n./v.)** -- spray | to spray

4128 -- **squish (v.)** -- (of sth soft) to be crushed | to make a sound of sth soft being crushed

4129 -- **squishy (adj.)** -- spongy

4130 -- **staccato (adj.)** -- having short and sharp sounds

4131 -- **stagger (n./v.)** -- unsteady walk; a start that is not concurrent ; great surprise; | to walk unsteadily; to not start at the same time; to shock sb || related words: **staggered (adj.)**

4132 -- **staggering (adj.)** -- amazing or shocking || related word: **staggeringly (adv.)**

4133 -- **stagnant (adj.)** -- inactive, still

4134 -- **stagnate (v.)** -- to be idle; to be still || related words: **stagnant (adj.), stagnation (n.)**

4135 -- **staid (adj.)** -- dull

4136 -- **stalemate (n.)** -- deadlock

4137 -- **stalker (n.)** -- a person who chases sb annoyingly || related words: **stalking (n.)**

4138 -- **stalwart (adj./n.)** -- loyal | strong supporter

4139 -- **stammer (v.)** -- to speak unclearly with repeating letters or sounds || related word: **stammerer (n.)**

4140 -- **stance (n.)** -- your opinions or views

4141 -- **stand-off (n.)** -- deadlock

4142 -- **standout (adj./n.)** -- different from others; noticeable | sb/sth that is different from others

4143 -- **standpoint (n.)** -- opinion; viewpoint

4144 -- **standstill (n.)** -- idle

4145 -- **stand-to (n.)** -- fully prepared to attack

4146 -- **starchy (adj.)** -- unfriendly

4147 -- **star-crossed (adj.)** -- having very bad luck

4148 -- **stark (adj.)** -- severe; without having any hope | complete || related words: **starkly (adv.), starkness (n.)**

4149 -- **starry-eyed (adj.)** -- too optimistic; too hopeful

4150 -- **startle (v.)** -- to surprise sb too much || related words: **startled (adj.), startling (adj.), startlingly (adv.)**

4151 -- **starve (v.)** -- to go very hungry

4152 -- **stash (n./v.)** -- sth that has been stored in secret way | to hide sth secretly

4153 -- **stasis (n.)** -- stillness

4154 -- **state of the art (n.)** -- modern

4155 -- **statecraft (n.)** -- skill in dealing with political matters

4156 -- **stately (adj.)** -- grand; very impressive || related word: **stateliness (n.)**

4157 -- **statesman (n.)** -- highly respected political leader || related words: **statesmanlike (adj.), statesmanship (n.)**

4158 -- **statuesque (adj.)** -- tall, beautiful and attractive

4159 -- **status quo (n.)** -- current or original situation

4160 -- **staunch (adj.)** -- loyal || related words: **staunchly (adv.), staunchness (n.)**

4161 -- **steadfast (adj.)** -- firm || related words: **steadfastly (adv.), steadfastness (n.)**

4162 -- **stealth (n.)** -- secrecy

4163 -- **steamroller (v.)** -- to use your power violently

4164 -- **stellar (adj.)** -- excellent

4165 -- **stench (n.)** -- very unpleasant smell

4166 -- **stentorian (adj.)** -- very loud and effective

4167 -- **stereotype (n./v.)** -- a particular type of thinking about sb/sth | to make a particular type of thinking about sb/sth || related words: **stereotyped (adj.), stereotypical (adj.), stereotypically (adv.), stereotyping (n.)**

4168 -- **sterling (adj.)** -- excellent

4169 -- **stern (adj.)** -- strict || related words: **sternly (adv.), sternness (n.)**

4170 -- **stew (v.)** -- to cook in a low or medium heat | to worry

4171 -- **stickability (n.)** -- persistence

4172 -- **stick-in-the-mud (n.)** -- sb who avoids sth new

4173 -- **stickler (n.)** -- very strict regarding rules

4174 -- **stiffen (v.)** -- to strengthen or harden

4175 -- **stifle (v.)** -- to suppress or suffocate || related words: **stifling (adj.), stiflingly (adv.)**

4176 -- **stigma (n.)** -- disgrace

4177 -- **stigmatize (v.)** -- to treat sb very badly || related word: **stigmatization (n.)**

4178 -- **stillborn (adj.)** -- unsuccessful | born dead

4179 -- **stilted (adj.)** -- unnatural; overformal || related word: **stiltedly (adv.)**

4180 -- **stimulate (v.)** -- to encourage or excite || related words: **stimulating (adj.), stimulation (n.)**

4181 -- **stingy (adj.)** -- not generous with money; miserly || related word: **stinginess (n.)**

4182 -- stink (n./v.) -- horrible smell; deep trouble or anger | to have horrible smell; to reek; to be too bad || related word: **stinky (adj.)**

4183 -- stinker (n.) -- extremely unpleasant person

4184 -- stinking (adj./adv.) -- reeking; filled with anger; very unpleasant | too much

4185 -- stint (n./v.) -- job period | to use sth in very small amount

4186 -- stipple (v.) -- to make dotted marks || related word: **stippling (n.)**

4187 -- stipulate (v.) -- to specify || related word: **stipulation (n.)**

4188 -- stir (n./v.) -- action of mixing a substance in liquid; excitement | to mix; to excite

4189 -- stockpile (n./v.) -- large supply | to keep sth in large amount

4190 -- stocktaking (n.) -- careful review of your situation

4191 -- stocky (adj.) -- having strong and sold body || related word: **stockily (adv.)**

4192 -- stodgy (adj.) -- difficult to digest | dull

4193 -- stoic (n.) -- a person who doesn't make complaint about its suffering || related words: **stoically (adv.), stoicism (n.)**

4194 -- stoke (v.) -- to fuel | to encourage, to strengthen; to excite || related word: **stoked (adj.)**

4195 -- stomp (v.) -- to tramp

4196 -- stone dead (adj.) -- completely dead or ruined

4197 -- stone deaf (adj.) -- completely deaf

4198 -- stoned (adj.) -- unable to behave normally because of effects of drugs

4199 -- stonewall (v.) -- to unnecessarily delay a decision

4200 -- stonker (n.) -- sth that is grand and impressive || related word: **stonking (adj.)**

4201 -- stony (adv.) -- unsympathetic || related word: **stonily (adv.)**

4202 -- **stony-faced (adj.)** -- unfriendly

4203 -- **stony-hearted (adj.)** -- cruel; having no feeling for anybody

4204 -- **stooge (n.)** -- silly and stupid person

4205 -- **stoop (v.)** -- to bend || related word: **stooped (adj.)**

4206 -- **stopgap (n.)** -- temporary substitute

4207 -- **stopover (n.)** -- short break in your journey

4208 -- **stout (adj.)** -- fat | strong | determined || related words: **stoutly (adv.), stoutness (n.)**

4209 -- **stow (v.)** -- to store safely

4210 -- **stowaway (n.)** -- sb who secretly travels in plain or ship without making payment

4211 -- **straddle (v.)** -- to be on both sides of sth

4212 -- **strafe (v.)** -- to make an airstrike from low height

4213 -- **straggle (v.)** -- to spread untidily | to leg behind

4214 -- **straggler (n.)** -- lazy person

4215 -- **straggly (adj.)** -- untidy

4216 -- **straitened (adj.)** -- without sufficient money; miserable

4217 -- **straitjacket (n.)** -- sth that prevents sth from making progress

4218 -- **straitlaced (adj.)** -- narrow-minded; old-fashioned

4219 -- **straits (n.)** -- state of not having enough money for your needs

4220 -- **strand (n./v.)** -- thread | a very small part of sth | to leave sb in a lonely place

4221 -- **strangle (v.)** -- to squeeze sb's throat in order to kill them | to hinder progress of sth

4222 -- **stranglehold (n.)** -- strong hold or total control

4223 -- **strangler (n.)** -- a person who throttles sb to death || related words: **strangulated (adj.), strangulation (n.)**

4224 -- **strapped (adj.)** -- poor; without enough money

4225 -- **strapping (adj.)** -- tall and strong

4226 -- **stratagem (n.)** -- clever trick

4227 -- **stratify (v.)** -- to arrange sth in layers

4228 -- **stratosphere (n.)** -- outer atmosphere of the earth || related word: **stratospheric (adj.)**

4229 -- **stray (adj./v.)** -- separated | to get lost

4230 -- **streak (v.)** -- to move fast | to run without wearing clothes

4231 -- **strenuous (adj.)** -- difficult and tiring || related word: **strenuously (adv.)**

4232 -- **strew (v.)** -- to litter or scatter

4233 -- **stricken (adj.)** -- seriously affected by sth unpleasant

4234 -- **stricture (n.)** -- restriction or criticism

4235 -- **stride (n./v.)** -- one long step | to move with long steps

4236 -- **strident (adj.)** -- loud | strong-minded || related words: **stridently (adv.), stridency (n.)**

4237 -- **strife (n.)** -- serious disagreement; conflict

4238 -- **stringent (adj.)** -- strict and severe || related words: **stringently (adv.), stringency (n.)**

4239 -- **stringy (adj.)** -- long and thin

4240 -- **stripe (n.)** -- strip | a particular category || related word: **stripped (adj.)**

4241 -- **strive (v.)** -- to struggle hard to achieve your goal || related word: **striving (n.)**

4242 -- **strobe (n.)** -- flashing lights at discos

4243 -- **stroll (n./v.)** -- leisurely walk | to walk in a slow and relaxed way || related word: **stroller (n.)**

4244 -- **stroppy (adj.)** -- loose-tempered; getting irritated on minor issues

4245 -- **strut (v.)** -- to walk in very proud or confident way; to swagger

4246 -- **stub (v.)** -- to accidently hit your toe against sth

4247 -- **stubble (n.)** -- short hair on man's face | lower part of stem ||
related word: **stubbly (adv.)**

4248 -- **stubby (adj.)** -- thick but short

4249 -- **stud (v.)** -- to fill sth with sth else || related word: **studded (adj.)**

4250 -- **studiously (adv.)** -- diligently

4251 -- **stuffed (adj.)** -- having had enough to eat your meal, etc.

4252 -- **stuffy (adj.)** -- unpleasantly warm; not fresh || related word:
stuffiness (n.)

4253 -- **stultify (v.)** -- to make sb feel very bored || related words:
stultifying (adj.), stultifyingly (adv.)

4254 -- **stumble (n./v.)** -- unsteady walk | to walk unsteadily

4255 -- **stumbling block (n.)** -- hurdle

4256 -- **stump (v.)** -- to confuse sb too much | to lead an election rally

4257 -- **stumpy (adj.)** -- thick but short

4258 -- **stun (v.)** -- to shock or impress; to astonish || related words:
stunned (adj.), stunning (adj.), stunningly (adv.)

4259 -- **stunt (v.)** -- to restrict || related word: **stunted (adj.)**

4260 -- **stupefy (v.)** -- to surprise sb too much || related words:
stupefying (adj.)

4261 -- **stupendous (adj.)** -- amazing || related word: **stupendously
(adv.)**

4262 -- **sturdy (adj.)** -- strong | determined || related words: **sturdily
(adv.), sturdiness (n.)**

4263 -- **stutter (v.)** -- to speak unclearly with repeating letters of sounds

4264 -- **stymie (v.)** -- to prevent sb from implementing their plan

4265 -- **suave (adj.)** -- confident || related word: **suavely (adv.)**

4266 -- **sub judice (adj.)** -- under trial

4267 -- **subdue (v.)** -- to suppress your feelings | to forcefully control
sb/sth

4268 -- **subdued (adj.)** -- quiet

4269 -- **subjugate (v.)** -- to control sb/sth; to overcome || related word: **subjugation (n.)**

4270 -- **sublet (v.)** -- to rent a rented property

4271 -- **sublime (adj.)** -- admiring || related words: **sublimely (adv.), sublimity (n.)**

4272 -- **subliminal (adj.)** -- subconscious || related word: **subliminally (adv.)**

4273 -- **submerge (v.)** -- to completely hide your feelings, etc. || related words: **submerged (adj.), submersion (n.)**

4274 -- **submissive (adj.)** -- meek || related words: **submissively (adv.), submissiveness (n.)**

4275 -- **subordinate (adj./n./v.)** -- less important | assistant; your junior | to not give enough importance to sb/sth || related word: **subordination (n.)**

4276 -- **suborn (v.)** -- to bribe sb to tell lies in court

4277 -- **subpoena (v.)** -- to summon sb to court as a witness

4278 -- **subsequent (adj.)** -- following; ensuing || related word: **subsequently (adv.)**

4279 -- **subservient (adj.)** -- meek || related word: **subservience (n.)**

4280 -- **subside (v.)** -- to drop or decrease

4281 -- **subsidiary (adj.)** -- additional

4282 -- **subsidize (v.)** -- to support sb/sth financially

4283 -- **subsist (v.)** -- to manage to survive with small amount of money or food | to be valid || related word: **subsistence (n.)**

4284 -- **substantiate (v.)** -- to verify || related word: **substantiation (n.)**

4285 -- **substantive (adj.)** -- serious and genuine

4286 -- **substratum (n.)** -- a layer below another layer

4287 -- **subsume (v.)** -- to consider sth as a whole; to include

4288 -- **subterfuge (n.)** -- dishonesty

4289 -- **subterranean (n.)** -- that is situated under the ground

4290 -- **subtle (adj.)** -- not easily noticeable | clever || related word: **subtlety (n.)**

4291 -- **subvention (n.)** -- financial assistance by the government

4292 -- **subversive (adj./n.)** -- destructing the political system | sb who tries to destroy the political system || related words: **subversively (adv.), subversiveness (n.)**

4293 -- **subvert (v.)** -- to try to attack political or religious system secretly; to try to attack sb's beliefs || related word: **subversion (n.)**

4294 -- **succession (n.)** -- chain; sequence

4295 -- **successor (n.)** -- heir

4296 -- **succinct (adj.)** -- to the point; brief || related words: **succinctly (adv.), succinctness (n.)**

4297 -- **succor (succour) (n./v.)** -- assistance to needy people | to assist a needy person

4298 -- **succulent (adj.)** -- juicy | related word: **succulence (n.)**

4299 -- **succumb (v.)** -- to accept your defeat; to give in

4300 -- **suds (n.)** -- bubbles

4301 -- **suffrage (n.)** -- your right to vote

4302 -- **suffuse (v.)** -- to spread or fill

4303 -- **sugary (adj.)** -- sentimental

4304 -- **suitor (n.)** -- sb who likes a particular woman very much and want to get married with her

4305 -- **sulk (v.)** -- to be very quiet and impolite to show your anger | related words: **sulky (adj.), sulkily (adv.), sulkiness (n.)**

4306 -- **sullen (adj.)** -- angry and quiet || related words: **sullenly (adv.), sullenness (n.)**

4307 -- **sully (v.)** -- to spoil

4308 -- **sultry (adj.)** -- too hot || related word: **sultriness (n.)**

4309 -- **summit (n.)** -- highest point; peak || official meeting between international leaders

4310 -- **sumptuous (adj.)** -- impressive and expensive || related word: **sumptuously (adv.), sumptuousness (n.)**

4311 -- **sunder (v.)** -- to break sth forcefully

4312 -- **superannuated (adj.)** -- too old

4313 -- **supercilious (adj.)** -- very proud || related words: **superciliously (adv.), superciliousness (n.)**

4314 -- **superficial (adj.)** -- obvious; apparent || related words: **superficially (adv.), superficiality (n.)**

4315 -- **superfluous (adj.)** -- unnecessary; extra || related words: **superfluously (adv.), superfluity (n.)**

4316 -- **supergrass (n.)** -- a criminal who is also a police informer

4317 -- **superimpose (v.)** -- to put sth on the top of another || related word: **superimposition (n.)**

4318 -- **superintend (v.)** -- to supervise || related word: **superintendence (n.)**

4319 -- **supernumerary (adj.)** -- more than is needed

4320 -- **superpose (v.)** -- to put sth on the top of another || related word: **superposition (n.)**

4321 -- **supersede (v.)** -- to exceed; to surpass

4322 -- **supine (n.)** -- unwilling to react; lazy || related word: **supinely (adv.)**

4323 -- **supper (n.)** -- a meal that you take at night or in late evening

4324 -- **supplant (v.)** -- to replace sth by sth new

4325 -- **supple (adj.)** -- flexible || related word: **suppleness (n.)**

4326 -- **supplicant (n.)** -- sb who makes request during prayer || related word: **supplication (n.)**

4327 -- **suppurate (v.)** -- to produce pus in a wound || related word: **suppuration (n.)**

4328 -- **supremacist (n.)** -- sb who has unreasonable beliefs about the greatness of their race

4329 -- **sure-fire (adj.)** -- certain; guaranteed

4330 -- **surefooted (adj.)** -- extremely confident

4331 -- **surfeit (n.)** -- surplus; excess

4332 -- **surge (n./v.)** -- sudden movement, increase, etc. | to rush; to increase suddenly; to excite

4333 -- **surly (adj.)** -- very impolite || related word: **surliness (n.)**

4334 -- **surmise (n./v.)** -- guess | to make a guess

4335 -- **surmount (v.)** -- to deal with sth complicated

4336 -- **surreal (surrealistic) (adj.)** -- too odd

4337 -- **surreptitious (adj.)** -- that is done in a secret way || related word: **surreptitiously (adv.)**

4338 -- **surrogate (adj./n.)** -- substitute | substitution

4339 -- **surveillance (n.)** -- close watch; supervision; observation

4340 -- **sustain (v.)** -- to continue | to uphold | to suffer | to provide || related words: **sustainable (adj.), sustainably (adv.), sustainability (n.)**

4341 -- **sustenance (n.)** -- nutrition | continuation

4342 -- **suture (n./v.)** -- stitch | to stitch a wound

4343 -- **suzerainty (n.)** -- ruling of one country over another country

4344 -- **svelte (adj.)** -- attractively thin

4345 -- **swaddle (v.)** -- to wrap

4346 -- **swag (n.)** -- stolen goods

4347 -- **swagger (n./v.)** -- proud and overconfident | to move or behave in a very proud manner

4348 -- **swamp (n./v.)** -- wet land; bog | to overfill || related word: **swampy (adj.)**

4349 -- **swank (v.)** -- to be overconfident

4350 -- **swanky (adj.)** -- impressive and stylish

4351 -- **swansong (n.)** -- the last performance given by an artist, etc.

4352 -- **swap (n./v.)** -- exchange | to exchange

4353 -- **sward (n.)** -- grass field

4354 -- **swarm (n./v.)** -- group | to move in a group

4355 -- **swarthy (adj.)** -- dark-skinned

4356 -- **swat (v.)** -- to hit sth with a flat object

4357 -- **swatch (n.)** -- a sample of a cloth

4358 -- **swathe (n./v.)** -- very large strip | to wrap

4359 -- **sway (n./v.)** -- side-to-side movement | to move side to side; to persuade

4360 -- **swearing-in (n.)** -- promise to be loyal; oath

4361 -- **sweeping (adj.)** -- extensive

4362 -- **sweepstake (n.)** -- lottery

4363 -- **swelter (v.)** -- to be too hot; to bake || related words: **sweltering (adj.), swelteringly (adv.)**

4364 -- **swerve (n./v.)** -- sudden turn | to turn in a sudden way

4365 -- **swig (n./v.)** -- alcoholic drink | to drink alcohol quickly

4366 -- **swill (n./v.)** -- poor quality food | to wash sth using water; to rinse

4367 -- **swindle (v.)** -- to cheat; to defraud

4368 -- **swine (n.)** -- unpleasant person or thing

4369 -- **swingeing (adj.)** -- critical; problematic

4370 -- **swinger (n.)** -- social person

4371 -- **swinging (adj.)** -- stylish; lively

4372 -- **swipe (n./v.)** -- action of hitting | to hit

4373 -- **swirl (n./v.)** -- spinning movement | to spin

4374 -- **swish (adj./n./v.)** -- stylish | movement with soft sound | to move making soft sound

4375 -- **swivel (v.)** -- to spin or swing

4376 -- **swoon (v.)** -- to be unconscious; to faint

4377 -- **swoop (n./v.)** -- sudden jump or move | to jump or move suddenly

4378 -- **swoosh (n./v.)** -- noisy movement through the air | to move through the air in noisy way

4379 -- **sworn (adj.)** -- under oath

4380 -- **swot (n./v.)** -- very studious person | to study very hard

4381 -- **sycophant (n.)** -- flatterer || related words: **sycophantic (adj.), sycophancy (n.)**

4382 -- **sylph (n.)** -- thin and attractive girl | ghost

4383 -- **sylvan (adj.)** -- related to trees

4384 -- **symbiosis (n.)** -- mutual relationship || related words: **symbiotic (adj.), symbiotically (adv.)**

4385 -- **symptomatic (adj.)** -- suggestive

4386 -- **synchronize (v.)** -- to happen at the same time as sth else || related word: **synchronization (n.)**

4387 -- **syncretism (n.)** -- mixing of different beliefs, etc.

4388 -- **syndicate (n./v.)** -- organization | to sell photos, etc. to news agencies || related word: **syndication (n.)**

4389 -- **synergy (n.)** -- extra power || related words: **synergistic (adj.), synergistically (adv.)**

4390 -- **systemic (adj.)** -- universal || related word: **systemically (adv.)**

Difficult English Words -- T

4391 -- **tacit (adj.)** -- understood; implied || related word: **tacitly (adv.)**

4392 -- **taciturn (adj.)** -- quiet in an unfriendly way || related word: **taciturnity (n.)**

4393 -- **tack (n./v.)** -- direction of your thoughts; direction of sail boats | (of sail boats) to change direction

4394 -- **tacky (adj.)** -- cheap; of low quality | sticky || related word: **tackiness (n.)**

4395 -- **tactile (adj.)** -- related to sense of touch

4396 -- **tad (n.)** -- small amount of sth; bit

4397 -- **tailback (n.)** -- traffic jam

4398 -- **tailgate (v.)** -- to drive very closely behind other car, bus, etc.

4399 -- **tailor-made (adj.)** -- fitting

4400 -- **tailspin (n.)** -- uncontrolled and aggravated situation

4401 -- **taint (n./v.)** -- unpleasant effect | to spoil

4402 -- **tamp (v.)** -- to compress

4403 -- **tang (n.)** -- sharp taste or smell of sth || related word: **tangy (adj.)**

4404 -- **tangential (adj.)** -- indirectly connected || related word: **tangentially (adv.)**

4405 -- **tangible (adj.)** -- touchable; noticeable || related word: **tangibly (adv.)**

4406 -- **tangle (n./v.)** -- disagreement; untidy mass | to make untidy mass of sth || related word: **tangled (adj.)**

4407 -- **tantalize (v.)** -- to entice || related words: **tantalizingly (adv.), tantalizing (n.)**

4408 -- **tantamount (adj.)** -- equivalent to sth bad

4409 -- **tantrum (n.)** -- angry behavior of small child

4410 -- **taper (v.)** -- to get thinner or narrower

4411 -- tardy (adj.) -- late || related words: **tardily (adv.), tardiness (n.)**

4412 -- tarnish (v.) -- to spoil sb's good reputation

4413 -- tarry (v.) -- to delay leaving a place

4414 -- tatters (n.) -- badly worn clothes

4415 -- taut (adj.) -- firm || related words: **tautly (adv.), tautness (n.)**

4416 -- tawdry (adj.) -- showy; immoral || related word: **tawdriness (n.)**

4417 -- technocrat (n.) -- expert in technical subject

4418 -- tedious (adj.) -- lasting too long; tiresome || related words: **tediously (adv.), tediousness (n.)**

4419 -- tedium (n.) -- dullness

4420 -- teed off (adj.) -- very angry

4421 -- teem (v.) -- to pour

4422 -- teeming (adj.) -- present in large numbers

4423 -- teeter (v.) -- to shake unsteadily

4424 -- teetotal (adj.) -- strictly avoiding alcohol || related words: **teetotaler (teetotaller) (n.), teetotalism (n.)**

4425 -- telling-off (n.) -- reprimand; scolding

4426 -- telltale (adj./n.) -- appearing to be existed | complaining child

4427 -- temerity (n.) -- boldness; rudeness

4428 -- temperamental (adj.) -- moody | connected with sb's personality || related word: **temperamentally (adv.)**

4429 -- temperance (n.) -- strict prohibition of alcohol due to morality

4430 -- temperate (adj.) -- having mild temperature | having polite behavior || related word: **temperately (adv.)**

4431 -- tempest (n.) -- storm

4432 -- tempo (n.) -- rhythm or pace

4433 -- temporal (adj.) -- related to time | related to physical world

4434 -- tempt (v.) -- to attract | to try to persuade || related words: **tempting (adj.), temptingly (adv.), temptation (n.), tempter (n.)**

4435 -- **tenacious (adj.)** -- firm | continual || related words: **tenaciously (adv.), tenaciousness (n.)**

4436 -- **tendentious (adj.)** -- controversial || related words: **tendentiously (adv.), tendentiousness (n.)**

4437 -- **tenderfoot (n.)** -- inexperienced person; beginner

4438 -- **tendril (n.)** -- stem | curl of hair

4439 -- **tenement (n.)** -- a large building with flats

4440 -- **tenet (n.)** -- belief or principle

4441 -- **tenor (n.)** -- meaning

4442 -- **tensile (adj.)** -- stretchable

4443 -- **tentative (adj.)** -- hesitant or uncertain || related words: **tentatively (adv.), tentativeness (n.)**

4444 -- **tenuous (adj.)** -- weak || related word: **tenuously (adv.)**

4445 -- **tenure (n.)** -- job period | right to stay somewhere permanently

4446 -- **tepid (adj.)** -- uncaring | slightly warm

4447 -- **terse (adj.)** -- brief and rude || related words: **tersely (adv.), terseness (n.)**

4448 -- **testament (n.)** -- evidence

4449 -- **testify (v.)** -- to be a witness in court; to provide evidence

4450 -- **testimony (n.)** -- proof | formal statement given in court

4451 -- **testy (adj.)** -- irritable || related word: **testily (adv.)**

4452 -- **tether (v.)** -- to tie an animal

4453 -- **thaw (v.)** -- to melt | to improve relationship

4454 -- **therapeutic (adj.)** -- healing; relaxing || related word: **therapeutically (adv.)**

4455 -- **thicket (n.)** -- undergrowth

4456 -- **thrash (v.)** -- to beat or defeat || related word: **thrashing (n.)**

4457 -- **threadbare (adj.)** -- thin | ineffective

4458 -- **threshold (n.)** -- a particular level | doorstep

4459 -- **thrifty (adj.)** -- economical

4460 -- **thrive (v.)** -- to prosper || related word: **thriving (n.)**

4461 -- **throb (v.)** -- to pulsate

4462 -- **throes (adj.)** -- extreme pain

4463 -- **throng (n./v.)** -- crowd | to move in a crowd

4464 -- **throughput (n.)** -- amount or number related to a particular activity in a particular period of time

4465 -- **throwaway (adj.)** -- disposable | casual

4466 -- **throwback (n.)** -- duplicate

4467 -- **thrust (n./v.)** -- sudden push | to push violently

4468 -- **thud (n./v.)** -- sound of sth heavy falling | to fall violently and noisily

4469 -- **thump (n./v.)** -- hard hit | to hit hard

4470 -- **thumping (adj.)** -- huge

4471 -- **thwack (n./v.)** -- hard hit | to hit or strike strongly

4472 -- **thwart (v.)** -- to spoil sb's effort

4473 -- **ticking off (n.)** -- rebuke

4474 -- **tickle (n./v.)** -- an itchy feeling | to make an itchy feeling in your body parts; to amuse

4475 -- **ticklish (adj.)** -- difficult and complicated

4476 -- **tidbit (titbit) (n.)** -- a piece of a food

4477 -- **tide (n.)** -- rush

4478 -- **tiff (n.)** -- minor disagreement

4479 -- **tillage (n.)** -- activity of growing crops

4480 -- **timorous (adj.)** -- fearful || related word: **timorously (adv.)**

4481 -- **tinder (n.)** -- dry grass, etc. that is used to light a fire

4482 -- **tinge (n./v.)** -- small amount of color, feelings, etc. | to add color, feelings, etc. in small amount

4483 -- **tingle (n.)** -- itch; uncomfortable feeling of particular emotion | to itch; to feel a particular emotion in uncomfortable way || related word: **tingly (adj.)**

4484 -- **tinker (v.)** -- to repair with minor improvements

4485 -- **tinkle (n./v.)** -- ringing sound | to make ringing sound

4486 -- **tint (n./v.)** -- shade or color | to add shade or color in small amount || related word: **tinted (adj.)**

4487 -- **tipple (n./v.)** -- alcoholic drink | to drink alcohol || related word: **tippler (n.)**

4488 -- **tipster (n.)** -- informer

4489 -- **tipsy (adj.)** -- drunk

4490 -- **tiptoe (v.)** -- to walk using your toes

4491 -- **tirade (n.)** -- strong criticism

4492 -- **titan (adj.)** -- huge, impressive or complicated

4493 -- **titillate (v.)** -- to excite || related word: **titillation (n.)**

4494 -- **titivate (v.)** -- to make minor improvements in your appearance

4495 -- **titter (n./v.)** -- a quiet laugh | to laugh quietly

4496 -- **tittle-tattle (n.)** -- gossip

4497 -- **titular (adj.)** -- in name only; without having real power

4498 -- **tizzy (n.)** -- panic

4499 -- **toddler (n.)** -- a very young child who can walk

4500 -- **toehold (n.)** -- grip

4501 -- **toil (n./v.)** -- tiring work | to do a lot of physical work

4502 -- **tome (n.)** -- huge volume of a book

4503 -- **topography (n.)** -- landscape || related words: **topographical (adj.), topographically (adv.)**

4504 -- **topple (v.)** -- to overthrow

4505 -- **topsy-turvy (adj.)** -- disordered

4506 -- **torment (adj./v.)** -- suffering | to torture; to cause trouble

4507 -- **torpor (n.)** -- inactivity

4508 -- **torque (n.)** -- a type of force that rotates a machine

4509 -- **torrent (n.)** -- water in large amount; flood || related word: **torrential (adj.)**

4510 -- **torrid (adj.)** -- hot | difficult | passionate

4511 -- **toss-up (n.)** -- fifty-fifty

4512 -- **tote (v.)** -- to carry sth heavy

4513 -- **totter (v.)** -- to walk unsteadily | to be likely to fall

4514 -- **touchy (adj.)** -- too sensitive || related word: **touchiness (n.)**

4515 -- **tousle (v.)** -- to make a mess of sb's hair

4516 -- **tout (v.)** -- to sell tickets illegally | to persuade

4517 -- **tow (v.)** -- to drag a vehicle using other vehicle

4518 -- **tract (n.)** -- region

4519 -- **trailblazer (n.)** -- a person who initiates sth; pioneer || related word: **trailblazing (n.)**

4520 -- **traipse (v.)** -- to walk with difficulty

4521 -- **traitor (n.)** -- sb who conspires against their own country || related words: **traitorous (adj.), traitorously (adv.)**

4522 -- **trammel (v.)** -- to restrict sb's freedom

4523 -- **tramp (v.)** -- to walk with heavy steps

4524 -- **trample (v.)** -- to put your feet over sth in order to crush it || to ignore sb's concerns

4525 -- **tranquil (adj.)** -- calm; peace || related words: **tranquilly (adv.), tranquility (n.)**

4526 -- **transcend (v.)** -- to exceed; to surpass || related words: **transcendent (adj.), transcendence (n.)**

4527 -- **transfix (v.)** -- to fascinate sb

4528 -- **transgenic (adj.)** -- genetically modified || related word: **transgenically (adv.)**

4529 -- **transgress (v.)** -- to cross your limits; to do sth unlawful || related words: **transgression (n.), transgressor (n.)**

4530 -- **transient (adj.)** -- temporary; short-lived || related word: **transience (n.)**

4531 -- **transition (n.)** -- conversion || related word: **transitional (adj.)**

4532 -- **transitory (adj.)** -- momentary

4533 -- **translucent (adj.)** -- semi-transparent || related word: **translucence (n.)**

4534 -- **transmigration (n.)** -- entering of a soul into sb's body

4535 -- **transmogrify (v.)** -- to make major changes in sth, especially in a surprising way || related word: **transmogrification (n.)**

4536 -- **transpire (v.)** -- to become known | to let the vapor pass out

4537 -- **transpose (v.)** -- to rearrange or reorder || related word: **transposition (n.)**

4538 -- **transvestite (n.)** -- a man who likes wearing women's dress

4539 -- **travail (n.)** -- great suffering

4540 -- **traverse (v.)** -- to pass though a road, etc.

4541 -- **travesty (n.)** -- mockery

4542 -- **trawl (v.)** -- to probe

4543 -- **treacherous (adj.)** -- deceitful or untrustworthy || related words: **treacherously (adv.), treachery (n.)**

4544 -- **treadmill (n.)** -- boring way of life

4545 -- **treason (n.)** -- disloyalty towards your own country || related word: **treasonable (adj.)**

4546 -- **treatise (n.)** -- an article or important topic

4547 -- **treble (v.)** -- to triple

4548 -- **tremble (v.)** -- to shake; to be worried || related word: **trembly (adj.)**

4549 -- **tremulous (adj.)** -- shaking because of anxiety || related word: **tremulously (adv.)**

4550 -- **trench (n.)** -- a long deep hole

4551 -- **trenchant (adj.)** -- showing critical views || related word: **trenchantly (adv.)**

4552 -- **trepidation (n.)** -- anxiety

4553 -- trespass (v.) -- to enter sb's land without permission || related word: **trespasser (n.)**

4554 -- tresses (n.) -- long hair of woman

4555 -- tribulation (n.) -- too much suffering

4556 -- tributary (n.) -- stream or river

4557 -- trickle (n./v.) -- flowing liquid; small amount or quantity of sth moving gradually | to ooze, to flow; to move slowly

4558 -- trifle (n.) -- insignificant thing || related word: **trifling (adj.)**

4559 -- trinity (n.) -- a group of three

4560 -- trinket (n.) -- an inexpensive ornament

4561 -- trite (adj.) -- too ordinary and insignificant

4562 -- triumvirate (n.) -- a group of three people with special powers to control sth

4563 -- trivia (n.) -- insignificant details

4564 -- trivial (adj.) -- insignificant || related words: **trivially (adv.), triviality (n.), trivialization (n.), trivialize (v.)**

4565 -- trot (v.) -- to walk fast

4566 -- trounce (v.) -- to beat or defeat

4567 -- trousseau (n.) -- collection of clothes and other objects by would-be married woman

4568 -- trout (n.) -- an irritating woman

4569 -- truant (n./v.) -- a child who bunks classes | to bunk classes

4570 -- truce (n.) -- ceasefire

4571 -- truculent (adj.) -- bad-tempered; quarrelsome || related words: **truculently (adv.), truculence (n.)**

4572 -- trudge (n./v.) -- a tiring walk | to walk with heavy steps

4573 -- truncate (v.) -- to shorten || related word: **truncation (n.)**

4574 -- trundle (v.) -- to move noisily | to walk with heavy steps

4575 -- truss (v.) -- to tie

4576 -- trying (adj.) -- irritating

4577 -- tryst (n.) -- a meeting between lovers

4578 -- tuck (v.) -- to put or push

4579 -- tuft (n.) -- bunch || related word: **tufted (adj.)**

4580 -- tumble (n./v.) -- fall | to fall down

4581 -- tumult (n.) -- great confusion || related word: **tumultuous (adj.)**

4582 -- turbid (n.) -- muddy or dirty || related word: **turbidity (n.)**

4583 -- turbulent (adj.) -- disorderly

4584 -- turmoil (n.) -- chaos

4585 -- turncoat (n.) -- deserter

4586 -- turpitude (n.) -- evilness

4587 -- tussle (n./v.) -- fight or struggle to get sth | to fight or struggle

4588 -- tutelage (n.) -- guidance

4589 -- tweak (n./v.) -- a twist or pull | to twist or pull

4590 -- twiddle (n./v.) -- a twist or turn | to twist or turn

4591 -- twinge (n.) -- sudden pain or other feeling

4592 -- twirl (v.) -- to curl

4593 -- twitch (n./v.) -- uncontrollable movement | to move uncontrollably || related word: **twitchy (adj.)**

4594 -- typify (v.) -- to exemplify

4595 -- tyrant (n.) -- dictator || related words: **tyrannical (adj.), tyrannize (v.)**

Difficult English Words -- U

4596 -- **ubiquitous (adj.)** -- everywhere and ever-present || related words: **ubiquitously (adv.), ubiquity (n.)**

4597 -- **ultra vires (adv.)** -- beyond legal power

4598 -- **ululate (v.)** -- to cry loudly || related word: **ululation (n.)**

4599 -- **umpteen (pronoun & determiner)** -- a lot of

4600 -- **unabashed (adj.)** -- shameless || related word: **unabashedly (adv.)**

4601 -- **unabated (adj.)** -- with full strength

4602 -- **unabridged (adj.)** -- complete; full-length

4603 -- **unaccounted for (adj.)** -- than cannot be found or is unexplained

4604 -- **unaccustomed (adj.)** -- unusual; unfamiliar

4605 -- **unacquainted (adj.)** -- without having knowledge of a particular thing; unfamiliar

4606 -- **unadorned (adj.)** -- that has no decoration; plain

4607 -- **unadulterated (adj.)** -- pure | complete

4608 -- **unalloyed (adj.)** -- completely pure

4609 -- **unapologetic (adj.)** -- not sorry; unrepentant || related word: **unapologetically (adv.)**

4610 -- **unappetizing (adj.)** -- tasteless

4611 -- **unavailing (adj.)** -- unsuccessful; ineffective

4612 -- **unbecoming (adj.)** -- unsuitable or unacceptable

4613 -- **unbefitting (adj.)** -- unsuitable

4614 -- **unbeknown (adj.)** -- without sb mentioned knowing

4615 -- **unbend (v.)** -- to become straight | to become less strict

4616 -- **unbending (adj.)** -- inflexible in his/her own views; obstinate

4617 -- **unbidden (adj.)** -- without being asked

4618 -- **unblemished (adj.)** -- that is not damaged, perfect

4619 -- **unbridled (adj.)** -- uncontrolled

4620 -- **uncalled-for (adj.)** -- unnecessary; unfair

4621 -- **uncanny (adj.)** -- strange and inexplicable || related word: **uncannily (adv.)**

4622 -- **unceasing (adj.)** -- never-ending || related word: **unceasingly (adv.)**

4623 -- **unceremonious (adj.)** -- uncaring, insulting || related word: **unceremoniously (adv.)**

4624 -- **uncluttered (adj.)** -- without unnecessary items; tidy

4625 -- **uncomprehending (adj.)** -- that cannot be understood || related word: **uncomprehendingly (adv.)**

4626 -- **uncompromising (adj.)** -- stubborn || related word: **uncompromisingly (adv.)**

4627 -- **unconscionable (adj.)** -- extremely bad | excessive

4628 -- **uncontaminated (adj.)** -- clean or pure

4629 -- **uncorroborated (adj.)** -- that cannot be confirmed

4630 -- **uncouth (adj.)** -- impolite; rude

4631 -- **unctuous (adj.)** -- friendly but not sincere || related word: **unctuously (adv.)**

4632 -- **undaunted (adj.)** -- fearless

4633 -- **underbelly (n.)** -- the weakest part of sth that is prone to easy attack

4634 -- **underclass (n.)** -- people without any status

4635 -- **undercover (adj./adv.)** -- in a secret way | secretly

4636 -- **undercurrent (n.)** -- sth that is unexpressed but noticeable; hint

4637 -- **underdog (n.)** -- a team, person, etc. that seems to be weak

4638 -- **undergo (v.)** -- to experience sth bad

4639 -- **undergrowth (n.)** -- bushes that grow under trees

4640 -- **underhand (adj.)** -- deceitful and secret

4641 -- **underline (v.)** -- to highlight

4642 -- **underling (n.)** -- sb who has low status

4643 -- **underlying (adj.)** -- basic or primary

4644 -- **underneath (adv./prep.)** -- below

4645 -- **underpin (v.)** -- to support || related word: **underpinning (n.)**

4646 -- **underplay (v.)** -- to take something too lightly

4647 -- **undertake (v.)** -- to take responsibility for a work, etc; to promise || related word: **undertaking (n.)**

4648 -- **undertone (n.)** -- indirect remark, hint, etc.

4649 -- **underwrite (v.)** -- to guarantee

4650 -- **undismayed (adj.)** -- unworried; undisturbed

4651 -- **undoing (n.)** -- the cause of your failure, ruin, etc.

4652 -- **undulate (v.)** -- to move or swell like waves || related word: **undulation (n.)**

4653 -- **unduly (adv.)** -- excessively

4654 -- **undying (adj.)** -- never-ending

4655 -- **unedifying (adj.)** -- unpleasant and disapproving

4656 -- **unenviable (adj.)** -- unpleasant and undesirable

4657 -- **unequivocal (adj.)** -- very clear in opinion; obvious || related word: **unequivocally (adv.)**

4658 -- **unerring (adj.)** -- without having any mistake || related word: **unerringly (adv.)**

4659 -- **unfathomable (adj.)** -- that cannot be understood

4660 -- **unfazed (adj.)** -- unsurprised or unworried in the events that happen unexpectedly

4661 -- **unfettered (adj.)** -- unrestricted

4662 -- **unflagging (adj.)** -- determined; tireless

4663 -- **unflappable (adj.)** -- calm; composed

4664 -- **unflattering (adj.)** -- unfavorable

4665 -- **unflinching (adj.)** -- determined and firm || related word: **unflinchingly (adv.)**

4666 -- **unfold (v.)** -- to clarify in a gradual way

4667 -- **unformed (adj.)** -- undeveloped

4668 -- **unforthcoming (adj.)** -- uncommunicative; reserved

4669 -- **ungainly (adj.)** -- moving in an awkward way

4670 -- **unglamorous (adj.)** -- simple or dull

4671 -- **ungodly (adj.)** -- irreligious or evil

4672 -- **unheralded (adj.)** -- unexpected

4673 -- **unhindered (adj.)** -- unrestricted

4674 -- **unhinge (v.)** -- to mentally disturb sb

4675 -- **unhitch (v.)** -- to untie

4676 -- **unicameral (adj.)** -- having one parliamentary body

4677 -- **unify (v.)** -- to unite || related word: **unification (n.)**

4678 -- **unimpaired (adj.)** -- without any damage

4679 -- **unimpeachable (adj.)** -- doubtless; conclusive

4680 -- **unimpeded (adj.)** -- unblocked; unrestricted

4681 -- **uninhibited (adj.)** -- expressing your feelings, skills, etc. openly

4682 -- **uninitiated (adj.)** -- inexperienced or unskilled

4683 -- **unkempt (adj.)** -- in a mess; untidy

4684 -- **unknowing (adj.)** -- unaware || related words: **unknowable (adj.), unknowingly (adv.)**

4685 -- **unleash (v.)** -- to set free

4686 -- **unlettered (adj.)** -- unable to read

4687 -- **unmindful (adj.)** -- careless

4688 -- **unmitigated (adj.)** -- (of sth bad) absolute; complete

4689 -- **unmoved (adj.)** -- without feelings; insensitive; unaffected

4690 -- **unnerve (v.)** -- to scare or terrify || related words: **unnerving (adj.), unnervingly (adv.)**

4691 -- **unobtrusive (adj.)** -- that is not disturbing; modest || related word: **unobtrusively (adv.)**

4692 -- **unpalatable (adj.)** -- not tasty | unacceptable

4693 -- **unparalleled (adj.)** -- better than all others; unmatched

4694 -- **unperturbed (adj.)** -- without any worry; calm

4695 -- **unprecedented (adj.)** -- that has occurred first-time; extraordinary || related word: **unprecedentedly (adv.)**

4696 -- **unprepossessing (adj.)** -- unattractive

4697 -- **unprincipled (adj.)** -- immoral

4698 -- **unpromising (adj.)** -- likely to be failed; appearing to be bad; doubtful; depressing

4699 -- **unputdownable (adj.)** -- that you cannot stop reading because of its being very interesting

4700 -- **unquenchable (adj.)** -- that cannot be satisfied; insatiable

4701 -- **unregenerate (adj.)** -- not wanting to improve your personality

4702 -- **unrelenting (adj.)** -- merciless

4703 -- **unremitting (adj.)** -- constant || related word: **unremittingly (adv.)**

4704 -- **unrequited (adj.)** -- unreturned

4705 -- **unrivalled (adj.)** -- better than all

4706 -- **unruffled (adj.)** -- (of a person) relaxed

4707 -- **unruly (adj.)** -- uncontrollable || related word: **unruliness (n.)**

4708 -- **unscrupulous (adj.)** -- dishonest; immoral; unfair || related words: **unscrupulously (adv.), unscrupulousness (n.)**

4709 -- **unseemly (adj.)** -- rude

4710 -- **unsettled (adj.)** -- not fixed or relaxed || related word: **unsettling (adj.)**

4711 -- **unsightly (adj.)** -- horrible; ugly

4712 -- **unsolicited (adj.)** -- unwanted

4712 -- **unsparing (adj.)** -- generous || related word: **unsparingly (adv.)**

4714 -- **unstinting (adj.)** -- giving openhandedly || related word: **unstintingly (adv.)**

4715 -- **unsullied (adj.)** -- pure

4716 -- **unsurpassed (adj.)** -- supreme; best

4717 -- **unswerving (adj.)** -- constant; reliable

4718 -- **untapped (adj.)** -- unused

4719 -- **untenable (adj.)** -- that cannot be defended

4720 -- **untoward (adj.)** -- awkward and unpleasant

4721 -- **untrammeled (untrammelled) (adj.)** -- unrestricted

4722 -- **unvarying (adj.)** -- constant; consistent

4723 -- **unveil (v.)** -- to expose; to disclose

4724 -- **unvoiced (adj.)** -- that has been thought about but is still unexpressed

4725 -- **unwarranted (adj.)** -- unsuitable and unnecessary

4726 -- **unwary (adj.)** -- not careful or cautious

4727 -- **unwavering (adj.)** -- steady || related word: **unwaveringly (adv.)**

4728 -- **unwind (v.)** -- to undo | to calm down

4729 -- **unwonted (adj.)** -- unexpected

4730 -- **unyielding (adj.)** -- obstinate

4731 -- **upbeat (adj.)** -- cheerful, enthusiastic or optimistic

4732 -- **upbraid (v.)** -- to criticize

4733 -- **upbringing (n.)** -- the way your childhood is shaped

4734 -- **upend (v.)** -- to overturn

4735 -- **upfront (adj.)** -- bold and honest

4736 -- **upheaval (n.)** -- disturbance

4737 -- **uphill (adj./adv.)** -- sloping upwards | towards the top of a hill/slope

4738 -- **uphold (v.)** -- to maintain a decision; to support || related word: **upholder (n.)**

4739 -- **upholster (v.)** -- to cover a furniture with padding, etc. || related words: **upholsterer (n.), upholstery (n.)**

4740 -- **upkeep (n.)** -- maintenance

4741 -- **uplift (adj./v.)** -- great joy | to fill sb with joy || related word: **uplifted (adj.)**

4742 -- **uppity (adj.)** -- too proud

4743 -- **upright (adj.)** -- behaving in a moral way; honest

4744 -- **uprising (n.)** -- revolution

4745 -- **uproar (n.)** -- angry reaction by public; chaos

4746 -- **uproarious (adj.)** -- extremely funny | full of noise || related word: **uproariously (adv.)**

4747 -- **uproot (v.)** -- to dig up | to leave

4748 -- **uprush (n.)** -- an exciting feeling

4749 -- **upshot (n.)** -- result

4750 -- **upstanding (adj.)** -- behaving in a moral way; honest

4751 -- **upstart (n.)** -- insignificant person; minion

4752 -- **upstream (adv.)** -- along a river

4753 -- **upsurge (n.)** -- swift increase in sth

4754 -- **upswell (n.)** -- increase of emotions, feelings, etc.

4755 -- **upswing (n.)** -- period of improvement

4756 -- **uptight (adj.)** -- anxious

4757 -- **upturn (n.)** -- period of improvement

4758 -- **upturned (adj.)** -- upside down; reversed

4759 -- **urchin (n.)** -- homeless child

4760 -- usher (v.) -- to tell sb where they should go

4761 -- usurer (n.) -- sb who lends money at too high interest rates || related word: **usurious (adj.)**

4762 -- usurp (v.) -- to seize || related words: **usurpation (n.), usurper (n.)**

4763 -- usury (n.) -- practice of lending money at very high rate of interest

4764 -- utilitarianism (n.) -- great happiness for large number of people

4765 -- utmost (adj./n.) -- maximum | maximum amount

4766 -- utopia (n.) -- perfect place || related word: **utopian (adj.)**

4767 -- utter (adj./v.) -- total | to say sth || related word: **utterly (adv.)**

Difficult English Words -- V

4768 -- **vacillate (v.)** -- to keep on changing your opinions || related word: **vacillation (n.)**

4769 -- **vacuous (adj.)** -- not having important thoughts; unintelligent || related words: **vacuity (n.), vacuously (adv.), vacuousness (n.)**

4770 -- **vade mecum (n.)** -- very useful guide

4771 -- **vagabond (n.)** -- homeless person

4772 -- **vagaries (n.)** -- unpredictable changes

4773 -- **vagrant (n.)** -- homeless beggar

4774 -- **vain (adj.)** -- proud | useless

4775 -- **vainglorious (adj.)** -- proud || related word: **vainglory (n.)**

4776 -- **vainly (adv.)** -- unsuccessfully

4777 -- **valediction (n.)** -- farewell; goodbye || related word: **valedictory (adj.)**

4778 -- **valiant (adj.)** -- brave || related word: **valiantly (adv.)**

4779 -- **validate (v.)** -- to confirm || related word: **validation (n.)**

4780 -- **valor (valour) (n.)** -- courage || related word: **valorous (adj.)**

4781 -- **vamp (n.)** -- dominating woman

4782 -- **vampire (n.)** -- blood-sucking dead person

4783 -- **vandalize (v.)** -- to damage or spoil public property || related words: **vandalism (n.), vandal (n.)**

4784 -- **vanguard (n.)** -- a group of leaders; forerunner

4785 -- **vanish (v.)** -- to disappear

4786 -- **vanity (n.)** -- pride

4787 -- **vanquish (v.)** -- to defeat || related word: **vanquished (n.)**

4788 -- **vantage-point (n.)** -- a situation from where you consider sth that occurred in past

4789 -- **vapid (adj.)** -- lifeless; boring || related word: **vapidity (n.)**

4790 -- **variegated (adj.)** -- having different sorts of things, etc. | having spots

4791 -- **vassal (n.)** -- a country that is controlled by another country

4792 -- **veer (v.)** -- to change or turn in a sudden way

4793 -- **vegetative (adj.)** -- connected with plant life

4794 -- **vehement (adj.)** -- passionate || related words: **vehemently (adv.), vehemence (n.)**

4795 -- **vein (n.)** -- an amount of quality | method or style

4796 -- **venal (adj.)** -- corrupt || related word: **venality (n.)**

4797 -- **vendetta (n.)** -- serious or violent dispute or disagreement between two groups

4798 -- **veneer (n.)** -- layer (outer appearance)

4799 -- **venerate (v.)** -- to respect sb very much || related words: **venerable (adj.), veneration (n.)**

4800 -- **venereal (adj.)** -- connected with diseases which spreads through 'physical' contact

4801 -- **vengeance (n.)** -- revenge

4802 -- **vengeful (adj.)** -- unforgiving || related word: **vengefully (adv.)**

4803 -- **vent (v.)** -- to show anger or other strong feelings

4804 -- **ventriloquism (n.)** -- ability to speak without moving your lips || related word: **ventriloquist (n.)**

4805 -- **venture (n./v.)** -- risky task | to do risky things

4806 -- **veracity (n.)** -- truth

4807 -- **verbatim (adj./adv.)** -- word for word

4808 -- **verbose (adj.)** -- talkative || related word: **verbosity (n.)**

4809 -- **verdant (adj.)** -- fresh and green

4810 -- **verily (adv.)** -- truly

4811 -- **verisimilitude (n.)** -- accuracy; genuineness

4812 -- **veritable (adj.)** -- authentic

4813 -- verity (n.) -- truth

4814 -- vernal (adj.) -- related to the season of spring

4815 -- versatile (adj.) -- having different uses or skills || related word: versatility (n.)

4816 -- verve (n.) -- energy

4817 -- vestige (n.) -- sign or trace || related word: vestigial (adj.)

4818 -- vet (v.) -- to investigate

4819 -- vex (v.) -- to annoy || related words: vexatious (adj.), vexed (adj.), vexation (n.)

4820 -- vibrant (adj.) -- lively || related words: vibrantly (adv.), vibrancy (n.)

4821 -- vicarious (adj.) -- felt by activities of others || related word: vicariously (adv.)

4822 -- vice (n.) -- immoral behavior

4823 -- vicious (adj.) -- brutal or extremely bad || related words: viciously (adv.), viciousness (n.)

4824 -- vicissitude (n.) -- problems and changes in daily life

4825 -- vie (v.) -- to compete

4826 -- vignette (n.) -- small picture or short piece of writing to depict sb

4827 -- vigor (vigour) (n.) -- life energy || related word: vigorous (adj.), vigorously (adv.)

4828 -- vile (adj.) -- evil || related words: vilely (adv.), vileness (n.)

4829 -- vilify (v.) -- to try to spoil reputation of sb by saying bad things about them; to malign || related word: vilification (n.)

4830 -- vim (n.) -- enthusiasm

4831 -- vindicate (v.) -- to justify || related word: vindication (n.)

4832 -- vindictive (adj.) -- very unkind; trying to take revenge || related words: vindictively (adv.), vindictiveness (n.)

4833 -- **virago (n.)** -- aggressive and dominating woman

4834 -- **virile (adj.)** -- (of men) full of energy || related word: **virility (n.)**

4835 -- **virtual (adj.)** -- almost real || related word: **virtually (adv.)**

4836 -- **virtue (n.)** -- positive quality

4837 -- **virtuosity (n.)** -- skill

4838 -- **virtuous (adj.)** -- having moral attitude || related word: **virtuously (adv.)**

4839 -- **virulent (adj.)** -- dangerous or critical || related words: **virulently (adv.), virulence (n.)**

4840 -- **visage (n.)** -- facial features

4841 -- **vis-a-vis (prep.)** -- in relation to

4842 -- **visceral (adj.)** -- resulting from emotions

4843 -- **viscid (adj.)** -- sticky and slippery

4844 -- **viscous (adj.)** -- thick and sticky; gluey || related word: **viscosity (n.)**

4845 -- **vista (n.)** -- outlook; prospect | landscape

4846 -- **vitiate (v.)** -- to spoil

4847 -- **vitrify (v.)** -- to transform into glass

4848 -- **vitreous (adj.)** -- hard and completely transparent

4849 -- **vitriol (n.)** -- bitter comments or statements || related word: **vitriolic (adj.)**

4850 -- **vituperation (n.)** -- angry criticism || related word: **vituperative (adj.)**

4851 -- **vivacious (adj.)** -- cheerful || related words: **vivaciously (adv.), vivacity (n.)**

4852 -- **vivid (adj.)** -- very clear or bright || related words: **vividly (adv.), vividness (n.)**

4853 -- **vivisection (n.)** -- experiment on living beings

4854 -- **vociferous (adj.)** -- expressing clearly; determined || related word: **vociferously (adv.)**

4855 -- **vogue (n.)** -- fashion

4856 -- **volatile (adj.)** -- unstable || related word: **volatility (n.)**

4857 -- **volition (n.)** -- independence

4858 -- **volley (n./v.)** -- strong criticism | to lob

4859 -- **volte-face (n.)** -- reversal

4860 -- **voluble (adj.)** -- clearly articulated or expressed || related word: **volubly (adv.)**

4861 -- **voluptuous (adj.)** -- (of woman) having attractive figure || related words: **voluptuously (adv.), voluptuousness (n.)**

4862 -- **voracious (adj.)** -- greedy or very eager || related words: **voraciously (adv.), voracity (n.)**

4863 -- **vortex (n.)** -- spinning mass of water or air | unavoidable situation

4864 -- **votary (n.)** -- supporter or worshipper

4865 -- **voyeur (n.)** -- a person who enjoys sb's problems || related words: **voyeuristic (adj.), voyeurism (n.)**

Difficult English Words -- W

4866 -- **wacky (adj.)** -- amusing and crazy

4867 -- **waddle (v.)** -- to walk like a duck

4868 -- **wade (v.)** -- to walk with an effort

4869 -- **wafer-thin (adj.)** -- very thin

4870 -- **waffle (n./v.)** -- senseless talk | to talk nonsense

4871 -- **waft (v.)** -- to float

4872 -- **wag (v.)** -- to move or wave from side to side

4873 -- **wager (n./v.)** -- bet | to bet

4874 -- **waggish (adj.)** -- amusing

4875 -- **waggle (n./v.)** -- side to side movement | to move side to side; to make sth move side to side

4876 -- **waif (n.)** -- weak and thin child

4877 -- **wail (n./v.)** -- loud cry; groan | to weep || related word: **wailing (n.)**

4878 -- **wallop (n./v.)** -- hit | to hit or defeat

4879 -- **walloping (adj./n.)** -- very big | defeat

4880 -- **wallow (n./v.)** -- pleasurable activity | to enjoy pleasurable activity

4881 -- **wally (n.)** -- silly person

4882 -- **waltz (v.)** -- to walk confidentially; to finish your task easily

4883 -- **wan (adj.)** -- very weak || related word: **wanly (adv.)**

4884 -- **wane (v.)** -- to fade; to diminish

4885 -- **wangle (v.)** -- to obtain sth in a clever way

4886 -- **wannabe (n.)** -- aspirant

4887 -- **wanton (adj.)** -- immoral or unacceptable || related words: **wantonly (adv.), wantonness (n.)**

4888 -- **warfare (n.)** -- aggressive competition

4889 -- warp (v.) -- to bend or twist | to influence unacceptably || related word: **warped (adj.)**

4890 -- warrant (v.) -- to justify

4891 -- wary (adj.) -- cautious || related words: **warily (adv.), wariness (n.)**

4892 -- washout (n.) -- complete failure

4893 -- waspish (adj.) -- annoying || related word: **waspishly (adv.)**

4894 -- watershed (n.) -- time of important changes

4895 -- waver (v.) -- to hesitate || related word: **waverer (n.)**

4896 -- wax (v.) -- to expand

4897 -- waylay (v.) -- to stop sb with a view to attack them or talk to them

4898 -- wayward (adj.) -- uncontrollable || related word: **waywardness (n.)**

4899 -- wean (v.) -- to start giving a child solid food

4900 -- weary (adj./v.) -- completely tired | to tire || related words **wearing (adj.), wearily (adv.), weariness (n.), wearisome (n.)**

4901 -- wee (adj./n./v.) -- little | urine | to urinate

4902 -- weird (adj.) -- odd || related words: **weirdly (adv.), weirdness (n.)**

4903 -- weirdo (n.) -- strange person

4904 -- well disposed (adj.) -- in favor

4905 -- well oiled (adj.) -- working well

4906 -- welsh (v.) -- to break your promise

4907 -- welt (n.) -- raised mark on the skin

4908 -- welter (n.) -- large amount

4909 -- wend (v.) -- to move slowly

4910 -- whack (n./v.) -- hard hit; an amount of sth | to hit hard

4911 -- whacked (adj.) -- tired

4912 -- whacking (adj.) -- very big

4913 -- **whammy (n.)** -- unpleasant and unfavorable situation

4914 -- **wheeze (n./v.)** -- trick | to breath with difficulty || related words: **wheezy (adj.), wheezily (adv.), wheeziness (n.)**

4915 -- **wherewithal (n.)** -- things that are needed to do sth

4916 -- **whiff (n./v.)** -- trace or smell | to smell bad || related word: **whiffy (adj.)**

4917 -- **whim (n.)** -- desire to do sth unusual

4918 -- **whimper (n./v.)** -- weak cry | to cry in weak voice

4919 -- **whimsical (adj.)** -- amusing and not serious || related words: **whimsically (adv.), whimsy (n.)**

4920 -- **whine (v.)** -- to complain | to make long high sound; to moan || related word: **whiny (adj.)**

4921 -- **whinge (n./v.)** -- complaint | to complain annoyingly || related word: **whinger (n.)**

4922 -- **whinny (v.)** -- to make a quiet and long high sound

4923 -- **whirlwind (adj./n.)** -- happening quickly | a situation of many things happening quickly

4924 -- **whirr (n./v.)** -- repeated low sound | to make repeated low sounds

4925 -- **whisk (v.)** -- to mix eggs, etc. using a kitchen tool

4926 -- **whistle-blower (n.)** -- informer within an organization

4927 -- **whit (n.)** -- small amount

4928 -- **whittle (v.)** -- to cut pieces of wood in order to give It a particular shape

4929 -- **whizz (n./v.)** -- expert | to move or do sth quickly

4930 -- **whizz-kid (n.)** -- kid or youth who is extraordinarily intelligent

4931 -- **whizzy (adj.)** -- using advanced technology

4932 -- **whoosh (n./v.)** -- quick movement | to move quickly

4933 -- **whopper (n.)** -- huge thing; giant || related word: **whopping (adj.)**

4934 -- whorl (n.) -- a ring or circle

4935 -- wield (v.) -- to hold | to exercise your authority

4936 -- wiggle (n./v.) -- side to side movement | to move from side to side

4937 -- wiles (n.) -- tricks

4938 -- wilt (v.) -- (of plants) to bend because of deficiency of water

4939 -- wily (adj.) -- cunning

4940 -- wimp (n.) -- coward person || related word: **wimpish (adj.)**

4941 -- wince (n./v.) -- strange facial expression | to show pain, embarrassment and similar feelings with your facial expressions.

4942 -- windfall (n.) -- money that you gain suddenly

4943 -- winnow (v.) -- to remove chaff of grain by blowing air through it.

4944 -- winsome (adj.) -- charming || related word: **winsomely (adv.)**

4945 -- wiry (adj.) -- thin

4946 -- wisecrack (n.) -- joke

4947 -- wisp (n.) -- thin piece; curl || related word: **wispy (adj.)**

4948 -- wistful (adj.) -- sad || related words: **wistfully (adv.), wistfulness (n.)**

4949 -- withering (adj.) -- arrogant || related word: **witheringly (adv.)**

4950 -- withstand (v.) -- to survive

4951 -- witter (v.) -- to keep on talking annoyingly

4952 -- wizened (adj.) -- wrinkled

4953 -- wobble (n./v.) -- unsteady movement | to shake || related word: **wobbly (adj.)**

4954 -- woe (n.) -- misery || related word: **woeful (adj.)**

4955 -- wonk (n.) -- hard-working and boring person

4956 -- wonky (adj.) -- unsteady

4957 -- wont (adj./n.) -- habituated | habit

4958 -- woolly (adj.) -- unclear || related word: **woolliness (n.)**

4959 -- woozy (adj.) -- confused and unclear

4960 -- wraith (n.) -- spirit

4961 -- wrangle (n./v.) -- complicated argument | to keep on arguing angrily || related word: **wrangling (n.)**

4962 -- wrath (n.) -- too much anger; rage || related words: **wrathful (adj.), wrathfully (adv.)**

4963 -- wreak (v.) -- to destruct

4964 -- wreath (n.) -- garland

4965 -- wreathe (v.) -- to cover or coil

4966 -- wreck (n./v.) -- damaged car, ship, etc. | to damage or spoil || related word: **wrecked (adj.)**

4967 -- wreckage (n.) -- debris

4968 -- wrench (v.) -- to pull; to twist

4969 -- wretch (n.) -- evil person

4970 -- wretched (adj.) -- miserable || related words: **wretchedly (adv.), wretchedness (n.)**

4971 -- wriggle (n./v.) -- twisting movement | to twist with sudden movements

4972 -- wringing wet (adj.) -- completely wet

4973 -- write-down (n.) -- reduction in value of sth, especially assets

4974 -- write-up (n.) -- review

4975 -- writhe (v.) -- to twist your body because you are feeling severe pain

4976 -- wrought (v.) -- caused something to change

4977 -- wry (adj.) -- showing feeling of amusement or disappointment || related words: **wryly (adv.), wryness (n.)**

Difficult English Words -- XYZ

4978 -- xenophobia (n.) -- fear of foreigners || related word: **xenophobic (adj.)**

4979 -- yak (v.) -- to talk about unimportant things

4980 -- yank (n./v.) -- sudden pull | to suddenly pull sth

4981 -- yardstick (n.) -- standard for measuring sth

4982 -- yarn (n.) -- false story

4983 -- yaw (n./v.) -- (of a plane or ship) unsteady movement | to change direction unsteadily

4984 -- yearn (v.) -- to desire for sth that is not easy to get || related word: **yearning (n.)**

4985 -- yell (n./v.) -- shout | to shout

4986 -- yen (n.) -- a desire that is felt strongly

4987 -- yield (n./v.) -- profit | to produce sth profitable; to give up; to move in a particular direction || related word: **yielding (adj.)**

4988 -- yob (n.) -- violent boy or man || related word: **yobbish (adj.)**

4989 -- yoke (n./v.) -- bondage | to join

4990 -- yucky (adj.) -- extremely unpleasant

4991 -- yummy (adj.) -- delicious

4992 -- zany (adj.) -- crazy and amusing

4993 -- zeal (n.) -- massive interest or energy; keenness or enthusiasm || related words: **zealous (adj.), zealously (adv.)**

4994 -- zealot (n.) -- sb who is too much interested about religion or politics; enthusiast | related word: **zealotry (adv.)**

4995 -- zenith (n.) -- the time of being most successful, powerful, strongest, etc; peak | highest point

4996 -- zilch (n.) -- nothing

4997 -- zing (n./v.) -- energy or liveliness | to move in a sudden way making loud sound; to criticize

4998 -- zinger (n.) -- amusing remark

4999 -- zombie (n.) -- a dead person who becomes alive again by magic | a person who has no feelings

5000 -- zoom (v.) -- to move very fast; (of prices) to increase suddenly

****

About the Author

Manik Joshi, the author of this book was born on **Jan 26, 1979** at Ranikhet and is permanent resident of Haldwani, Kumaon zone of India. He is an Internet Marketer by profession. He is interested in domaining (business of buying and selling domain names), web designing (creating websites), and various online jobs (including 'self-publishing'). He is science graduate with ZBC (zoology, botany, and chemistry) subjects. He is also an MBA (with specialization in marketing). He has done three diploma courses in computer too. **ManikJoshi.com** is the personal website of the author.

Amazon Author Page of Manik Joshi:
https://www.amazon.com/author/manikjoshi

Email:
mail@manikjoshi.com

****

BIBLIOGRAPHY

'ENGLISH DAILY USE' TITLES BY MANIK JOSHI

01. How to Start a Sentence
02. English Interrogative Sentences
03. English Imperative Sentences
04. Negative Forms in English
05. Learn English Exclamations
06. English Causative Sentences
07. English Conditional Sentences
08. Creating Long Sentences in English
09. How to Use Numbers in Conversation
10. Making Comparisons in English
11. Examples of English Correlatives
12. Interchange of Active and Passive Voice
13. Repetition of Words
14. Remarks in English Language
15. Using Tenses in English
16. English Grammar- Am, Is, Are, Was, Were
17. English Grammar- Do, Does, Did
18. English Grammar- Have, Has, Had
19. English Grammar- Be and Have
20. English Modal Auxiliary Verbs
21. Direct and Indirect Speech
22. Get- Popular English Verb
23. Ending Sentences with Prepositions
24. Popular Sentences in English
25. Common English Sentences
26. Daily Use English Sentences
27. Speak English Sentences Everyday
28. Popular English Idioms and Phrases
29. Common English Phrases
30. Daily English- Important Notes

'ENGLISH WORD POWER' TITLES BY MANIK JOSHI

01. Dictionary of English Synonyms
02. Dictionary of English Antonyms
03. Homonyms, Homophones and Homographs
04. Dictionary of English Capitonyms
05. Dictionary of Prefixes and Suffixes
06. Dictionary of Combining Forms
07. Dictionary of Literary Words
08. Dictionary of Old-fashioned Words
09. Dictionary of Humorous Words
10. Compound Words in English
11. Dictionary of Informal Words
12. Dictionary of Category Words
13. Dictionary of One-word Substitution
14. Hypernyms and Hyponyms
15. Holonyms and Meronyms
16. Oronym Words in English
17. Dictionary of Root Words
18. Dictionary of English Idioms
19. Dictionary of Phrasal Verbs
20. Dictionary of Difficult Words

OTHER TITLES BY MANIK

01. English Word Exercises (Part 1)
02. English Word Exercises (Part 2)
03. English Word Exercises (Part 3)
04. English Sentence Exercises
05. Test Your English
06. Match the Two Parts of the Words
07. Letter-Order In Words
08. Simple, Compound, Complex, & Compound-Complex Sentences
09. Transitional Words and Phrases
10. Regular and Irregular Verbs

****

28265173R00137

Made in the USA
Columbia, SC
07 October 2018